ARE YOUR PARENTS DRIVING YOU NUTS?

- Are holidays nearly impossible to get through?
- Do you avoid family gatherings?
- Are you going crazy trying to take care of your folks?
- Are they still busy trying to take care of you?
- Do your parents still disapprove of your husband, wife, lover, friends?
- Are you sick and tired of hearing advice? Of feeling manipulated and guilty?
- Do you just want to feel closer to your parents?

You're not alone. Most people have trouble dealing with their parents even after they themselves have grown up.

This guide offers real solutions. Through careful planning, sensitive communication—and love—you can learn to enjoy your parents. You can make the most of your relationship with the people who brought you into the world. This book will take you step by step through the rewarding healing process!

HOW TO DEAL WITH YOUR PARENTS WHEN THEY STILL TREAT YOU LIKE A CHILD

How To Deal With Your Parents

When They Still Treat You Like a Child

By,

LYNN OSTERKAMP, Ph.D.

BERKLEY BOOKS, NEW YORK

HOW TO DEAL WITH YOUR PARENTS
WHEN THEY STILL TREAT YOU LIKE A CHILD

A Berkley Book / published by arrangement with
the author

PRINTING HISTORY
Berkley edition / January 1992

ISBN: 0-425-13137-8

A BERKLEY BOOK ® TM 757,375
Berkley Books are published by The Berkley Publishing Group,
200 Madison Avenue, New York, New York 10016.
The name "BERKLEY" and the "B" logo
are trademarks belonging to Berkley Publishing Corporation.

PRINTED IN THE UNITED STATES OF AMERICA

10 9 8 7 6 5 4 3 2 1

CONTENTS

ACKNOWLEDGMENTS

Lots of people contributed to this book. I acknowledge my debt to them and I am pleased to be able to thank them publicly for their help.

Hundreds of adults filled out long questionnaires in which they described difficult interactions with their parents, discussed their attempts to change those situations, and spoke about how they would ideally like to get along with their parents. Many gave even more generously of their time in personal interviews. Without the input of these "grown children," this book would not exist. Because I promised them that they would remain anonymous, I have changed their names, locations and other identifying characteristics. Although I cannot thank them by name, I genuinely appreciate their willingness to share their feelings and experiences.

My special friend and colleague, Susan Baile, gave me the initial encouragement I needed to move this project along from an idea to a reality. She is uniquely able to help me clarify my priorities. I sincerely value her friendship.

My literary agent, Elizabeth Trupin, believed in this book when it was merely an outline and a sample chapter. Her support and her straightforward, optimistic approach to selling the book gave me the motivation to finish the manuscript. I feel truly fortunate to have her representing my interests.

My son, Jeffrey, a journalist who never compromises his standards in the quality of his writing, took time out of his busy schedule to read and comment on an early draft of this book. I appreciate and always learn from his insistence that the craft of writing has no tolerance for careless style.

My sister, Betty Ann, has always been a loyal booster of my endeavors. She not only read and commented on the book's first draft, but also insisted on seeing all the revisions and additions as it progressed. She also introduced me to people and shared personal stories that became an integral part of this book. I appreciate her belief in me.

My daughter, Laurel, knows me so well she can almost finish my sentences. Thus, she is able to add her own creative insights to my ideas in a way that enhances my views without compromising their basic identity. Her comments and suggestions for changes in the first draft of the book added significantly, to the final version.

But, even with all this help and support, I doubt this book would exist if I had not had the consistent encouragement and assistance of my husband, Allan Press. He read every word of every draft, sometimes again and again. A social psychologist, he contributed ideas, references and new perspectives on tricky issues. He helped me collect material and offered suggestions for analyzing and incorporating it. He tolerated my ups and downs through the long process of writing, selling and rewriting this book. He always believes in me and pushes me to take the risks I need to take to move my creative projects along. There is nothing I can say that will adequately express the gratitude I feel for his contribution to this book and to every part of my life.

HOW TO DEAL WITH YOUR PARENTS

When They Still Treat You Like a Child

PART ONE

Desires and Expectations

CHAPTER 1

Why Are So Many Grown-Up People Still Worrying About What Their Parents Think?

"Even though I'm 40 years old and my parents are each 62, they are still very quick with advice and slow to give me credit for having thought through my own problems and difficulties. Their disapproval spoils a lot of the time we spend together. For example, our whole family gathers at their house for the holidays. Mom spends weeks baking before we come, but those 'treats' always become a source of argument and hurt feelings between us. I'm the heaviest person in my family, and in hundreds of subtle and not so subtle ways I am told that while most of the family can handle this stuff, I need to be more conscious of my health, and I'm continually being asked 'Weren't you on a diet?' I end up feeling that if my own parents can't love and approve of me, there must be something wrong with me." (Pat, age 40)*

We are our parents' children for a long time. Even when we are grown up, we are still their children. Most adults have stores of horror stories like Pat's. These are not tales of abuse, nor are they pathological, but they do hurt. We complain, we compare stories with our friends, we may even cry or yell, but basically we tolerate the situation or adapt to it. Why? Partly because old patterns are difficult to change and partly because we are not sure what we really want or what we are willing to risk.

*Names and identifying characteristics have been changed throughout this book.

How Should an Adult Child Behave?

For the first time in American history, a typical married couple in their forties has more living parents than children.[1] As our population ages, the length of time people fill the role of "adult child" is increasing. Yet most adults are uncertain as to how an "adult child" should behave. In fact the term itself is a paradox that conveys much of the confusion that accompanies the role.

Many capable, independent adults report that they feel instantly childish again when they are around their parents. The character Allie on the sitcom *Kate and Allie* spoke for many with her remark: "When I'm around my mother she makes me feel like I'm ten years old with braces on my teeth and gum in my hair."

Parents are major figures in our lives. We want their love and approval, and we worry about disappointing or hurting them. From the college student who tells her parents she wants to go home with a friend for Thanksgiving and then hears, "Don't worry about us, Dad and I will just eat a bologna sandwich," to the forty-five-year-old man who is worried sick about how to tell his parents he has just been laid off from the job he's held for 20 years, we share a common frustration. We want to improve our relationships with our parents, but we don't know how.

In fact, we often have difficulty knowing how to talk to our parents as adults, especially if they do not treat us as adults. For example:

- A thirty-five-year-old man says: "My wife and I took my father out boating, and although he's never owned a boat in his life, he felt compelled to instruct me on how to dock a boat."
- A twenty-six-year-old new mother complains: "My mother acts as if I am too young or immature to care for my daughter properly. We were at her house for dinner and I was changing the baby and she said, 'Oh, you don't know how to do that,' and she just took over."
- A thirty-nine-year-old woman who had just bought a new car recalls: "My seventy-two-year-old father called me up to

remind me to take care of the license and insurance for my car. He also reminded me on my birthday to check and see whether my driver's license needs to be renewed. Doesn't he think I've learned anything over the years?"

- A forty-two-year-old man found out that his sixty-six-year-old mother had had a mastectomy when another relative mentioned it two months later, assuming he knew. He says: "They do not inform me until after the fact, and sometimes not even then, when something bad has happened, because 'You'll just worry and you shouldn't.' When do they think I'll be old enough for them to stop protecting me?"

- A forty-two-year-old woman says: "If I go in their house and kick off my shoes, my father will stare at my feet because I'm in the living room without my shoes on. He won't say anything, he'll look at my feet. And I know I should go put my shoes on. Here I am in my forties and I have to go find my shoes when my feet are hot."

- A twenty-eight-year-old woman's mother came to visit, cleaned out her daughter's refrigerator, and rearranged her kitchen cabinets. "Then, when I got home from work," the daughter complains, "she told me I should clean up my room and rearrange my closet."

- A thirty-six-year-old man happened to mention to his mother in a weekend phone conversation that he was on a diet. "She called me long-distance in the middle of the week to find out what I was eating and make sure I was getting enough nourishment and hot food."

- A twenty-eight-year-old woman from the midwest flew to Phoenix to visit her parents who were there for the winter. When she got there, "they didn't want me to drive their car because the sun is so bright here and the roads are so wide that it's hard to see the traffic very well."

Somehow it takes you back to the times when your mother would say, "Pin your gloves to your coat so you don't lose them." Or your father would remind you to "look both ways before you cross the street." As an adult, it is hard to know how to respond. As children, we receive messages like, "Don't talk back to your father," or, "Don't talk to your mother that way." Even as adults we may still hear, "Don't forget I'm still your mother [or father]," or "I'm only concerned for you and

I *am* your parent." Can we ever escape these old parent-child interactions and begin to feel like adults in conversations with our parents?

Today more than ever before, this question has an urgent ring. As our population ages, creating an increasing overlap between generations, we are challenging the old myth that once we are grown up our relationships with our parents are set and relatively unimportant in our lives.

The Changing American Family

We are witnessing a basic change in the American family structure. It is aging as our population ages. People over sixty-five are the fastest growing segment of our population; the number increased by 4.3 million, or 17 percent, since 1980, compared to an increase of 6 percent for the under-sixty-five population. Between 1970 and 1984, the median age of all Americans jumped from twenty-eight to 31.3 years and the portion of the population over age eighteen grew from 65 percent to 73 percent. In fact, during the 1970's the elderly population of the United States increased at a higher rate than the total population of India.[2]

If more Americans have surviving parents than ever before, then we are adult children for more years than ever before. In 1963, only 25 percent of people over the age of forty-five had a surviving parent. By the early 1970's, 25 percent of people in their late fifties had a surviving parent; by 1980, 40 percent of people in their late fifties had at least one surviving parent.[3]

Today parents and children can anticipate sharing nearly half a century of their lives. For about half that time, the child may also be a parent, linking several family generations. A fifty-year-old woman today has a life expectancy of more than thirty-one years, and her seventy-five-year-old mother more than twelve.[4]

Even though we are a mobile society, parents and adult children tend to have regular contact. For example, a 1984 study found that four of every five older persons had living children. Two-thirds of these older parents lived within 30 minutes of an adult child; 62 percent had at least weekly visits with children and 76 percent talked on the phone with children at least weekly.[5]

Frequency of contact, however, says little about the *quality* of interaction between adult children and their parents. In fact our society has conflicting ideas about what form these contacts should ideally take. On the one hand we expect grown children to "break away," to establish independence from their parents, and to make it on their own. Similarly, we expect parents to let go and to find their own meaningful activities, rather than "living through their children." This would seem to argue for somewhat distant, autonomous relationships between adult children and parents, preferably without any dependence in either direction.

Yet Americans also value looking out for our own. Nothing replaces the family when it comes to willingness and/or obligation to tolerate and care for someone who is sick, disabled, or otherwise unable to carry their own weight. We expect adults to see their parents regularly if distance permits, to help them if they need it, and to offer emotional support. We expect parents to continue to help their grown children in times of trouble and even to invite them to move back home for a while if necessary. All this implies a level of emotional closeness and involvement that seems to contradict the importance of independence.

No wonder relationships between adult children and parents are confusing. If we subscribe to both these conflicting values we may feel dissatisfied or guilty no matter what we do. We might feel that we are either too involved with our parents or that we are neglecting them.[6]

Our communication mirrors these conflicting values. Parents and adult children each want closeness without giving up independence. Gerontologists predict that as our population ages, relations between adult children and parents will become increasingly complex and possibly more emotionally stressful.[7] Already Americans are looking more closely at family life and beginning to explore new possibilities for improving relationships between the generations.

Do We Have a Generation Gap?

How wide the gulf looks depends on where you are standing. Research shows that parents tend to minimize the differences between themselves and their adult children, while children do the reverse. Parents tend to see (and want) more emotional closeness than adult children do. Adult children are more likely to see the relationships in terms of exchanges of help or services.

Researchers suggest that because parents see their children as one way of continuing their personal histories and validating their own lives, they have a greater stake in minimizing the differences between generations. Thus parents actually see better communication and understanding in the relationship than their children do.[8] Larry is thirty-two, lives about 700 miles from his parents, sees them about twice a year and talks to them by phone once or twice a month. He finds it hard to have much of a conversation with his mother because she will not accept any disagreement with her ideas. She makes judgments about people and what they should do and gives opinions about what happened in the news and expects him to agree with her. Larry finds it frustrating, but his mother seems unaware of the problem: "My mother thinks she and I have great give-and-take conversations about everything under the sun. But actually those conversations drive me crazy. I can't discuss anything with her unless I say she's right. If I disagree and say so, that is outrageous to her."

Like Larry, adult children seem to feel freer to notice and describe dissatisfactions in their interactions with their parents. In fact, adults who have living parents as well as children of their own tend to report more difficulties in their relationships with their parents than with their children. In data a colleague and I have collected on the stresses and satisfactions of adults aged twenty-two to seventy, a group of 513 people have one or more children and at least one surviving parent. These adults:

- reported significantly more dissatisfactions in their relationships with their parents than in their relationships with their children.
- were more likely to say they enjoyed being with their children than with their parents.
- were more likely to say they had a good relationship with their children than with their parents.
- were more likely to say they found their parents annoying than that they found their children annoying.

What Do We Expect?

Family therapists note that we all think our parents are uniquely impossible. Yet many adults have seen the same difficult patterns between their parents and their grandparents that they find in their own communication with their parents. For example, forty-two-year-old Sara says that her sixty-eight-year-old mother is following a family tradition when she gives advice:

"My mother is pretty opinionated and sometimes she gets carried away with giving advice, but she comes by it naturally because her mother was *really* good at it. I'll never forget the time when I was still living at home and the operator interrupted a phone call I was on to say there was an emergency call for my mother and could I please hang up. Well, I did and here comes the emergency call: my grandmother with advice on how to cook the meat that was in the oven."

Comics make entire routines out of such stories. We laugh because they are so universal. Few of us have escaped parental lines such as:

- Money doesn't grow on trees.
- Wait until you have children of your own.
- If I had talked to my parents the way you talk to me . . .
- I don't want to hear another word about it.
- I'm your mother and you owe it to me.

Just knowing that so many parents communicate this way is enough to apply another "wise" parental saying to the whole situation: "Don't expect too much, then you won't be disappointed."

Thus many adults do not expect communication with their parents to improve. Nevertheless, this does not mean that adult children are satisfied with the status quo.

What Adults Say They Want From Their Parents

In our data, more than 30 percent of adults say they often or almost always feel their parents do not really know them. Another 24 percent sometimes feel this way. Nearly half report that at least some of the time their parents expect too much, are not enjoyable to be with, or make them feel guilty. More than a third say that their parents try to control them at least some of the time.

Not surprisingly, what adult children say they want from their parents is different behavior. For example, here are some adults' responses to questions about changes they would like in their interactions with their parents and about the role they would ideally like their parents to play in their lives now:

- "What I would like most of all is simply to be given the equal opportunity to express what I feel and think. It has always been a one-sided affair—with them sharing what they think and feel about their selected topics. Also, I would like my mother to quit making judgment statements about my affairs and trying to control my decisions." (Female, age 44)
- "I wish my mother would not worry so much so that we could discuss problems with her and get the benefit of her years of experience and also her emotional support." (Female, age 58)
- "I would like to be able to share everything with them and be able to have better conversations between the three of us." (Female, age 23)
- "I would like to feel comfortable about talking about subjects such as raising children without it becoming a fight or a one-sided conversation." (Male, age 31)
- "I would like to share feelings with my dad and get off the material stuff. I'd like to simply talk about what life means to us and what our hopes for the future are, acknowledging that each of us has feelings. I just want to share life without judgments." (Female, age 25)
- "My mom expects more from me than I want to or can give. I wish she were not so demanding. For example, when I visit my hometown she expects me to spend all my time with her. Also, I would like her not to expect me to call her every weekend at the same time." (Male, age 35)
- "I would like it if my mother wouldn't 'suffer' so much when I'm needing her to listen and accept what I'm saying about my feelings when I'm having a rough time. Also, I'd like her to reach outside of her tragic world she's carefully cultivated

and ask me a question that she really wants to hear the answer to." (Female, age 34)

- "I wish my father could have a better understanding of the importance of my feelings and my point of view." (Male, age 49)
- "I would like them to be trusted adult friends. I would like to be able to be open with them without the fear that they would be personally offended or that they would disclose my personal revelations to others." (Female, age 31)
- "I would like my father to speak to me as an adult rather than as a child. I don't like his obsession to control my life and to treat me as if I were born yesterday." (Female, age 25)
- "I wish I could be less guarded in my conversations with my mother and she would quit trying to manage my decisions. I see her as being very manipulative and wanting to be in control. I want her to treat me as a capable adult friend without giving unsolicited advice or opinions on my actions or using guilt or money to coerce me." (Female, age 49)
- "I would like to feel that I could talk to them more openly about my own personal issues and about issues with them." (Male, age 40)
- "I wish my parents would see things the way I see things more often." (Female, age 32)
- "I wish we were more affectionate with each other. We rarely hug or verbalize our love for one another." (Female, age 31)
- "I would like them to be less judgmental and to not hold grudges. I would also like us all to be able to be more direct with each other." (Male, age 27)
- "I would like us to be friends. We have shared nearly 40 years of life together. I would like the emotional support I give and expect from my friends—and I wish we could be more honest." (Female, age 39)

What Most Parents Want

Overall, research finds that parents want continued contact with their children along with continued independence. They want to help their adult children when they can, and they definitely do not want to feel dependent on their children. They want respect and dignity.

Parents want to feel included in their adult children's lives, to share experiences, and to have a continued important role. They want to feel useful to their children and to believe that even after they die, their teachings and values will continue to influence their children.[9]

Unfortunately, from an adult child's point of view, parents' communication often seems to create feelings in opposition to these desires. Even though parents want their adult children to *choose* to spend time with them and to enjoy sharing their lives, their children may feel more *obligation* than desire in their reasons for being together. How does this happen?

Usually it is a long process of reactions that build up over time. Parents and their adult children each act on the basis of their own needs and desires, then they react to the other's actions, and the process goes on and on. Consider Joan's situation:

Joan: It's Getting Harder To Be Nice

I was the middle child in my family. When my older brother and my younger sister fought, I never took sides. I was "the sweet one" and "the peacemaker." I just tried to be nice to everyone. My parents always praised me for not being any trouble, for being agreeable and helpful.

I got married young, which they didn't like, but they accepted it. What they couldn't accept was my divorce. I tried to stay in that marriage even after I knew it was a mistake, partly because I worried about how they would react. I could never talk to them about how moody and demanding my husband was, because they would have just told me to find a way to make him happy.

I've had a hard time since the divorce, raising my son alone, working as a secretary, and living on very little money. I've changed a lot, too. I don't feel that I have to keep everyone happy all the time like I used to. I do always try to be as cheerful and nice as ever around my parents because I know they expect it, but it's getting a lot harder to do.

They don't give me much credit for anything. They keep telling me I could get a better job if I tried. They even show me ads. They tell me my apartment is too expensive for what it is. They say my five-year-old son

Chris stays up too late, eats the wrong food, watches too much TV, and on and on. I'm furious when they do this, but I don't say anything angry. I just pretend to listen, try to ignore what they are telling me, and go on living my own way.

When I'm around them, I feel guilty. I can't seem to please them anymore, even though I try. Even worse, I have a new boyfriend now who has moved in with Chris and me, but I haven't told my parents. They've only met him once. They'll be so worried that I'm making another mistake, that I'm going to get hurt, or that having my boyfriend here will be bad for Chris.

Lately I've been spending less time with them. I don't invite them here even though they only live sixty-five miles away. I know they want to come, but I pretend not to notice their hints. I really do love them, but a lot of the time I can't stand to be around them. I wish we could enjoy each other more.

Five Major Issues That Cause Trouble

Joan's complaints and reactions exemplify the types of conflicts that many adults report in their relationships with their parents. Most of the arguments and stress between adults and their parents center around five trouble zones.

Understanding. Joan wants her parents to know her as the person she feels she really is and to love and accept her as that person. She would like them to hear and understand the struggles she has faced, but not to base their love for her on her successes or failures in these situations. She wants to feel that she does not have to live up to some perfect image in order to keep their love. But Joan does not know how to tell them who she "really" is. She is afraid they will not listen and afraid of their reactions if they do listen.

Approval. Joan wants her parents to respect her as a capable adult who can make her own decisions. She does not want their advice about what job she should have, how to raise her son, or where she should live. She wants to feel that they give her credit for being grown-up enough to make her own choices.

But she cannot find a way to stop their criticism and advice or to hear it as anything but disapproval.

Guilt. Joan resents her parents' comments, but she feels guilty about this anger. She feels unable to meet their expectations and uncomfortable that she is not trying harder to be the person they want her to be. She feels that she has let them down already and that if they knew about her new relationship they would worry even more about her. She would like to tell them that she needs more independence, but she does not know how to do it without feeling guilty.

Change. Joan is and is not the same person she was as a child. She carries with her all her past history of relating to her parents—her role as "the sweet one," the unwritten rule of not expressing anger, her easy acceptance of their authority. Although Joan has changed in her daily life, when she is with her parents she slips back into her old role and her habitual family communication style. She would like to communicate with them in a more adult way, but she has not been able to change her old habits.

Power. Joan is struggling with her parents over who is in charge. They tell her how to live, but she ignores their advice. She keeps secrets from them but feels guilty about not being more open. She wants unconditional acceptance, but they impose conditions. They want more involvement in her life, but she holds back. They would all like more closeness, but the power struggle creates distance instead.

Is It Possible to Resolve These Issues?

Conflicts, misunderstandings, anger, and resentments that have developed over the years will not evaporate overnight. They certainly will not disappear if you, like Joan, cannot be honest with your parents. This does not mean you should unleash all your stored-up anger on your parents or tell them about every embarrassing deed in your past. It does mean you probably can improve your relationship with them by making some changes in the way you communicate.

As you read through this book, you will find specific

techniques to help you improve your communication with your parents. With all of these methods, one point is crucial: You must know what you want. If you want your parents to agree with you and tell you that you are right, you may make very little progress toward your goals. You may be quite convinced that it is your parents who need to change, not you, because you are right and they are wrong. You will need to let go of that view to improve your communication with them. As long as you are trying to prove you are right, the struggles will only intensify.

However, if your goals are to feel more adult in your interactions with your parents, to be able to free yourself from the old patterns that you know and hate, and to have a more open, honest relationship with them, you should be able to make major changes with these techniques. The process will not be a simple one, because it takes a lot of practice and energy to change long-standing routines. Nevertheless, the outcome can be well worth the effort.

Why Bother to Change?

By now you may be asking yourself whether it is worth the trouble to try to improve your relationship with your parents. After all, you have a busy life. Why not let *them* make the first move?

Remember that adult children have some compelling reasons to want to transform relationships with parents:

- As long as your parents live, which may be a long time, you will probably continue to talk with them and spend time with them. Family ties are very strong; you cannot divorce your parents. Since this relationship is likely to be part of your life for years, you can benefit from improving it.
- You are likely to have more dissatisfactions with the relationship than your parents do, as the research shows. If so, you have the most to gain from the change.
- You will probably outlive your parents. If you do not at least try to have the relationship with them that you really want, you will be the one living with the regrets later when it is too late.
- You may need to help your parents in some major ways if

they become ill or frail in their later years. If you feel manipulated, misunderstood, or unappreciated by your parents now, you are likely to experience these feelings even more intensely when your parents are depending on you for help. Assisting them will be much easier if all of you have resolved old conflicts and worked out a comfortable communication style.

• Some adult children eventually bring a chronically ill or disabled parent into their home because they want to provide care for a parent with whom they have had a close, loving relationship. Others, who have not had an open, loving relationship with their parent, may bring the sick parent into their home in an attempt to resolve feelings of guilt or inadequacy about this lack of closeness. This second motive usually leads to a very stressful situation, since relationships rarely improve when one person is ill and dependent. If you do what you can to improve the relationship before such a crisis arises, you are less likely to make caregiving decisions based on guilt and more likely to be able to enlist your parent's cooperation for whatever arrangement you propose.

Learning New Ways of Talking to Your Parents

As adults, we often find that the path to a smooth relationship with our parents is as elusive and mysterious as the maze Alice confronted in Wonderland, where, as we also typically discover, "all ways here are the Queen's ways." But fortunately, change *is* possible if you decide to make the effort. Part of this process is taking a close look at your communication with your parents and deciding what you care enough about to change and what you are willing to forget. Another important element is knowing how you got where you are and how you can get out.

If you ask them, most grown children will tell you that ideally they would like to interact differently with their parents. If you share their feelings, you would say that you love your parents, but wish you could be more open with them without feeling judged or worrying about hurting their feelings. Over the years you have probably found it easier to find new ways of relating to other significant people in your life than to change your old patterns with your parents.

This book will help you analyze, understand, and improve your everyday interactions with your parents. It is a skills-oriented book that approaches the adult child/parent relationship from a communication perspective, with a focus on interaction rather than on pathology. It will explain and illustrate new ways of behaving that you can begin to try out. As you experiment with unfamiliar ways of communicating, you can examine the effects and incorporate the most successful ones into your ongoing interactions with your parents. Specifically, you will find ways to:

- Tell them what you want and what you are willing and unwilling to accept.
- Stop keeping secrets from them to protect them from worry or save yourself uncomfortable explanations.
- Let them know that while you appreciate their desire to help you avoid mistakes you want to take the chance of trying out your own plans.
- Negotiate with them for new ways to discuss controversial topics.
- Help them see you as the different person you are by withdrawing from old struggles and stepping back from the typical family arguments.
- Escape the tyranny of unwritten family rules.
- Get to know them as people rather than as parents by learning to see the world through their eyes.
- Free yourself from guilt and manipulation.
- Handle sticky situations that arise during visits, holidays, or family gatherings.
- Eliminate mixed messages you may be sending them.
- Stay out of family power struggles and "no-win" games.
- Avoid being drawn into struggles or disagreements between them.
- Stop blaming them for old hurts.
- Help them without sacrificing your own life to do it.
- Decide what type of relationship you want to have with them now and what you can do to get it.
- Let them know you love them.

CHAPTER 2

Why Can't You Talk to Them the Way You Talk to Other People?

"I never discuss anything with my parents that I think will hurt them. When I have problems in my life, I don't tell them until *after* I have everything worked out. When I don't follow that rule, I regret it. For example, last summer I told them about a health problem. A week later my mother told me about how much she had worried, hadn't been able to sleep, and had had stomachaches due to concern. So, usually when I feel down or depressed or have a problem, I keep it to myself so my parents won't worry."

(Maria, age 37)

Even though you have known your parents longer than you have known anyone else on earth, and even though you have shared plenty of ups and downs with them, it may still be very difficult to tell them what is going on in your life or how you truly feel. When asked what they would most like to change about their relationships with their parents, adults tend to mention the lack of candor. Most people feel some desire to be more open and honest with their parents, but they also feel stuck in the old familiar family ways.

The Tyranny of Unwritten Family Rules

Moving toward more open communication with your parents may require changing some long-standing patterns of interaction within your family. Family systems theorists and family therapists point out that unwritten rules or unspoken agree-

18

ments usually exist among family members that prescribe how the family is to function and what is acceptable to talk about. Furthermore, families do not discuss these rules, but act as if they are unaware any rules even exist. The "forbidden" topics simply do not come up.[1]

Even though they may not talk about family rules, most adults can describe their parents' unwritten code of acceptable versus unacceptable topics. For example:

- "The · overall message is, 'Don't share any negatives.' Personal struggles and even health problems are to be endured but not discussed. My marriage almost fell apart a couple of years ago and my parents have never talked with me about it."
- "We don't cross certain lines, and we especially don't get emotional around my father. If anyone gets emotional around him, he will withdraw, and if you try to talk about it, he just withdraws more."
- "The subject of sex if forbidden. We never talked about it, even when I was a teenager. Since I'm not married, I always hide my birth control pills when I visit—not because I don't want them to know I take them, but because I don't want the subject to ever have to be brought up."
- "We can't discuss any difficulties in our communication patterns. If I bring it up, they respond in denial and insist that they are not experiencing any problem whatsoever and I am simply worrying too much about insignificant things."
- "We were raised by strict religious beliefs. It is unacceptable to talk about any contrary beliefs. If we have to, we will go so far as to lie to them about what we do or don't believe."
- "We don't talk about past conflicts. Somehow admitting that we've had these problems seems very threatening. My brother and my father haven't gotten along for years, but somehow we all just pretend not to notice."
- "We make believe we are having fun at family holiday gatherings. I don't think any of us really has a good time, but we could never say so."

Analyze Your Family Rules

If you think carefully about your interactions with your parents over the years, you will probably be able to come up with a list of the unwritten rules that govern your communication. Do any of the following unwritten rules operate in your family?

___ Never ask for help.
___ Don't raise your voice around Mother.
___ It is important to be logical.
___ Don't talk about Grandfather's (or anyone's) drinking.
___ Always defend family members over outsiders.
___ Don't talk about money.
___ Don't talk about sex.
___ Only Mom and Dad are allowed to complain.
___ Dad is always right on political issues.
___ Never admit you are afraid.
___ Don't notice when Mom and Dad fight.
___ Don't make mistakes.
___ Don't ask questions if a family member acts strangely.
___ Don't show anger.
___ Don't express affection openly.

You can probably add to this list with specific unwritten rules from your family that restrict what you can talk about and how you can express your thoughts and feelings. Just try completing the sentence: "In my family we never _____ ," or the sentence: "In my family we always _____ ."

Five Paralyzing Fears

You may want to break the rules, to be able to talk about more than the weather or your parents' latest projects, but going beyond such safe subjects seems to lead to trouble. If you feel this way, it is probably based on unpleasant experiences you have had with your parents over the years. The fears that people say stand in the way of talking more openly with their parents usually fall into one of five categories:

1. *Fear of disappointing them.*
   "I feel as though they expect so much from me that I am always on guard and cannot fully be myself. When I lost my job, they acted like I'd committed a crime. If I had it to do

over again, I would wait until I found a new job and then just tell them I had decided to switch."

2. *Fear of their anger.*
"I can't discuss my ideas on issues like religion or politics with my parents unless I want a big argument. Usually I water down my beliefs or completely avoid these subjects or just listen to them without really voicing any opinion."

3. *Fear of hurting them.*
"I don't usually tell them when I am upset because they worry so much. Once when I was having a hard time at work and I told them about it, they called me every day, worrying about all the terrible things that might happen. I felt terrible for upsetting them so much."

4. *Fear that they will reject you.*
"My mother always has to be right. If I say anything she doesn't accept, she just makes a condescending remark as if I don't know any better. I know her beliefs and I'm careful not to contradict them."

5. *Fear that they will take over.*
"Even though I am forty, my parents still see themselves as 'fixers' who are responsible for me. If I tell them about a problem I am having, they give me exact directions about how to handle it and then call back to see if I have taken their advice."

For many grown children the desire to speak more frankly with their parents is not strong enough to overcome these negative experiences from the past. It seems easier to play by their rules than to take a chance on making everything worse. But some adults are sick of being limited by the old rules and would really like to get rid of them.

How Hard Is It to Change the Rules?

Because family rules are a force for stability and predictability in the family, they are not easy to change.[2] Over the years we learn to predict the effects our comments or actions will have on our parents and we adjust our behavior to get the responses we want. Parents often react quite negatively if adult children talk about topics that are off limits or behave in forbidden ways. Even when the rules seem long out-of-date, breaking out of the established patterns can seem virtually impossible. Consider the case of Tony, age fifty-one, and his widowed mother, who is now seventy-six.

Tony: I Can't Communicate With A Stone Wall.

My parents always demanded absolute respect, honor, and deference to their authority. This means they were always right, they always knew best, and their children were not allowed to talk back, to argue a point, or to question a judgment in any circumstance.

They were always Bible fundamentalists. My mother still believes in the creation story as reflected in the book of Genesis. Once one of my children made a remark about something relating to evolution and prehistoric times, and my mother picked up on it. I knew this was forbidden territory, but I tried to update her. As far as she was concerned I was headed straight to hell and taking my children with me.

I wish I could be more open and honest with her. I'd like to be able to talk to her and feel she understands. I hate the feeling of having to "walk on eggs" around her and needing to shield my family from the possible repercussions of any implications that we don't believe everything in the Bible exactly as it was written. I also hate the way she sometimes just refuses to hear what I am saying.

My mother will not listen to anything that interferes with what she sees as our duty to her. Recently when we were having a crisis with our own teenage daughter and we needed to be available for her, I explained to my mother why I couldn't come to visit her every Sunday afternoon as she expected me to do. She simply told me, "I don't want to hear your problems. I'm old and they might upset me. I don't think there is *any reason* why you can't spend your Sundays with me."

Why Bother to Try to Change the System?

Based on these disagreeable encounters, deciding to protect himself against more of the same may seem the safest, most sensible course for Tony. Unfortunately, superficiality may not be as safe as it seems. If Tony makes the decision not to tell his mother the truth, he is also keeping her at a distance. His primary gain from this choice is avoiding unpleasantness. Even if he tells himself he is acting selflessly and considerately to save his mother from knowledge that might worry or upset her, he also knows he is protecting himself from having to deal with her reactions. When he is trying to avoid her anger, rejection, or control, he is also clearly saving himself from trouble.

His primary loss is the openness he says he wants with his mother. If Tony continues to "walk on eggs" by withholding his true thoughts and feelings from his mother, he limits the level of closeness or intimacy he can have with her. While this sort of superficial interaction is appropriate for a casual acquaintance or co-worker, it is not a good basis for the sort of relationship he says he wants with her.

If Tony really wants more open, honest communication with his mother, he will have to take more chances. To have a close personal relationship with someone, you must trust them enough to be willing to risk sharing yourself at a deeper level than may feel easily comfortable to you. Psychologist Carl Rogers once said that he had found that the elements that "cannot be shared" in a close relationship are those that are the most important and rewarding to share.[3] So, even though your parents, like Tony's mother, may have shown over the years that being open with them is a risk hardly worth taking, you might still want to look for a way to change that.

Risk Without Regrets

Our biggest fear when we contemplate taking a risk is that the outcome will be so disastrous that we will wish we had left well enough alone. The key to coping with this hesitation is not complete avoidance of risk, but rather careful calculation of a strategy that will allow you to choose your risks so as to come out with as few regrets as possible, whether you win or lose.

For example, a person who is offered an exciting new career opportunity in a different city will need to decide whether to give up present security for possible future gain. Most of us would do a reasonable amount of comparing and balancing present costs against potential future rewards. We would probably ask ourselves questions such as: "What if I'm not good at the new job? How will I know how much I'll like it if I don't try? What are my chances of success if I make the move? How much will it cost me to do it? What will my choices be if after I try it, I decide I don't like it?"

The overall question here is, "Is this risk worth taking?" That is also the question Tony and all adult children face in contemplating taking the necessary steps to communicate more openly with their parents. In answer to this question, Tony might say, "After all, my mother is seventy-six. We've lived this way for all these years. Why go through the trouble of trying to change it now?" On the other hand, he might say, "My mother is seventy-six. She probably won't be around much longer. If she dies without ever really knowing me, I'll always regret it."

As you approach the possibility of changing the way you communicate with your parents, follow three recommendations derived from the study of risk analysis:

- *Make a conscious choice*. Regrets are more likely when we do not feel that we are in charge of our actions. If Tony feels that his mother is completely in charge of their relationship, he is likely to feel hopeless about it. But if he recognizes his right to choose the way he will operate in the relationship— even if that choice is to continue the present patterns—he is likely to feel much better. Of course his choices apply *only* to himself and his communication and behavior. His mother may or may not end up changing and he cannot control that.

  Once he has made his choice, Tony will need to remind himself that he is doing what he wants to do and what he thinks is best for his circumstances. If he decides to take the risk of change, he should proceed cautiously.

- *Decide how much discomfort you can accept*. Assessing the possible hazards clarifies the level of risk involved. Tony needs to consider how much unpleasantness he is willing to tolerate to change the way he and his mother communicate. Change is almost always messy. When doing major house-cleaning or remodeling, quite a bit of upheaval and disarray is necessary before anything looks much better. We decide to put up with that for a while so the house will look better in the long run.

  Changing your style in a relationship creates mess because

the other person can no longer count on you to follow the rules, or even predict your behavior. This means that the other person will have to expend more energy interacting with you and will probably have to make some changes in his or her communication to accommodate your new style. Since you are the one initiating the change, you must remember that the other person may not want to change and may resist strenuously.

Certainly this is what Tony must expect. His mother has given *no* indication that she wants, or will even accept, a more open style of communication with him. He has already seen her reaction to his attempts to break the rules. Now he must decide whether to stay with the status quo or push forward despite the difficulties. *There is no right decision for Tony in this matter.* Only he can decide what he wants and what he is willing to risk to get it.

• *Analyze the costs versus benefits.* If Tony simply drifts along wishing for a more open, honest relationship with his mother, but not doing anything about it, or if he periodically jumps in in an unplanned way, he is not playing the odds in his favor. Any successful businessman knows the importance of deciding how much you are willing to risk, estimating the possible payoff, and plotting a strategy to maximize the odds in your favor.

To help himself analyze the level of risk involved, Tony should ask himself four important questions: 1) What could go wrong if I take this risk? 2) How likely is it that these undesirable consequences will result? 3) What benefits could come from making this change? 4) Do the possible benefits outweigh the possible costs?

Although most people cannot give clear-cut answers to the questions, going through the process of analyzing the costs and benefits clarifies the situation. You will find that you can make a more objective decision about what you want to attempt in your communication with your parents after you go through this type of reasoning. It can also be useful to actually try a more frank approach with them and then reevaluate the costs and benefits.

You may decide that the costs of change are so high that you would rather stay with the type of communication they prefer. As one forty-four-year-old woman said of her communication with her seventy-year-old mother: "I no longer try to force communication on a topic my mother doesn't want to hear. Although this certainly hasn't improved our communication, I don't feel as much anger toward her anymore. I guess I've accepted the status quo. In the past I would continue to talk about whatever she didn't want to hear and we'd end up angry at each other. This current approach isn't very satisfying, but it is more peaceful."

Or, you may find the benefits are surprisingly high as one twenty-seven-year-old woman reported: "I have had a terrific relationship with my parents since I started telling them more about how I feel. We understand one another better and can talk more openly and be more relaxed. I've found it's easier to bring out feelings and 'lay the cards on the table' rather than hold feelings in and let the stress build up. It's better for everyone in the end."

Starting on the Right Foot

If you do choose to make a change, it is important to begin this new period of honest communication from a positive position. It will not improve your relationship with your parents to dredge up old hurts, blame them for past mistakes, or try to make them apologize or admit they were wrong. While these goals may have some appeal, taking this approach is almost bound to make them angry and defensive.

If you want them to be more open, try changing the position you operate from in the family. We all fall into roles in our families, and we make our communication fit. Perhaps you are the quiet one in your family, or the rebellious one, or the baby, or the one who is in charge. Or, maybe, like Steve, you're the one who is always wrong:

Steve: They Always Liked Jason Best.
    When I was growing up, my brother Jason was always the one who did things right, and I was the one who messed up. Even though I am two years older than he is, he's always been held up to me as an example. Now that we're both in our forties, it seems like nothing much has changed.
    School never was easy for me. I had a hard time

learning to read, and it seems like everything was an uphill struggle from there. But Jason just breezed through. He never got into trouble like I did, and he was the big tennis star and got a scholarship to college and everything.

But still I did okay. I made it through high school and I got on with the post office and now I have seniority for the good routes, and I usually get Saturdays off. My wife is a legal secretary, and we both like our work. We make enough to give our kids what they need, and we own our own house, so wouldn't you think that would make my folks happy?

But they're still comparing me to Jason. He's an electrical engineer with a fancy big salary, and his wife teaches history in high school. My parents still talk about what a shame it is that I didn't go to college and how I could have done so much better if I had tried harder. See, all they can see is what *they* want for me. They have this picture of how their kids should be—like Jason, not like me.

They always pay more attention to his opinions than mine, even when we're talking about something that doesn't have anything to do with stuff he particularly knows about. Like when they were looking into the possibility of selling their house and buying a condominium for retirement. They kept asking Jason what he thought about this and what he thought about that. It's not like engineers are exactly experts on real estate. They didn't seem to care at all what I thought. I guess they figure someone who didn't go to college never will have anything worthwhile to say.

So when I'm around them I don't say much. Usually if I try to talk to them I just end up getting mad. I wish I could talk to them without worrying about how they are judging everything I say. I feel like they don't know me at all and they probably never will. I wish it could be different between us.

Giving up Old Struggles

"Mom always liked you best." The old favorite Tommy Smothers crack always brings a laugh. We find it humorous because the feeling is so universal. When we're growing up we measure it by who gets the biggest piece of cake, the best birthday present, or the most privileges. As adults, we're still counting. Do they treat one of us as more capable, more successful, more acceptable? Do they like our spouse or our children equally?

Once we get into this role, it can be very hard to let go. We see evidence everywhere to support our position. "I can tell by the look on her face that my mother still thinks my sister is better looking than I am," complains one attractive thirty-year-old woman. "My father never asks my brother if everything is going all right at work," another young woman complains. "I know he asks me that because he thinks I can't really handle my job."

Nevertheless, your best chance for moving your communication with your parents to a level of trust where you feel comfortable being honest with them is to let go of these long-standing hurts and resentments. Steve, for example, is convinced that his parents are treating him unfairly—and he may well be correct. Every time his parents compare him to Jason or take Jason's advice over his, all the old pain from childhood comes rushing back to crumple his self-esteem. But as long as he keeps focusing on trying to even the score with his brother, Steve will continue to be angry and defensive whenever he perceives a slight from his parents. He will continually be trying to prove himself and looking for acknowledgment that he has "made it." If Steve can let go of this struggle long enough to see his parents as simply two people who are confined by their own restrictive values, he can begin to see the situation differently. He can see that the issue really is not whether or not he is a success or a failure, but whether his parents can change their outlook enough to see that success comes in many forms. And, if they cannot or will not expand their views, he may be able to accept that as *their* limitation, rather than seeing it as an indictment of himself.

Once you have relinquished your stake in an enduring feud with your parents, you will feel much freer to be yourself around them. If you can assume—or pretend if necessary—that they want to know you better, but that they do not know how to change the old ways either, you can take the first step by starting off with today and letting yesterday go. You can begin to talk to them like you would to a friend, starting slowly and giving them time to get to know the person you are now.

Steve could begin by talking about his own projects, activities, and interests simply to share information. He can look for enjoyable ways to involve his parents in his family's activities, perhaps in contexts that are different from those that bring up the usual old arguments. He can put his energy into creating the new relationship he wants with them, rather than winning an old struggle.

As time goes along, he can begin to tell them more about his desire for approval from them and why this is so important to him. The next chapter will give you some specific techniques for doing that. Of course, Steve cannot predict his parents' reactions to these changes, but his new behavior will certainly improve his odds of getting the relationship he wants with them, as compared to his chances if he continues his old pattern.

Treat Them Like Adults

To develop a more open, honest relationship with your parents, you also must be willing to let them take some risks. If you are protecting them by not telling them the truth because you think they cannot handle it, you may be building unnecessary walls.

If you exclude them from your problems, such as loss of a job, illness, or financial setbacks, you will find yourself pretending more and more when you talk to them. This is especially tempting when you do not see them often. After all, why worry them when there is really nothing they can do? But when you keep a major aspect of your life secret from them, you are bound to feel nervous being around them. This adds more distance to your relationship. And, if they find out about the problem later, they will probably be upset that you did not tell them right away.

If they discover you have deceived them, they are likely to be worried and suspicious in the future that your life is not going as well as you say it is. You will hear comments like, "I know you're hiding something," or "I can tell by the look on your face that something's wrong," or, "You don't sound fine—are you sure you're okay?"

Remember that your parents are adults who are most likely more capable of handling bad news than you think they are. Most of them have been through hard times and have survived. Generally parents would rather cope with the worry of knowing about your bad times than feel excluded from important parts of your life.

Expect them to respond as a trusted friend would when you share a problem. If they overreact or begin telling you how upset *they* are about your problem, point out to them that their panic only adds to your difficulties. As one suddenly unemployed young man said to his parents, "I know I can't support two children on unemployment, but worrying about you staying awake nights stewing over my situation doesn't make my job search any easier."

Treat Yourself Like an Adult

Remember that now that you are grown they cannot control you through anger and bossiness unless you let them. Instead of hiding your problems from them to avoid their anger, blame, or advice, you can be honest but remind them that you do not want their analysis of the situation unless you ask for it. Then let them know what you do want.

One woman, whose mother responded to the news of her impending divorce with a list of all the mistakes the daughter had made that probably caused the divorce, said, "Mother, this is a difficult time for me. Even if you do think I am at fault, how do you think it will help me for you to tell me that?" Her mother was so surprised that she asked what the daughter did want her to say. The daughter said, "I guess what I really want is for you to just listen and believe that I am doing my best and that I can handle this even though it is hard." Her mother thought about it and responded with the suggestion that they walk to a nearby park where she likes to go when she has a problem to think about. That walk was the start of a new chapter in their relationship, where for the first time they were able to talk over personal problems as two adults.

Love Is Not the Same as Agreement

Overall the risk of being open can be worth the trouble and perhaps less frightening than it seems when you realize that the true prize is acknowledging the mutual love you and your parents feel for one another. What else keeps us coming back again and again, even when we feel miserable about what happens when we are together? Why else do we care so much about what they think? We love our parents and we want to know that they love us.

What we need to realize is that we can love them and they can love us even though we may disagree on everything else. We need to find ways of being together and communicating that will allow us to express and receive that love even though our parents may disapprove of many of the choices we have made in life. George, thirty-three, has finally reached that point with his sixty-nine-year-old mother and his seventy-two-year-old father.

George: Love Is Worth Working For.

In my home, growing up, I could never openly discuss my homosexuality. Once when I was a young teenager, my father at the dinner table was discussing one of his clients who had a confrontation with police officers who were trying to get into his apartment. The client yelled, "Leave me alone. You are only after me because I'm queer." My father said, "If someone had that problem, why the hell would he want anyone to know about it?"

But over the years we have grown to be pretty good friends. They have had serious health problems and seem to have become more accepting and easygoing. I have become more sure of myself and more willing to take risks and to share. I feel like we interact pretty well today, although we still do not talk about my sexual orientation.

I wish I could express to my father with words my homosexuality and my affection for my male partners. I know this is understood, and we discuss circumstances and skirt the issue often. I also wish Dad and I could look each other in the eye and verbalize "I love you."

But I love my parents and I know that they love me. Just asking them for help has changed a lot of things. It has made them more aware of difficulties I face, and when obstacles or problems are overcome, we share a sense of achievement and accomplishment. I also help them with physical chores like moving things, heavy yardwork, or snow removal. And we find things to do together to simply spend time together, like going over to their house to watch TV for a while or dropping in sometimes for a meal.

I think no matter what situation you have gone through growing up, it is worth trying to achieve a healthy relationship with your parents. It may be a long, slow process, but I think love is worth it.

PART TWO

Old Patterns and Struggles

CHAPTER 3

What Can You Say That Will Satisfy Them?

"My parents were always proud of me for doing well in school until I got to college. When I decided to go into engineering my mother was terribly upset. She kept telling me that boys don't like girls who are so smart, that I should go out more instead of studying so much, and that a career is no good if you're lonely all your life. My father, too, he'd yell at me—things like, 'If you're so smart, you should know no man wants to sleep with a genius.'"

(Gloria, age 28)

It's hard to listen when the message is that you're not measuring up to someone's expectations. When the person who is disappointed in you is a parent, the words may feel especially painful. Somehow most of us feel a stronger need to hear approving comments from our parents than from other people, yet it often seems that our parents feel more free than others to tell us how much they disapprove of our actions.

Messages of Disapproval

Do any of these remarks sound familiar?

- "You always were sloppy."
- "Don't you think it's about time you started paying more attention to the future?"
- "Why are you always so selfish? Can't you think about anyone but yourself?"

- "Your problem is that you never really take life seriously."
- "You could be so pretty if you'd just lose a few pounds and spend a little more time on your appearance."

Why do they say these things? What is the message? Do they really mean, "You should do everything my way," or "I think everything you do is wrong"? Probably not. In fact, most parents when describing their adult children to others outside the family are highly complimentary of their offspring's accomplishments.[1] So why do they seem so hard to please?

Many adults report that they feel hopeless around their parents, like they can never measure up. Somehow their parents seem to overlook everything they've done that's good, focusing instead on the problems or on what they haven't done. One woman in her mid-twenties complains that her parents continually lecture her about going to church regularly. They remind her that she was brought up going to church and that she should be going now. She says, "When they come to town they always bring church clothes and just assume that we will go to church even though I do not know anyone at the church."

Some parents seem to believe they need to "fix" certain aspects of their grown children to get their lives running smoothly. One thirty-nine-year-old woman who has returned to school to change careers after a divorce is tired of hearing her parents tell her, "If you don't lose weight, no one will hire you." She feels especially manipulated when they offer to buy her a new wardrobe or even a car if she will lose as much weight as they want her to lose.

Some parents apparently think they have the inside track on important information and that their children can never know as much. One man in his mid-thirties says that when he buys anything like an appliance or when he gets his car fixed, his father insists he made the wrong choice or paid too much. He says: "I would like my father to acknowledge that my views or positions are okay. He doesn't have to approve of everything I do, but I'm so tired of hearing about all the great tips he gets from 'Joe' or 'Bill' and why I should have done what this or that person did."

Some parents just seem to want to take over and fix up their grown children's lives. One forty-two-year-old man describes his difficulties with his parents who are in their late sixties: "I am an over-the-road driver, which they do not like because I am out on the road and away from my family so much. My father, who lives about five hundred miles away, asked me to furnish him a résumé of mine and he would contact people he knew and find me a different job."

What Do Parents Want?

What do parents want? Do they want to write a life script for each of their children to follow exactly, no surprises and certainly no slip-ups? Probably not. But on the other hand they'd clearly be delighted to have their grown-up children create life scripts on their own that meet or even exceed parental expectations. Why? Because if your life is proceeding according to your parents' expectations, they feel better in several ways:

- They don't have to worry about you and your future, because your life is on track and you're doing okay.
- They don't have to feel embarrassed when their friends and relatives ask about you. "Oh, Sally's book just won the Pulitzer prize" is so much more satisfying than "Sally's working as a waitress and writing in her spare time."
- They can feel successful as parents. After all, if you turned out just the way they wanted you to, they must have done a good job. If you didn't, it may be their fault—or other people may think it's their fault.
- They can feel that they've accomplished something extra in the world through you—especially if you're able to achieve something they always wanted to do but never managed to pull off.
- They can understand you and relate to you more easily because your goals and values are similar to theirs. They don't find themselves getting into frequent arguments with you over values, life-styles, and goals.
- They feel validated by you. After all, if you follow a life script based on their values, you are demonstrating clear approval for the people they are and the choices they've made.

Of course most parents know somewhere deep inside that their children will not follow this ideal life script. Actually,

most wouldn't even say they want this. They'll just say they
want their kids to be happy or successful or some other vague
descriptive term. And they'll say that what they want from
their grown-up kids is love and respect, certainly not obligation.[2]

Somehow, though, they forget this in daily life and slip back
into wishing for more. Parents who have lost a child to war,
accident, or illness will clearly tell you that if they could only
have that child returned, that would be all they'd ask. They
wouldn't care what choices that child made. Surely they do feel
that way, but just as surely if they really had the kid back, it
wouldn't be too long before they'd be suggesting job opportunities or ways of improving physical appearance. Ellen, for
example, feels that her parents will never be satisfied with her.

*Ellen: They Want Me to Change, But They Don't Want Me
to Change.*

Sometimes I feel like there's no way I can ever satisfy
them. I don't really even know what they want. It seems
like whatever I do is never what they want. They'd like
me to settle down—whatever that means—and show them
I'm mature and can take care of myself. Well, I can take
care of myself. I've been doing it for more than ten years
now. Just because I'm divorced and I've changed jobs a
lot they see me as somehow not taking care of myself.

They're always talking about the future. Don't I want to
have children? How can my career ever get anywhere
when I keep changing jobs? And on and on. Well, yes, I
want to have children, but I'd like to be married first. And
right now I'm not in a relationship that is ready for
marriage. My field is advertising, and it's a very up and
down sort of area. You have to switch jobs often to get
anywhere. I suppose it is unstable, but I'm supporting
only myself so I don't see the problem.

Then there's the issue of visits. Because we live
hundreds of miles apart, they want me to spend all my
vacations visiting them. It's not that I don't want to see
them—I do. But their life-style is very different from
mine, and long visits get difficult to handle. The first
couple of days are fine, but then if I want to do something
different or go somewhere new, they start with, "Why

would you want to do that?" or "I always thought you liked eating early," or whatever.

My mother has very specific ideas of the way everything should go, and she's used to planning all the family activities. My father either goes along or has some good excuse to do something else he *has* to do. But he doesn't let me get away with that. "You know how much your mother enjoys shopping with you," and so on. They seem to expect me to be the exact same person I've always been, to like to do everything just the way we always did it, and never to change at all or want anything else. Don't they realize that I spend most of my life living away from them, that I'm grown-up now, that I've changed and am still changing?

It's weird. They want me to change and grow up in some ways—like being "successful" with a career, marriage, and a family; but they don't want me to change in the way I relate to them. Now I don't think that's possible. If you change, you change. It affects who you are in your whole life.

How can you or Ellen remind your parents that your first priority has to be meeting your own expectations for yourself, rather than becoming the person they want you to be? And how can you avoid an unpleasant scene in the process?

What Do You Want?

To begin, you must be clear about what you want and what is most important to you. For example, in Ellen's case: Does she want her parents to say they don't care whether or not she has children, or does she just want them not to mention the subject? Would she be satisfied with having them acknowledge that while they personally would enjoy having grandchildren, they realize that her life is her life and that she must make her own choices? Could she accept a compromise where they agree not to discuss money with her unless she brings it up but are free to give their honest opinions if she does introduce the topic?

In any communication situation where you want to bring about some change having your goal clearly in mind is essential. Once you have decided on the modifications that will satisfy you, you can begin to plan the strategies you will use to achieve them. Ellen can begin by choosing one topic—say her career—and asking herself several questions:

- "What would I ideally like them to say to me about my career?"
- "What could they say that would satisfy me, even though it's not ideal?"
- "What do I find totally unacceptable?"

She might decide that while she would ideally like them to tell her that they are proud of her accomplishments, she would be willing to accept having them say that they understand she is struggling in a competitive field and that they support her efforts. She may conclude that she is unwilling to listen to comments that suggest that she is making inadequate progress or that her choices are frivolous or immature.

Ellen should also make sure that this topic is truly important to her and that it is her main priority at the moment. It does not work to make an issue over everything all at once. Sticking to one topic at a time will help you ask for what you want in a way your parents are most likely to find acceptable. If you spill out everything you have resented over many years, they will naturally begin to defend themselves rather than listen openly to what you have to say.

Helping Them Remember You Are Grown Up

Now you must find a way to tell your parents what you want without starting a battle or having them stalk off with injured feelings. One key is to make sure you are not feeling angry when you begin this conversation. While openly sharing feelings can create closeness, an angry attack will only make the situation worse. Don't try to have this discussion the next time they say something that you just can't tolerate. Wait until you feel calm. Choose a time and place that seems likely to allow for relaxed dialogue. Then plan what you want to say.

When you talk to them, take responsibility for what you want, rather than blaming them for their behavior. Make statements that begin with, "I want . . . ," "I feel . . . ,"

"I need . . . ," "I like . . . ," etc., rather than with, "You always . . . ," "You never . . . ," "You don't . . . ," etc. Think of the discussion as telling them something they may not realize about you, rather than accusing them of mistreating you.

Expect them to treat you as an adult. Treat them with respect, and expect the same from them. Make sure you let them know you care and that, in fact, your love for them is the main reason you want to improve your relationship with them. Be calm but firm about telling them what you want. While you should stay flexible enough to negotiate and compromise with them on areas of disagreement, you should not accept shouting or other forms of verbal abuse. If this happens, ask them calmly to stop; repeat the request if necessary. If they ignore your repeated requests, tell them you will continue the discussion some other time. Then leave the room or hang up the phone or otherwise remove yourself.

This communication style of mutual respect is one we tend to be accustomed to using in public, but not at home with the family. Changing your communication style with people with whom you have a long history is not simple. Usually it takes considerable practice. The results, however, are usually well worth the effort. To begin making such a major change, a specific set of steps to remember—such as "The Six As of Negotiating Approval"—can be very useful.

The Six A's of Negotiating Approval

Remind yourself that you are trying to change the level or type of disapproving messages you are getting from your parents. Keep in mind your goal: What you have decided will be acceptable to you, at least for now. Then try the following six negotiating steps:

- *Acknowledge their desires.* Everyone likes to know they have been heard. If you immediately resist your parents' suggestions, they may feel that you are simply not listening very well to their point of view. So they keep on repeating the suggestions. But if you stop and acknowledge their point of view even though you may not agree with it, they at least know you understand what they want. Ellen might say, "I know you really want me to have children. I'm sure you're looking forward to having grandchildren. You must find it very frustrating that I'm still not even planning to have children."

- *Assert your own preferences*. The next step is to make clear to them that what they want is not necessarily what you want. It helps if you also let them know you have thought about the issue and you have your own reasons for the choices you are making. Ellen might say, "I would like to have children but only when I feel like I'm in a stable marriage and ready to give them the support I think they need. So far in my life, I just haven't felt prepared for children."

- *Ask them if they really disapprove*. They may not realize how judgmental their comments seem to you. If you can calmly let them know how you feel when they criticize you, they may back off. Ellen might say, "You often ask me whether I want children, and you point out your friends who have grandchildren, and you tell me that at my age I need to start thinking about a family. When I hear these comments, I feel that you really disapprove of me because I don't have children. Do you basically see me as a failure because I'm not married with a family?"

- *Answer by letting them know how much their approval means to you*. If Ellen's parents respond to her question by telling her that they do not disapprove of her and do not mean to imply disapproval, Ellen can tell them how glad she is to hear that and how much she values their approval. If, however, they make comments like, "We just cannot understand why you're living the way you do," or "Sometimes we wonder if you'll ever settle down," Ellen will need to explain that she feels rejected when she hears these remarks. She might say, "When you say that, I feel that you don't accept me as I am. That's hard for me because I love you and what you think of me truly makes a difference."

- *Accept their positive intentions*. Although it is always tempting to try to change the other person, that's not an outcome you can count on. What you are working on here is letting them know how you see the situation and checking out what is going on to see whether or not you are accurately interpreting their messages. So, if they respond by telling you that they do not mean to be giving messages as harshly negative as you are hearing, you must take them at their word. They need acceptance, too. Once you have established what they are intending to communicate, you can work on changing the form of the message. Ellen might say, "I feel much better now that I know you don't see me as a failure just because I don't have children. I hope we can find a different way of talking about this subject in the future."

• *Agree on a new way of interacting on this topic.* Because this is your negotiation, you need to propose a solution. Make sure the solution offers some benefit to them as well as to you. Don't be locked in to this one outcome though; they need space to offer alternatives. Ellen might say, "I would feel much better if you would not discuss my having children in the future unless I bring it up. Could you accept that if I promise to let you know whenever my plans or feelings about having children change?" If they agree, she might also ask, "Do you mind if I remind you about this agreement, if you forget and bring up the subject later?" If they do not agree to this proposal, she needs to explore other solutions with them until they find one they can all accept. She could ask them to suggest some possibilities or ask them what they would recommend if they were in her shoes.

Changing Your Reactions to Criticism

What if you find yourself feeling so angry and disgusted at the continual barrage of criticism that you hardly know where to start negotiating? Consider the case of Keith:

Keith: I Hate His Criticism.

My father criticizes everything I do and say! I really mean everything. I remember once right after I got my answering machine, he called and left a message criticizing my message. "Keith, we're wasting money on a long-distance call listening to this silly message," my Dad complained. "What if someone was calling you about something really serious? How would they feel listening to this idiotic rambling?"

Can't he understand that I'm twenty-five years old and my life isn't deadly serious all the time? Just about every

time I talk to him, I end up getting mad. Then he criticizes
me for losing my temper.

Keith should first consider how he deals with criticism in
general. When people outside his family find fault with him,
does he lose his temper the way he says he does with his father?
Maybe if a friend had criticized his answering machine
message, Keith could have laughed and said, "He just has no
sense of humor," and let it go without feeling angry. By
looking at his reactions to critical comments from friends,
acquaintances, employers, or co-workers, Keith can decide
whether he needs to work on the way he copes with criticism
overall, or only on his reactions to parental criticism.

Certainly criticism can hurt. Ideally we can learn to examine
a critical message to decide whether it contains any useful
information. In the process, we should remind ourselves that
the comments are simply one person's point of view, and are
not necessarily an accurate picture of us or our behavior.

Unfortunately, criticism usually has the effect of bringing up
old negative feelings and self-doubts. Most people feel at least
some inadequacies—maybe about their physical appearance,
or their abilities and accomplishments, or their social life or
sexuality. If these feelings of inadequacy come flooding over
you whenever someone criticizes you, you probably will
respond with an angry attack on that person or with destructive
self-blame.

If Keith discovers that he has these difficulties in dealing
with criticism in general, he can work on reminding himself to
look for the specific message the person is giving him, rather
than hearing a global indictment of himself. For example, his
boss may want Keith to change a couple of his work habits, but
that does not necessarily mean he thinks Keith is incompetent.
Keeping a list of his accomplishments and of situations he feels
he handled well can help Keith restrain his self-doubts so that
critical comments don't leave him feeling personally dimin-
ished.

If Keith's strong reaction to criticism occurs mainly when
that criticism comes from his father, he must find a way to tell
his father that he needs love and approval, not continual
criticism and that he is no longer willing to accept his father's
tirades. Working through the steps of the "Six A's of Negoti-

ating Approval," Keith could begin by acknowledging his father's wish to have him be more serious and responsible, yet asserting his own desire to find enjoyment in life in his own way. When he tells his father how much he needs love and approval from him, Keith will need to be careful to avoid making statements that sound like blame.

He may need to remind his father often that the criticism is not helping him and that he feels hurt by these negative remarks. He will probably also need to practice not getting riled up over every critical comment, since defensiveness only adds fuel to the conflict. While it would be unrealistic to expect Keith's father to change dramatically overnight, their relationship will certainly improve if Keith continues his new way of responding. Even if his father never changes at all, Keith will feel better if he can learn to see the constant criticism as simply his father's bad habit, rather than as something he must react to and defend against.

Will Your Parents Change?

No one knows the answer to this question, not even your parents. Criticizing their children gets to be a habit for most parents, maybe because they're trying so hard to get their children to do what they think is best or because they want their children to avoid their mistakes. Habits are hard to change; consider what people go through to give up smoking or to change their eating habits. Change takes time and patience; relapses are common.

Furthermore, change requires motivation on the part of the person doing the changing. That means you cannot change your parents, they must change themselves. Of course by changing yourself and your reactions you can create a situation in which they want to change.

In a more encouraging vein, you may find that your parents don't need to change as much as you thought in order for you to feel quite differently. Just getting a few clear messages of approval from them may be enough to counteract a great deal of criticism. Consider the case of Marie.

Marie: I Just Needed to Hear Her Say She Was Proud.
    I came here alone from France when I was only

nineteen. I stayed with some cousins for a while and started going to college part-time. In about a year I got married to an American student, and we both worked to earn our way through school. Our son was born during my junior year, and it took me another two years to graduate after that. It was a real struggle, but I graduated with high grades and was considered one of the most promising students in my department.

My mother came over for my graduation. I was so excited to see her and have her share my happiness. But when she got here all she could talk about was how I should be spending more time with my son, how he was too young to be spending so much time with a sitter, and how I was missing out on so many of the joys of motherhood.

It all came to a head on the night of graduation when we were getting ready to take some pictures of me in my cap and gown. She made one more comment about my son, and I felt so frustrated that I turned to her and said, "Aren't you proud of me at all? Here I have a good marriage, I've done well in college in a foreign country, and I have a child who is healthy and happy. I thought you would be proud, but all you do is criticize."

To my surprise, she said of course she was proud and that she thought I knew that. She said she realized that my life was very different from hers and that it took some getting used to for her, but that she was very happy that I seemed to be doing so well. She said she hadn't realized that she was criticizing me so much.

The whole visit was different after that. I was able to talk to her about my concerns about having enough time for both my work and my family, and she understood. I'm so glad I told her that I needed her approval. If I hadn't said anything, she would have gone home assuming I knew how she felt, and I would have kept on feeling like I had let her down.

What If They Will Not Change?

Obviously not all parents will respond as Marie's mother did. Some will insist on clinging stubbornly to their attempts to change their grown children. These parents may be unwilling to give any messages of approval, even when you let them know that this is important to you.

The key at this point is to realize that their critical attitudes are lifelong habits that say much more about their way of looking at the world than about your worth as a person. They have developed the unfortunate habit of focusing on the negative, of constantly finding flaws that disturb or disappoint them. And, even worse, they feel compelled to point out any imperfections they find in others, somehow convinced that notifying people of their deficiencies will be good for them.

If your parents are so set on improving you or making you fit the mold they have selected for you that they cannot understand that their comments are crushing you, you will have to find ways to deflect their blows. If you cannot get any satisfaction from talking to them about the way you feel about their criticism, you will have to talk to yourself instead. Neil, for example, reminds himself of his accomplishments when his father berates him.

Neil: I Let His Judgments Fly Over My Shoulder.

My father is very authoritative and controlling. He thought I should be a pharmacist so I could always find a job. He barely tolerated my study of physical education. He has told me many times, "We wanted you to study something useful, but you insisted on physical education."

He thinks I should buy a house instead of renting, so he sends me articles about buying houses. He also sends me articles about what to buy or not to buy and how to manage and invest my money. Then he calls me later to see if I have followed the recommendations.

It really annoys him that I don't live the life he thinks I should lead. He tells me, "The difference between you and your sister is that she pays attention to what I have to say. You just ignore me and do exactly what *you* want to do."

I have tried to change his attitude by telling him that I want to make my own decisions and that I would like him to stop criticizing me and treat me as a capable adult. But he can't see it. So I have stopped expecting him to change.

Now I just basically ignore most of it. My wife suggested that I just let his judgments fly over my shoulder instead of buying in to them. So that is what I do now.

I remind myself that I have a job I like and a happy marriage. Even though we are not rich, we enjoy where we live and we have the life-style we want. The kids I teach like me and enjoy my classes, which to me is success. My wife and I have time for a lot of outdoor activity, which keeps us healthy and which we enjoy. So my father's ideas for how I should live are his problem, not mine. I like the way I live.

So the final word on how you can satisfy your parents is that you are not required to satisfy them. Once you are grown up, your primary concern must be making your own choices. Ideally, you can help them see that by working through the "Six A's of Negotiating Approval." But if not, you, like Neil, must learn to find that approval from other people and within yourself.

CHAPTER 4

Why Do You Keep Having the Same Arguments?

MOM: "Where have you been? Do you know what time it is?"

DAVE: "Of course I know what time it is. It's nine o'clock. I told you we wouldn't get here until after dinner."

MOM: "We had dinner hours ago. I had visions of you splattered all over the highway."

DAVE: "Why do you have to worry over nothing all the time? Why don't you wait until something really happens to start worrying?"

MOM: "All I'm asking for is a little common courtesy. You could have called to say you'd be late."

DAVE: "If I had called, you would have argued with me on the phone about why we didn't start earlier. You always have something to complain about."

MOM: "That's enough! I'm your mother and I don't have to listen to this kind of talk."

There they go again! When you find yourself caught up in an old familiar argument, you may feel like you are trapped in a barrel going over a waterfall with no way to avoid the crash. You know what is coming, you want to escape, but you do not see a possible way out. Why do these same fights keep cropping up with parents?

Feeling Stuck

Communication researchers at the University of Massachusetts have studied repetitive arguments, which they call "undesired repetitive patterns," and found them to be universal experiences. The fights consist of a particular sequence of comments that keep coming up between two specific people. Although the content of the arguments may vary, the pattern is stable and the outcome is predictable.[1]

When we are caught up in one of these recurrent disputes, we seem to operate as if we were following an internal code or rule book that tells us what sort of statement must follow a particular type of comment by the other person. We respond almost automatically, without consideration of the consequences, even though we know the outcome will be negative. The overwhelming feeling during the exchange is of being out of control.

Clearly the end result of Dave's argument with his mother is not the outcome he would have ideally chosen. Why drive to visit her only to end up in an argument the minute he arrived? If you asked him, Dave would probably say something like, "I couldn't help it. My mother drives me crazy sometimes. She always finds something to worry or complain about." If you probed further, you would probably find that although Dave does not see many choices of how to respond to his mother in these conversations, he hates having this locked-in feeling. And if you asked Mom how she felt, you would find that she also perceived herself as having been trapped in an unwanted exchange.

Thus, we begin to see that neither person deserves all the blame for a repetitive argument or angry debate. The problem is that they are both responding automatically, as they feel they must respond, rather than choosing a more thoughtful reply that is likely to stop the merry-go-round before it is too late. They each see the other's behavior as being the cause of their own conduct, and they each believe that their remarks express aspects of their personalities that are virtually impossible to change.

Specifically, in Dave and Mom's argument, Mom acts as if she were following these rules:

- "If Dave doesn't put my concerns ahead of his own, I have to complain."
- "If he doesn't seem contrite, I must keep telling him how inconsiderate he is until he shows he is sorry."
- "If he attacks me, I can terminate the discussion because I am his mother and he should show me respect at all times."

Dave, on the other hand, seems to be following another set of rules:

- "If Mom confronts me, I must defend myself to prove I am not in error."
- "If Mom accuses me of causing her worry, I must show her that she causes her own worry."
- "If Mom keeps criticizing me, I must keep arguing to prove I am right."

The rules you apply in choosing your responses in an argument with your parent depend on your interpretation of the parent's comment, which is influenced by your evaluation of your parent, your shared history, and your assessment of the specific situation.[2] Because we each construct our own set of rules, your parent will probably be operating according to a different set of rules. The pattern of your communication with your parent will be a product of each individual internal set of rules and of the way these rules mesh together.

Five Themes of Recurrent Arguments With Parents

Most adults can easily generate a list of familiar arguments with their parents, in which the topic may vary but the theme stays the same. Here are five especially common ones:

1. *You'd be better off today.* In this scenario the parent's theme is, "You should take my advice and I can prove that by showing how much better off you would be today if you had followed my advice in the past." The grown child counters with, "I can make my own decisions, the past has nothing to do with today, and you don't remember it the way it really was." For example:

MOTHER: "You should dress up more for work if you want anyone to take you seriously."

DAUGHTER: "How do you know they don't take me seriously?"

MOTHER: "You never did know how to pick the right clothes. I still remember that time you got sent home from high school because of some stupid outfit you wore. I told you not to wear it, but you never listen to me."

DAUGHTER: "I don't know why you always bring that up. It was a long time ago and anyway it was a protest so it has nothing to do with today."

MOTHER: "And what about the time you didn't get that summer office job when you went to the interview in that short skirt. I warned you, but you didn't pay any attention."

DAUGHTER: "I didn't get that job because I couldn't type well enough, as I told you at the time. Why do you always think you know more than I do about *my* life?"

2. *Think what I tell you to think.* Here the parent's message is, "You should share my values and agree with my opinions, and your life-style should show that you do. If you don't do this you are showing me disrespect and implying that I don't know anything." The grown child comes back with, "I've heard all this before and it never made sense. Your ideas are narrow-minded and out-of-date and you have no understanding of what my life is like." For example:

MOTHER: "I just don't understand how you can miss church on Sunday. Doesn't your conscience bother you?"

SON: "I have my own spiritual beliefs. I just don't believe that salvation hinges on being in a church on Sunday. I think the way I live and treat people is more important— not like some of the hypocrites who show up for church but don't care what they do the rest of the week."

MOTHER: "That's certainly not how you were brought up. You know we always went to church. Now people probably think your parents didn't teach you anything."

SON: "They don't think anything about it at all. They don't even notice. Most people I know don't go to church either."

MOTHER: "That's probably why you've gotten away from going to church, then. Maybe you should find some new friends."

3. *Prove you care.* In this argument, the parent is saying, "Because I am your parent you should always take my side and give me priority over your spouse - boyfriend - girlfriend - etc." The adult child responds with, "You always try to cause trouble between me and someone I am close to. You just want to keep me a child forever." For example:

FATHER: "Why didn't you call me on Sunday? I waited all day for you to call."

DAUGHTER: "Why were you waiting all day? I told you I was going to help Mark work on his neighborhood recycling project."

FATHER: "I thought surely you could find a few minutes for a phone call. I guess Mark is more important to you than your parents."

DAUGHTER: "That's ridiculous! I had a commitment and I even told you about it in advance. It has nothing to do with who is more important. Why do you always make everything a contest?"

FATHER: "All I'm asking is that you call us on Sundays. Is that too much to expect? It's not as if I'm asking for a lot of your precious time."

4. *I know best.* Here the parent says, "I've lived a lot longer than you, and I know what the world is like, so my ideas count more than yours do. You can't tell me anything I don't already know." The grown child argues back with, "You don't know as much as you think you do, and I can prove it by showing how you've been wrong in the past." For example:

FATHER: "You should buy an American car. Those foreign cars you always buy cost a fortune to get fixed."

SON: "What are you talking about? I still remember that Chrysler you had that practically ate you alive in repair bills."

FATHER: "That Chrysler was a great car. I seem to remember you liked driving it pretty well when you were in high school."

SON: "Well, you remember wrong. I drove it because it was all I had to drive then, but I'd sure rather have the car I have now. Anyway, you've never even owned a foreign car, so how can you compare?"

FATHER: "I was buying cars before you were born, so don't tell me what I know."

5. *When you get to be my age.* The parent says, "Your problems and concerns are trivial compared to what I've been through. When you get to be my age, you'll realize that what looks important to you now turns out to be insignificant." The adult child responds, "You never really listen to me or take me seriously. You only care about yourself." For example:

MOTHER: "You should call your brother and work things out with him. Someday you'll regret these hard feelings between you."

DAUGHTER: "You know he drinks too much, and every time I see him we get into a fight. I don't want to talk to him."

MOTHER: "When you get to be my age you'll realize how important family is. You can forgive a few mistakes to keep family together."

DAUGHTER: "I'm not talking about mistakes. He is impossible to be around. You want me to call him only so you can pretend it's all okay. You don't care how I feel about it."

MOTHER: I've put up with a lot more than a few drinks with my family over the years. You don't realize how lucky you are sometimes."

As you read these examples, you may notice that at least one of them sounds particularly familiar. Perhaps one or more of them resembles a conflict that hooks you in with one of your parents. Other situations may come to mind that also fit the pattern. Even though you might have thought that you do not have conversations with your parents in which you are out of control, you may discover that in some situations you do respond automatically in a way that escalates the conflict.

Do These Arguments Serve a Purpose?

You may have noticed that an underlying theme of all these conflicts is, "I'm right, you're wrong." Why do parents and their adult children keep trying to prove that to one another when the chance of succeeding is so slim?

Social pyschologists have proposed that people strive to maintain a state of balance in their relationships with their friends and loved ones.[3] For example, if I like you and you like me but we disagree on the issue of abortion, we will each try to influence the other to change in the direction of our own opinion in order to relieve this tension between us. Similarly, if we each like each other, but you like Sandra and I dislike Sandra, we will again feel imbalance. Too little balance between us will probably lead one or both of us to restore balance by deciding that we do not like the other after all. So we may no longer be friends or even see each other.

In the case of our parents, however, our options are more limited. Most adults do not want to stop seeing or talking to their parents, nor do parents want to give up contact with their children. So imbalanced situations must be resolved *within* the relationship or severe tension may result.

For example, if you and your parent disagree about how to budget money, you will probably each feel a need to convince the other that your way is right. If you still cannot agree, you may resolve your feelings of imbalance by deciding that it is acceptable and natural for parents and their children to disagree about spending money. Your parent, however, may still believe that parents and their children should agree about spending. So he or she continues to raise the subject. Now, you may find yourselves each trying to change the other's beliefs about the importance of agreement between parents and children on the issue of spending.

A related theory from social psychology that also explains some of these arguments is the idea that people dislike feeling inconsistent.[4] For example, if I think of myself as the sort of person who will not take on a disagreeable job just because it pays well, but I find myself with a disagreeable well-paying job, I feel a sense of inner conflict. I can resolve it by leaving the job, by changing my views about myself, or by deciding that the job really is not so disagreeable. Probably I will take the latter path because it is the easiest.

Parents may feel inconsistency when they believe that good parents teach their children proper values about spending money, they believe that they have been good parents, and yet their adult children do not accept or follow their parents' ideas about spending. If the parents decide that the easiest way to resolve their inner conflict would be to convince their children to change, the subject will keep coming up between them.

So this strain toward symmetry in relationships can create a situation between parents and adult children in which it is difficult to let some struggles go. Furthermore, both parents and adult children generally have groups of friends who agree with their positions and support them in trying to prove one another wrong.

How Do the Arguments Begin and End?

Because we are accustomed to thinking in linear terms, we tend to look for causes and results. Yet, family therapists point out that in family interactions, there is no obvious beginning or end to a communication sequence.[5] Thus it is never clear who bears responsibility for continuing a quarrel.

When you are involved in an argument, you usually see your statements as responses to the other person. But that person probably sees you as the cause. Actually, the problem is the interaction between you both, which is not solving the difficulty and may even be increasing it. Unfortunately, neither of you may be able to see other choices for responding.

To have conflict, at least two people must participate. Although an argument may start with a verbal attack, it is not a true conflict until the attack is followed by a counterattack.

Unfortunately, when one family member attacks another, the attacked member usually responds with a counterattack, says sociologist Samuel Vuchinich who has conducted extensive studies of family arguments.[6] He and his colleagues videotaped dinner conversations in 52 typical families to study the types of disputes that occurred. In analyzing the tapes, he looked first for instances where one person opposed or attacked another directly by disagreeing, insulting, correcting, or challenging the other. He found that while some initial attacks were ignored or accepted, most led to conflict.

And family members tend not to work through their differences in these arguments. Of the more than 200 conflicts that Vuchinich and his colleagues identified on their tapes of family dinners, fewer than one-tenth were resolved through compromise. Two out of three of the conflicts ended in a standoff, where the arguers dropped the dispute without resolving it. The remainder ended with one person withdrawing or with one giving in to another. If this is typical of family arguments, it is not surprising that so many conflicts appear over and over again.

Playing Our Parts During Conflict

One reason that conflicts do not get resolved, especially in families, is that we each tend to slip into our own characteristic communication styles once an argument gets going. These styles control the form the debate will take and usually the outcome as well. Unfortunately, the styles do not usually promote a mutually satisfying resolution of the disagreement because the people involved are not working together to resolve the issue. Rather, as Marsha describes, they are playing their parts.

Marsha: I'll Never Forget the Nightly Shoot-out.

For as long as I can remember, my parents have been vying for control. My father blames, accuses, evaluates, gives orders, and puts everyone down. My mother, who is more passive, complains, makes excuses, changes the subject, or refuses to answer. They fought frequently while we were growing up, my father yelling, my mother pouting and sometimes going for days in silence.

Because my mother chose to play the martyr, I chose to be her protector and took up the gauntlet of arguing with my father. If my father began cutting down my mother, I took him on, drawing his anger away from mother to myself. If she wouldn't stand up to him, I would.

My younger brother was, and still is, very sensitive. He always tried hard to please and frequently found himself being criticized by my father. Usually I took up his battle as well. I'll never forget the nightly shoot-out at the family dinner table. The four of us would sit down to eat, my brother or father would say something, and they would begin to argue. My mother would try to change the subject, I would defend my brother, and eventually there would be a blowup, with the dinner ending in silence.

Even though it has been more than twelve years since either my brother or I lived at home, it's not much different today when we're all four together. As soon as any disagreement comes up, we're each playing our parts just like we always did. Sometimes I can stay out of it if I sense an argument brewing and remember to back off, but it is always tempting to jump in like I'm used to doing.

Common Communication Styles That Perpetuate Family Arguments

When we see family conflicts portrayed in movies or television programs, the interactions often have a familiar ring. The reason arguments in fictional families seem real and recognizable is that some communication patterns seem to be almost universal when people are quarreling. Family therapist Virginia Satir's classification of these communication styles has become a classic explanation of the process. She says people tend to adopt one of four styles during a stressful argument[7]:

- *Placator*. The placator tries to please, agrees with whatever anyone else wants, and tries to keep everyone happy. This person is the martyr who apologizes and takes responsibility for whatever goes wrong.
- *Blamer*. The blamer finds fault, disagrees, dictates, and

never takes responsibility for problems. Whatever goes
wrong is always someone else's fault.
• *Computer*. The computer is reasonable, calm, and collected.
This person chooses words carefully, does not show feelings,
or react to others.
• *Distracter*. The distracter makes irrelevant comments, ignores the point of the discussion, does not answer others'
questions, and tries to change the subject.

Certainly these communication styles are not the only ones
a person can use during conflict. We use these and similar
styles to try to protect ourselves when we fear that we might
make a mistake, be rejected, be criticized, hurt someone's
feelings, or destroy a relationship. They are methods of saying
what we think will bring about the outcome we want, rather
than saying what we really feel or believe. For example, in
Marsha's family people criticize, apologize, or bring up new
topics because that is the part they play in family arguments.
They do not feel free to communicate in a way that is real for
the specific moment and issue. Father has trouble apologizing,
Mother is afraid to directly criticize, and Marsha has extreme
difficulty staying out of the argument, even when the issue
does not actually involve her.

These habits are hard to break. We may be able to avoid a
familiar pattern when we are feeling relaxed and secure, but
when we are tired, stressed, or threatened, we revert back.
Furthermore, the styles family members use tend to feed into
one another. For example, a blamer and a placator like
Marsha's parents can go on for years.

Probably you and your parents have been following particular patterns in your arguments for a long time. Your styles
may not correspond exactly with one of the types described
here, but if you think back to one or two especially upsetting
arguments between you and a parent, you will very likely
recognize predictable types of sequences that keep the conflict
going.

Changing the Arguments

All this is not to say that the situation is hopeless. Certainly
some conflict is inevitable in any close relationship. This is

especially true when the people are involved with one another over a long time or a wide variety of situations, and when each person in the relationship wants and expects support from the other. It would be unrealistic to believe that each person could always meet the other's expectations or that two people would continually agree. You must expect some disagreements to arise between you and your parents.

The goal is not to avoid conflict but rather to find ways of resolving it so that the relationship gets stronger rather than weaker. If a conflict is ignored or repeatedly allowed to end with explosion or withdrawal rather than resolution, feelings of anger, resentment, and distrust continue to build up between the people involved. This puts the relationship on a negative track that becomes increasingly difficult to reverse.

Five Steps Toward Resolving Conflict

Ideally, conflict should open up communication between people so that they begin to explore new and better ways of managing their differences. The result should be a situation where nobody loses, even though no one wins the whole battle. Fortunately, when we move away from searching for who is at fault in an ongoing struggle and begin to look for ways we can improve the situation, alternatives appear.

To begin, you must believe change is possible. You know that it is, because you can change your behavior and that will change the entire situation. If you do not play your usual part, the conflict cannot take its usual course. Of course, you cannot change your parents' behavior in any predictable way, but if you truly want better communication more than you want to win arguments, you are starting off on the right foot.

Next you must make some changes—possibly major ones—in your own communication. Most people find that the five steps below help them deal much more positively with conflict.

- *Stay Calm*. The more tired, stressed, or rushed you are, the more likely you are to get hooked in to an argument especially by someone you are vulnerable to and who knows where you are touchy—like a parent. If you have a history of conflict with one or both parents, it will be worth your while to do whatever you can to feel calm and relaxed when you are going to spend time with them or talk to them on the phone. If you try to squeeze in a quick phone call to Mom between a hard day at work and an evening meeting, you may have a hard time overlooking any comment she makes that strikes you the wrong way.

For example, Dave, in the example at the beginning of this chapter, may have had hassles at work, a tiring drive in traffic, and an argument with his wife before he ever got to his mother's house. This left him ripe for reacting angrily to his mother. If he had taken time off so that he could have left earlier in the day, or perhaps waited until the next morning when he was rested for the drive, or coped with some of his job and personal stress by exercising at noon, he probably would have been less easily caught up in the argument.

• *Think Before You React.* When you react to an attack, or what you perceive as an attack, by defending yourself or counterattacking, your response tends to cement your position and the other person's, too. When Dave responded to his mother's charges by asking, "Why do you have to worry all the time?" he jumped right in to one of their usual arguments where she accuses and he denies any problem. Then he and his mother were stuck in an argument over who was right, which obviously neither of them would win. Alternatively, he could have acknowledged her concern by saying something like, "It sounds like you were really worried."

We often feel reluctant to respond to an attack this way, because we feel that we are letting the other person win. But if what Dave wants is a pleasant evening, he wins if he does not rise to the bait and get into an angry argument with his mother. He does not necessarily need to apologize or say that he is wrong in order to defuse the fight; he just needs to step back and think about what he really wants to say.

• *Ask for Clarification.* When you find yourself caught up in an old argument, you may find that you are not actually clear as to what you are arguing about. One way to explore the real issue while at the same time avoiding some of your usual response patterns is to ask questions. The questions should be designed to gather information, however, not as simply another counterattack. For example, Dave's question, "Why don't you wait until something really happens to start worrying?" is clearly an attack. If he wanted information, he might have asked, "When did you start worrying?" or, "Was there any particular reason that you were especially worried this time?" or, "About what time did you think we would get here?" He might also check to see whether something else is going on by asking his mother if she is angry with him about something else, or upset about something not even involving him, or not feeling well, or so on.

By moving away from his usual response of pigeonholing his mother as a hopeless worrier and complainer, Dave could move toward freeing himself from his automatic reactions to her remarks. By finding out more about her worrying behavior, at least in regard to his travel, he may be able to discuss this issue with her later in a manner that leads them to a way of preventing this conflict the next time he visits.

• *Look for Resolution, not Victory.* Fighting and problem solving are not identical processes. When we fight verbally, we tend to use threats, name-calling, extreme statements, accusations of past wrongdoing, and any other tactics we can think of that seem to give us the upper hand. We choose such strategies because we want to defeat the other person, not because we think the tactics will help us resolve the issue. Dave, for example, accuses his mother with the extreme statement, "You always have something to complain about." Such a remark leaves little likelihood of a positive resolution of the problem.

If Dave truly wants to change his communication with his mother, he should try to engage her in exploring solutions. To do this, he needs to take responsibility for his own feelings, thoughts, and actions, rather than blaming her. For example, he might say, "Mom, I feel upset that we argue so much when I visit, but I'm not sure how to change that. Could we talk about it?" If she responds with accusations like, "Of course we argue when you're so inconsiderate," he can reply calmly in a way that keeps the discussion on track. He might say, "I would really like to find a way to arrange a visit where we don't have this argument. Do you have any suggestions?"

• *Be Flexible.* Mediators know that neither side in a dispute is going to get everything they want. But that idea is so difficult to accept, especially when you are upset, that it can be hard to listen to any alternatives to your position.

If you insist on only one solution, you leave yourself no room to negotiate. If you are open to at least considering other possibilities, the chances of a positive outcome are much greater. Sometimes a proposal that initially sounds unacceptable turns out to be more workable than you had thought it would be.

Dave may think that giving his mother a general time range for his arrival and expecting her not to worry or complain unless he deviates drastically from that time is the only way he can operate. He might find, however, that he could agree to give her the latest time he expects to arrive, with assurances that he will call if he will be later than that. If he were willing to make that agreement, she might promise that she would not complain about the actual time he plans to arrive and that she would be understanding about unforeseen delays. If she could do that, Dave might promise to make more of an effort to be realistic about his schedule so that his estimates would more accurately predict his arrival.

If Dave does decide to use these steps to resolve his conflicts with his mother, he will soon begin to feel more in control of his own responses when the two of them disagree. Even if his mother does not change, Dave can use these techniques to free himself from getting continually trapped in to those same old arguments.

CHAPTER 5

Are You and Your Parents Speaking the Same Language?

"When I told my mother I was getting a divorce, she was very upset. I tried to explain the situation to her and tell her about how unhappy I had been and why. She got a sad look on her face and began to cry, but all the concern she expressed was about my children and how sorry she felt for them. She did not even want to hear how bad the situation had been for me while I was married, or to entertain the notion that maybe my life would get better after I divorced. She operates from an old rule that says divorce is wrong and the divorced will go to hell."

(Maxine, age 43)

Many adults complain that they find it difficult or impossible to make as much contact with their parents as they would like, especially on important issues. They report many frustrations and disappointments in their attempts to have "grown-up" talks with their parents. Conversations rarely seem to go beyond gossip, empty talk, or predictable exchanges. These adults say that attempts to engage their parents in more meaningful discussions fail because their parents interrupt, change the subject, or refuse to acknowledge a problem or conflict.

Do Parents Really Want to Hear?

Based on their parents' responses, some adult children assume that their parents do not really want to hear what they have to say. Instead of paying attention to what their grown children are trying to say to them, these parents respond in one of several disappointing ways.

- *They want to talk only about themselves.* Betty complains that her mother seems to have no interest at all in hearing about Betty's life. "When I'm talking about my life, my mother will immediately begin discussing her own feelings or experiences, without addressing my concerns. She turns everything into a conversation about herself, her life, her friends. She loves to babble on, telling me in detail about all our relatives, people I used to know, and people I never knew."

- *They tell stories.* Jim is frustrated because his father seems to use whatever Jim says as a lead into one of his stories. "He never lets me finish a conversation or a statement without interruption," Jim says. "He always breaks in with, 'That reminds me of the time . . . ' and then he's off telling one of the same old stories again. He knows we've heard them all before, but that doesn't seem to matter to him one bit."

- *They hear only what they want to hear.* Janelle complains that her mother denies any problems in her own life and refuses to hear about anything negative in Janelle's life either. "My mother will not accept that I have my own feelings and emotions. If I say 'I have a headache,' she will say, 'No, you don't.' If I say, 'I had a bad day,' she says, 'It couldn't have been that bad.' When I tried to talk to her about some problems my husband and I were having in our marriage, she said, 'No one in our family has ever gotten a divorce.' Then she just left the room. We never talked about it again."

- *They already know everything.* Stan describes his interactions with his parents as almost always one-sided. "My parents make up their minds on matters based on very little information, and then they refuse to listen to any other view. My dad likes to tell me why the world is going down the tubes and how nothing will ever be as good as it used to be. My mom goes on about how children are growing up too fast today and know too much about sex. If I say anything that implies that I do not accept their outlook, they are offended that what they believe is being challenged."

- *They're too busy.* Matthew has a hard time getting and

keeping his parents' attention. "They always seem to be reading the paper, watching TV, or doing some task around the house when I'm talking to them. They'll never just stop and listen. Or when I am trying to tell them something, they interrupt and try to help me finish the story by guessing the answer. Then I lose track of my thoughts. I don't see why they can't take a few minutes to just listen to me."

Is It Hopeless?

These grown children are disappointed that their parents do not seem to want to hear about them. And they are exasperated that it seems impossible to engage their parents in an interesting conversation. So gradually the adult children tune out their parents, too, which compounds the difficulties between them.

When this happens between you and your parents, you feel hurt because you really do want to make contact with them. You want them to acknowledge you as an adult, to see you as a valuable and interesting person, and to care about your concerns. But you probably think to yourself, "What's the use? They'll never change."

The situation is rarely that hopeless, however. If you can begin to develop an understanding of why they respond the way they do, you can usually find approaches that ward off their irritating reactions.

For example, parents who continually talk about themselves, their activities, and their friends may need more acknowledgment from you that their interests and concerns are important. Nodding and occasionally saying "uh huh" will probably not do it. Look for an interesting aspect and respond with a comment that shows you have some idea of the importance of the issues in their lives. If their conversation is primarily a litany of complaints, you might also try a question that could divert it into a more positive direction. For example, you might say, "It must be difficult having the neighborhood change so much after all these years. Is there anything you like better about it now?"

Some of their annoying responses are simply old habits. To break out of these ruts you need to find a way to change the context so as to break the routine. If you are stuck listening to stories you have heard over and over again, you can try deflecting the storyteller with a question that changes the path, such as, "Wasn't that the time you hired the guy who walked in off the street without references? Do you think you'd be that trusting in today's world?" If you are having trouble getting their attention away from the television, suggest taking a walk or going out for coffee.

But what if you still cannot make contact? How can you tell them about serious matters in your life when they either refuse to listen or cut you off with useless advice? To begin, you need to examine their motives for responding as they do.

Are Parents Avoiding Touchy Issues?

Some adults report that their parents use predictable routines to avoid discussing certain issues or topics. For example, parents may help each other evade a potentially threatening conversation with comments such as, "Don't upset your mother," or "You know your father worries when he hears you talk this way." Or they may make contradictory statements like, "You know I want to hear about your problems, but don't tell me anything that will make me worry."

This sort of communication can be especially frustrating because while at one level you seem to be talking with your parents about feelings, at another level they seem to be preventing the conversation from continuing. In these situations, they usually do not directly acknowledge that they want to avoid an issue, but they still effectively block it out. For example, Tim feels like he and his mother live in different worlds at times.

Tim: She Drives Me Crazy.

My mother is a master at double-talk. She tells me she wants to know what I really think, but when I start to tell her what I think, she says she doesn't want to hear. For example, my sister has some real problems in her life, a lot of which are because she abuses drugs. So my mother will say, "Don't you think your sister is doing better? Don't you think this job will work out for her?" And I'll say, "Mom, do you really want my honest opinion about this?" And she'll say, "Yes, you see her more. How does she seem to you?" So I'll say, "Well, I think she's not going to get anywhere until she stops using drugs, and I haven't seen any improvement lately." Then my mother will get upset and say, "I don't understand how you can talk about your sister that way. You know how I worry about her. Why are you always so negative about her?"

Sometimes Mom makes me feel crazy. We both know what is really going on, but she acts like she's living in some different world. She just changes the facts around to be what she wants and then expects me to agree with her. She talks about a weekend last summer when we all went to the beach to celebrate my father's birthday and had such a great time. Well, actually, my sister was spaced-out, my father was yelling at her, and my mother was crying half the time. But now she wants me to remember it with her like some storybook family weekend.

Occasionally Mom is so convincing that I find myself wondering whether I can trust my own observations or memories. But most of the time I think we both know she's pretending. What's frustrating is that we can never talk about it.

Why Do Parents Avoid the Truth?

Although it may seem that parents who respond in these ways are deliberately refusing to hear or accept what they prefer to avoid, the situation is not that simple. In fact, from the parent's viewpoint, everything probably looks much different. For example, if we could hear Tim's mother's description of their interactions, she might explain it this way:

"Tim and his sister, Michelle, never got along when they were growing up and they still don't. I think a lot of that is my fault because I was never able to find a good way to stop them from competing for my attention. Somehow over the years it turned into a situation where Michelle gets attention by causing trouble and Tim gets it by doing well. I know Michelle has some problems in her life, but she is working on them and I see some real change. But Tim never wants to give her credit for anything and always wants to talk about what she's doing wrong.

"Sometimes I think Tim doesn't want us to get along. For example, last summer we all spent the weekend at the beach for my husband's birthday. We had a few arguments, but mostly we had fun being together. Now all Tim can remember are the conflicts. He refuses to even admit that it was an enjoyable family time. I wish he could be more forgiving."

We know that people observing a situation will have differing views of what is actually taking place. This is even more true for people who are actively involved in the interactions. Trying to sort out the truth is frustrating and probably not worth the effort it takes unless you are involved in a court case.

In fact, when it comes to human interaction, rather than one true description of what happened, there are various personal perspectives. The reason for the disparities has a lot to do with the way human beings process information.

Effects of Selective Filtering

Each person sees the world from a somewhat different frame of reference, just as windows in various rooms of a house provide different views of the same backyard. We selectively pay attention to certain dimensions of what is out there and exclude others. Such filtering is necessary so that we can selectively focus rather than being continually distracted by events that are irrelevant to us at the moment. Yet, our filtering also has the effect of defining for each of us an individual reality, which can create barriers in our communication with others.[1]

To consider how this occurs, imagine yourself living inside a box with only one window through which you can see the world. This window, which determines your view of the world, is your frame of reference. Your window's shape, angle, and clarity are determined by your experiences, emotions, physical state, needs, values, and so on. For example, if you are very hungry you will probably see food and not notice much else. Similarly, if you have certain strong beliefs, you are likely to pay particular attention to actions and comments that support those beliefs. Your view of any situation is specific to you at that particular moment and in those specific circumstances. It is not necessarily the same as the way you would perceive a similar situation in another time or circumstance, nor is it likely to be the same as the perspective of someone else who was in that same situation.

Nevertheless, we tend to accept our own perspectives as reality. It is easy and natural to fall into seeing your own view as the right, best, or only way of looking at a situation, rather than recognizing it as simply one of many possible views. Then when someone else describes the same situation very differently, you see that person as confused, wrong, or untruthful. It is very difficult to step back and consider how your own experiences and values have shaped your view and are affecting your communication. It is even more difficult to accept the possible validity of another person's perceptions when those views differ greatly from your own. Instead, you are likely to find yourself defending your view and trying to convince the other person that your perspective is the right one.

Effects of Historical Perspective

Parents and their adult children are particularly likely to have different perspectives because they have lived through quite different life experiences, which have shaped their values and beliefs. In fact, people from different generations may differ as much in outlook and attitude as do people from different social classes or ethnic groups. In the case of Tim and his mother, this difference in values is striking. Mom grew up in a time when the focus was on the image of the happy family and on the mother's responsibility for creating this harmony. When she was a young adult in the fifties, family togetherness was the ideal, open confrontation was avoided whenever possible, and creating a good impression was more important than sharing genuine personal feelings. Tim is a product of a different era. He reached adulthood in the seventies, a time when changing relationships were the norm, when talking things out honestly was highly valued, and when pretense was scorned. It is hardly surprising that they have trouble communicating.

For another example, consider thirty-six-year-old Joe, who was born in 1954, and his sixty-one-year-old father Harold, born in 1929. Harold was a young child during the Great Depression, a time of scarcity and economic insecurity. He was a teenager during World War II, a patriotic, duty-oriented time. Harold was a young adult in the post-war era; he graduated from high school in 1947, and turned twenty-one in 1950. Like most of his generation, Harold believes in hard work, sticking to a career path with single-minded dedication, and striving to reach the top.

Harold has always measured his success by the amount of money he makes and the prestige of his job. He keeps score by comparing himself to other people. Harold prides himself on knowing "how the system works," and on fulfilling his obligations to his family, his company, and society. He learned at an early age the value of devoting himself to duty and hard work and has prospered accordingly. He values material possessions above personal growth and believes that fun should be reserved for one's spare time after the work is done.

Joe was a young child during the fifties, a prosperous time in America. He was a teenager during the troubled Vietnam War era, when patriotism was at a low in this country. Joe values relationships, new challenges, and personal choice. He wants enjoyment as much as achievement and believes that his duty to himself to engage in work that is personally fulfilling comes before his obligation to the goals of the organization that employs him.

Because they grew up in such different times, Harold and his son Joe have had opposite outlooks in some areas. Harold has felt driven by duty and by worries of financial disaster, so he has followed the established path, carefully working himself up the career ladder. Joe has felt economically secure, yet confused by the array of personal choices available to his generation, so he has taken financial risks by switching careers in his search for one that is satisfying.[2]

Their different perspectives lead them into frequent arguments, mostly along the lines of the following:

HAROLD: "I'll never understand how you could leave a good managerial job in a successful company to start a photography business where you have to work night and day just to get by."

JOE: "I've told you before, Dad, I just didn't enjoy that job. I was always doing what someone else thought was important. Now I'm doing work I like and I make my own choices. It's fun to go to work in the morning."

HAROLD: "What does fun have to do with it? We're talking about work here. Don't you feel any sense of responsibility? What about all the money you owe the bank for starting that business? Don't you worry about being so far in debt?"

JOE: "I'll pay the money back one way or another. Anyway, it's not your problem. Why can't you let me do the worrying?"

HAROLD: "You never worry about anything, that's why. As long as you're having fun, everything is okay by you. But one of these days you're going to find out that that's not the way the world works. And then where will you be?"

Becoming Reacquainted With Your Parents

If Harold and Joe each had a less biased understanding of the other's point of view, they would have a better chance of breaking out of this cycle. If they could suddenly change places with each other for a day or so, like the movie characters in *Freaky Friday* or *18 Again,* they would quickly see that the world is a much different place when you walk in someone else's shoes.

Then they could realize that, rather than one of them being right and the other wrong about issues such as the importance of climbing the career ladder, they simply have different perspectives. Once they are each able to move beyond seeing their own perspective as reality, they will not feel such a strong need to defend their views. Then they can move from argument to discussion.

Because Joe and Harold do not have magic available to allow them to switch places, they will need to devote some time and energy to learning about each other's views. If you want to learn more about your parents' frame of reference and help them understand yours, you also will need to make a conscious effort to do so. The process will take time and possibly some extra patience, but it can be exciting and rewarding. Here are five suggestions to help you proceed.

• *Start by listening to them.* It may be tempting to begin by making sure they understand your perspective. But remember, they have been alive during your entire life, while you have only been around for part of theirs. Even though that does not mean they understand you any better than you understand them, it does mean you probably have more catching up to do on background. Furthermore, it can be interesting to discover the people your parents were before you came along.

Probably your parents occasionally tell tales about their youth, but you may have long ago learned to tune out these stories, which often seem to contain a lesson you would rather not hear. The old joke about the parent who recalls having walked five miles everyday to school—in the snow . . . uphill . . . both ways—rings a bell with many adult children. But, if you decide to ignore the moral lessons and exaggerations and simply listen without evaluating, you will learn quite a bit from these stories. You may not learn what really happened, because memories are always shaped by selective filtering. But you will learn about how these events felt to your parents and about the experiences that shaped their values. You will also get a picture of what life was like in the time and place of their youth. This will help you understand their perspective and realize why it may differ significantly from your own.

• *Ask questions.* If you want to get beyond surface sermons, clichés, and platitudes, ask questions to encourage your parents to give more details. When asking questions, it is important not to phrase them in a way that invites a defensive response. Think of yourself as an information gatherer; ask for specifics, but not for explanations.

As an example, imagine that you have just met someone from another community and you want to know as much as you can about that community and what living there feels like to this person. When he says he lives in a small town, you might ask him: How many people live there? Who are the major employers? How many schools and parks does the town have? What do the residents do for recreation? What do you enjoy most about living there? He will probably feel comfortable with such questions and will soon provide you with a detailed picture of the town and its residents. Ideally you would avoid questions that make him feel he must justify or defend his community, such as: Why do you live in such a small town? Is there anything to do there? Do most people have to commute to get jobs?

Similarly, when you are asking your parents about their

pasts, ask questions that will help you get as full a description as possible, but avoid any hints of challenge or judgment. Do not ask "why" questions, because they imply a request to justify. If your parent says, "I was very unhappy as a teenager," ask, "What were you unhappy about?" not, "Why were you unhappy?" Keeping asking questions that will bring out more details. If your parent responds with, "Oh, I guess I had the usual teenage problems," you could ask, "Who did you have problems with?" or, "What are some of the major problems you remember?" or, "How did you deal with the problems?"

Pick times when you and they feel relaxed and free of time pressure. Sometimes personal talks are easier when you are working together on a household task, gardening, taking a walk, or engaging in some similar familiar activity.

• *Accept their responses without judgment.* It is important to make sure your parents know you will love them just as much if they are less than perfect. They may be ashamed of parts of their past and worried that hearing about these times may lower their status in your eyes. Let them know it is okay to be honest with you.

One way to do this is to create for yourself a frame of mind where you are listening nonjudgmentally. Try to see the situations your parents describe from their frame of reference and to sense the hurt or pleasure they associate with the experiences. Imagine yourself in their shoes, as if you were living their lives for a little while. This will help you to be sensitive to their feelings and to accept them as people who have done as well as they could in difficult or confusing situations, just as you have.

Pay attention to extra cues that will help you tune in to their feelings, such as tone of voice, gestures, and bodily movements. Be an active, searching listener, gathering but not analyzing information.

• *Try to respond to their feelings.* Check out your understanding of their feelings by communicating what you are picking up and asking them whether you are getting the right message. Comments such as, "It sounds like you really didn't feel you had much choice about taking that job," or "So you were really upset that your father didn't want you to date a Catholic," give them a chance to confirm or correct your understanding. These statements also create an atmosphere of togetherness, a sense that you are sharing their experience.

This sort of response will also help you understand their reactions to events in their lives today. If you take time to listen carefully and respond to the emotions they show as well as to their words, you will come to see their world more clearly. For example, one woman reported, "Last winter my parents attended four funerals of friends and relatives in six weeks. Rather than simply talk with them about the deceased people, I expressed how hard it must be to be their age, grieving for so many people and continually experiencing loss. Each parent shared their depression, sadness, and sense of hopelessness, and I felt much closer to them."

• *Be open with them about your own concerns.* Your parents need your help to be able to understand your perspective. Be honest with them. Don't protect them from the bad news. Think out loud now and then when you are working through a problem. Let them know how you arrived at decisions, rather than giving them the finished product. When you feel some nervousness about the future, admit it rather than pretending that you have everything figured out. If they know you have given a subject serious thought, they may be less likely to be upset even when they disagree.

Joe and Harold Try Again

If Joe were to follow these suggestions in a conversation with Harold, he might be surprised to find his usually "bull-headed" father responding quite differently. For example:

HAROLD: "I'll never understand how you could leave a good managerial job in a successful company to start a photography business where you have to work night and day just to get by."

JOE: "I guess that must be hard for you to understand. I know you have always felt a lot of responsibility for providing for all of us. Did you ever have times where you wished you could try another career?"

HAROLD: "Well, you know I always loved playing the clarinet. But I kept that for my spare time. Sure, I would have liked playing in a group, but I never even considered throwing over everything I had for some silly dream."

JOE: "It sounds like you didn't feel you had the freedom to make any changes once you got started in your career. I guess what I'm doing must seem very risky to you. You probably wonder if I'll ever be anywhere near as successful as you are."

HAROLD: "Well, I do worry about all the money you borrowed to start this business."

JOE: "I'm concerned about that, too, but it is really important to me to try doing what I really enjoy doing. I know I'll have to put in more time and work harder to make it in this business, but I'm willing to do that because I really love it. I do want you to know that I am taking the business and the loan seriously."

HAROLD: "Well, at least you know the risks. I hate to see you putting yourself under so much pressure, but I guess you think it's worth it. I know I never have wanted to be in such an insecure financial situation."

In this conversation Joe and his father each learned something about each other's point of view and ended up a little closer in the process. By listening, exploring, and accepting rather than defending himself, Joe opened the door for his father to break out of his old pattern of responses.

Unfreezing Old Misunderstandings

Setting out to learn about the people who are your parents will dislodge some old patterns of interaction, especially if you can begin to see what has shaped their attitudes and beliefs. While understanding cannot change the past, it can change the way you feel now about difficult times you have had with your parents in the past and the way you respond to similar times today. Sharon discovered why her life-style threatens her parents' image of themselves as good parents.

Sharon: They Raised Me to Be a "Good Kid."
My parents often feel that I have failed them in some

ways. I am not their ideal concept of a lady, in that I am not yet married and I have a career of my own. They can't understand how I basically trust people, because they raised me never to trust others. Also, they can't understand my work as a social worker who, as they say, "goes around helping people who don't deserve it." My father has repeatedly told me that "social workers are crazy to think that they can improve people who are on welfare. People on welfare are only sick people who cheat and use us decent people."

I have spent a lot of time justifying myself to them and trying to prove that I have made good choices, but that hasn't changed anything. Recently, over Thanksgiving weekend I spent some time asking them about how they raised me and what influenced them in their parenting. As a result of these discussions, which were both emotional and informative, I have a much better understanding of why they raised me in the protective way that they did and why they are so disapproving of my life today.

Both of my parents were raised in strict, conservative farm families of German background. They grew up believing in very clearly defined roles for men and women. A woman should be a wife, very domestic, and passive, but able to endure a lot of strain and complete her tasks. A man should be hard-working, aggressive, and proud. He is the financial provider for the family, and if he can't provide he is seen as a failure.

They were taught that children need a lot of support and guidance to keep them out of trouble. They feel that kids are a result of their parents; bad parents have bad kids, good parents have good kids. They truly believe that they wouldn't be who they are if their own parents hadn't guided them in the right direction.

Now they feel that I am wasting my time on a misguided career, when I should be married and raising children. They feel that I don't listen enough to older people, which my mother feels is her fault. They wonder why I have taken the route I have and worry that I will ultimately fail.

I can understand their concerns given their values and upbringing and the paths they have taken. If I had grown

up when they did, I probably would have followed my
parents' direction just as they did. But somehow, what I
saw in society versus what they taught me raised enough
conflict in me that I searched for my own identity. They
probably won't change their views, but maybe if they
keep seeing that I am happy, they will worry less. I can
see why my living so differently from them is upsetting to
them, but I hope they can gradually begin to realize that
I am doing fine.

Now that Sharon understands her parents' perspectives, she
can communicate with them a bit more easily. She will
probably still feel that they are in different worlds much of the
time, but at least now she knows more about the differences.
When she tells them about her life, she can begin by acknowledging the contrasts between her life-style and their expectations and admitting that she knows it is difficult for them to
accept her choices. By offering this respect, she sets the tone
for an atmosphere of acceptance rather than defensiveness,
which increases the likelihood that her parents will listen and
begin to understand her views.

CHAPTER 6

What Can You Do With All That Advice You Didn't Ask For?

"I don't think my parents ever pass up a chance to give me advice. My mother saves newspaper articles about healthy eating for me to read. Usually I just throw them in the trash. My father is always giving me advice on financial matters, like insurance and retirement. He thought I should remain at a job where I was depressed and unhappy, just because it offered a good retirement plan. I was twenty-five years old at the time and couldn't have cared less about retirement. I wish they would realize I can think for myself."

(Mike, age 27)

Perhaps Mike's parents, who are now in their mid-fifties, forget that retirement plans and healthy eating are of greater concern to them and others their age than to young people in their twenties. Or they may be looking back to their own twenties and wishing they had been more foresighted. So, they are trying to give Mike the benefit of their newfound wisdom.

But Mike not only does not want their advice on these matters, he actively resents it. Why does he react so negatively?

The "Hidden" Message Behind Advice

When someone speaks to us, we listen at two levels. We hear not only the content of the communication, but also a message about our relationship with the speaker and/or about what the speaker wants us to think or do. When Mike's mother

79

tells him that eating hamburgers and french fries in fast-food restaurants is likely to raise his cholesterol level, he hears more than a piece of information on nutrition. Mike also hears that his mother thinks he is not responsible about his food choices, that she is telling him where and what he should eat, and that she still feels she must watch over him like she did when he was a child.

Unfortunately, Mike's mother may not realize that his need to feel that she sees him as a competent adult far outweighs his need for information about cholesterol. She also probably does not understand that Mike will very likely ignore her advice because he feels that she is judging him and trying to control his choices. He feels that if he changes his behavior based on her comments, he will be giving up some of his autonomy.

Mike is also experiencing another uncomfortable aspect of a situation in which one person is giving another advice: the feeling of an uneven balance of power. This imbalance can be fine if one accepts the other person's authority on a particular topic and seeks advice, as in a doctor-patient relationship. But Mike does not accept his mother as an authority on his eating habits nor did he solicit her advice on this matter. He probably feels that she is trying to keep him in a childish role where she is in charge.

Mike feels that he is an adult now and thus should be able to relate to his parents as an equal. When his parents persist in giving him advice he has not asked for, he interprets that as a denial of his adult status.

As further evidence of his unequal status, Mike has no doubt observed that advice generally flows mainly in one direction in his relationship with his parents—from them to him. Experience and research supports this view. Researchers at the University of Chicago interviewed members of three adult generations in 148 families about how the family members related to one another and what they talked about. The interviewers showed each family member a set of cards and asked if they had discussed the topics on the cards with a specific member of the other generation. If the answer was yes, the interviewers asked follow-up questions to find out whether one of the pair had tried to influence the other on that subject. The trend that emerged was one of parents giving their children far more advice than their children gave them.

Familiar Forms of Parental Advice

Parents seem to be full of advice on a variety of topics, but some themes are especially familiar to grown children. How to select and keep the ideal job or spouse, how to take care of your money or your health, and what to buy and how much to pay for it are recurring subjects. Adult children complain that their parents never seem to accept that they know enough to make these decisions without help:

- "My mother thinks I choose the men in my life wrong. She says I am choosing men like she did, and she wants me to learn from her mistakes not my own. If I bring a new man to meet her, she'll say things like, 'He's just like your father. Don't make the same mistake I did.' It makes me feel really bad." (Female, age 25)
- "Recently my father purchased a used car for me and my family because ours has over one hundred thousand miles on it. He was not going to give it to us. He expected us to buy this car from him which he felt would solve our problem. As you know, a car is a personal item that most of us like to choose for ourselves." (Male, age 42)
- "My parents keep telling me that if my wife and I would just be more frugal and learn the value of money, we could buy the house we want. They have no understanding of how hard it is to afford to buy a house today. They say if we followed their example and 'put money aside every week,' we'd have plenty. They can't see that the economy has changed. They only see that 'young people today just don't know how to do without.'" (Male, age 34)
- "My mother wants me to marry someone prestigious like a doctor or a lawyer. Right now I am considering going back to school to get a master's degree in business administration. She thinks it is a big mistake, that I will be 'too educated' to attract a man. She tells me, 'The way to keep a man is to keep something good cooking in the oven.'" (Female, age 29)
- "My father hates the fact that I have my own business. He says it is insecure and that I should get a government job with security and good benefits. I tell him I have no interest in

working for the government and I don't feel my business is insecure. But he keeps sending me articles about small businesses going under and information about government jobs." (Male, age 36)

Why Do Parents Give So Much Advice?

Somehow parents seem to be forever stuck in an advice-giving mode no matter how old their children get. We laugh when we hear stories of eighty-year-old parents reminding their sixty-year-old children to drive carefully or to get their eyes checked. We snicker at tales of successful middle-aged professional men and women facing advice from their parents on everything from finances to relationships. Yet the tradition continues.

Parents persevere as authority figures, even when they know that their adult children are more likely to reject than accept unsolicited advice. Why do parents insist on staying parents even though their children are grown up? They have a number of reasons, most of which are well-intentioned.

- *They want to pass on the wisdom they have acquired from their own experience.* Shirley got married at eighteen, had her daughter, Kristi, at nineteen, got divorced at twenty, and spent ten years as a struggling single mother with no child support. Now thirty-seven, Shirley is happily remarried, working part-time, and going to college to get a degree so she can get a job she likes better. But she is devastated that eighteen-year-old Kristi has dropped out of her first semester of college to get married, with plans to work full-time to help her new husband finish school. "She's too young," Shirley groans, "and I know the mistake she's making because I've *been there.* I can't just sit by and watch her mess up her life this way."

- *They knew you when you did not know so much and find it hard to change their earlier perceptions.* Peter can talk for hours about his daughter Rebecca's financial irresponsibility. He remembers how in high school she spent more money than she had on clothes; how he had to give her a weekly rather than monthly allowances in college so she would have money at the end of the month; and how he had to help her out during her first few years out of college because she never had any money for emergencies like car repair or dental expenses. So, even though Rebecca is thirty now, has a good job, and has not asked him for money for years, Peter still gives her constant advice about financial matters. In his eyes Rebecca is still the teenager who "spends two dollars for every one you give her." After so many years of seeing her that way, it is hard for him to change his image of her. He may automatically think of her as a spendthrift, or he may try to see her differently but lapse back into the old view.

- *They worry about you.* Once you grow up and move away from home, your parents worry that you will not take care of yourself, that you will make disastrous mistakes, and that something will happen to you. Probably they are remembering all the dumb things they did when they were younger. Somehow they seem to feel they will worry less, or have less to worry about, if they remind you to be careful. As one sixty-three-year-old mother commented, "My daughter is forty years old and I know she's grown up, but I want to be sure she doesn't put off getting regular mammograms and pap smears, so I nag her about that now and then."

- *They want to feel needed.* In the beginning, children need their parents for everything. Ideally, in the course of 20 years or so, this unequal relationship is gradually transformed into more of a partnership. But some parents find it very difficult to let go of that feeling of being needed by their children. As Edith commented, "I like to give my son Dan food to take home with him when he visits. He's not married and I know he doesn't cook much. But he keeps telling me not to bother, that he mostly eats out anyway. I tell him that my food is better for him than restaurant food and it's not good for him to eat out so much. And, anyway, it's no bother. There's so little I can do for him anymore."

- *They believe that advising you is still their responsibility as parents.* In a study in which researchers interviewed young adults and older adults, a clear conflict emerged in this area. The older people interviewed felt that it was a parent's right and duty to advise their grown children, while the younger people felt that grown children should not have to accept or even listen to parental advice unless they had sought it.[2] Because the boundaries are not clear, the situation remains frustrating for both parties. As one twenty-seven-year-old woman complains: "My mother seems to feel it is her duty to ask me if I am getting enough rest, sleeping well, eating the right food, and so on. I always seem to have a lot to learn. My father reminds me that he has lived a lot longer than I have, so he knows more about everything. I will never reach adulthood in their eyes!"

• *They want to control you.* Some parents unfortunately feel a need or desire to actually manage their children's lives. Perhaps they grew up in this tradition themselves and simply expect to continue it or possibly they are extremely powerful people accustomed to controlling all aspects of their lives. Whatever their reasons, these parents' advice-giving goes beyond being frustrating or irritating. Their domination may feel so overwhelming that breaking free seems impossible.

An interesting case is that of Florence Nightingale, the founder of modern nursing. Her wealthy mother, Fanny, was so opposed to Florence's desire to study nursing that for years she forbade Florence from any mention of the subject. When Florence finally began formal study of nursing at age thirty, her family was furiously resentful and would hardly speak to her. In 1850, Florence wrote: "My present life is suicide; in my thirty-first year I see nothing desirable but death. What am I that their life is not good enough for me? O God, what am I? . . . Why, Oh my God, cannot I be satisfied with the life that satisfies so many people?"[3]

The fact that Florence did not succumb to her mother's domination despite the anguish of her struggle is encouraging. Yet her difficulty in her thirties in seeing her own choices as legitimate in the face of parental opposition shows the power some adults concede to their parents.

Solution-Giving as a Problem-Solving Style

Although the parental role seems to bring out the advice-giver in everyone now and then, some people are clearly more directive than others. When it comes to helping another person deal with a challenge or problem in life, people have two basic styles of operating. Some people are primarily *facilitators*, others are most often *solution-givers*. To illustrate, imagine that two friends of yours, John and Linda, a married couple, are trying to decide whether to move to another state so that John can accept a promotion with his company. This would be their second move in five years, but would mean a much higher salary for John. If they move, Linda would have to find another new job and their children would have to change schools again. What would you suggest to John and Linda?

If your suggestions focus mainly on what you think is best for John and Linda, what you think is the correct or right thing to do in this situation, or what specific choice you would make in their shoes, then your style of helping is acting as a *solution-giver*. Some examples of the suggestions other solution-givers made to this situation include:[4]

- John should go ahead and take the job. His wife could find another job and make new friends. The children would adjust.
- I think John would be extremely selfish and inconsiderate to take another position and cause hardship on his family again.
- It doesn't make sense to stay in one place if a better job offer comes along.

If your suggestions focus mainly on suggesting ways John and Linda could decide what is best for them, on listing factors they should consider, or questions they should ask themselves as they decide, or on reminding them that they must consider their own values and make their own choice, then your style of helping is acting as a *facilitator*. Examples of suggestions made by other facilitators:

- My advice to Linda and John is to sit down together with pen and paper and put two separate headings on the paper—advantages and disadvantages—to both of them.
- The family should decide what is important to them as a unit, but the individuals must also decide what is important to them.

• I think John and Linda have to deal with the question, "What is life all about, and what is true happiness?"

If one or both of your parents generally take the solution-giving approach to solving problems when you are looking for someone to listen and help you think through a situation, you may find discussions with them very frustrating. Carol and her Dad have very different ideas of what is helpful, and this disagreement is a problem for them. Carol complains:

"My job is stressful right now because of new responsibilities and changes. I don't need stress from my Dad, too, but somehow I'm getting it. It starts when I tell Dad about a problem I'm having at work that I'm not sure what to do about. Right away he explains to me exactly how I should handle it. Usually I don't want to take his advice, and I find myself telling him why I think his solution won't work. Then he jumps in and tells me why taking his advice is the most logical, most reasonable thing to do, and before I know it we end up in a fight.

"When I'm worried, I want to tell him, and often I would welcome some help in resolving the situation, but somehow our discussions just seem to make me feel worse. Maybe I should keep my problems to myself."

Carol's father is also concerned about the fights, but he sees the problem somewhat differently:

"I know Carol is under a lot of stress at her job lately, and I've been making an effort to listen carefully to her problems so that I can help her. She doesn't have anyone else she can talk to about these issues, and because I've been in a situation similar to hers, I think I really can help her. I'm not just talking off the top of my head. I consider all the pros and cons of a solution before I suggest it, and I think I have some decent ideas.

"But no matter what I suggest, it isn't good enough for Carol. Right away she starts telling me why my idea won't work, and if I mention some points she's overlooked, she gets mad. I honestly don't understand what she expects from me. If she doesn't want my help, I wish she wouldn't ask for it."

Confronted with another person's dilemma, Carol's father, a solution-giver, considers the situation and evaluates the pros and cons using his own criteria. Then he suggests the course of action he believes to be the best and explains why he favors that solution. He sees his point of view as the correct one, and defends it as the most rational alternative for anyone in that situation.

Fights develop when what Carol wants from her father is understanding and assistance in considering alternatives, but what she gets is ready-made solutions. Their fights escalate when what Dad wants from Carol is acknowledgment of the merit of his proposed solution, but what he gets is resistance.

Responding to Solution-Givers

Facilitation is generally more helpful than advice. Professional helpers are trained to listen, provide an accepting atmosphere, and help people reach their own solutions. Untrained people, however, are more apt to give advice than to assist you in solving your own problems. If you think about your friends' responses, you may discover that many of them also tend to be solution-givers. You may have simply been less aware of their advice because it does not annoy you as much as advice from your parents.

No matter who is giving you advice, the way you interpret the suggestions will significantly affect the interaction between you. When presented with ready-made solutions they have not asked for, people tend to feel pressured to comply and then resist the pressure. Advice can also feel like judgment. You may feel as if the advice-giver sees you as inferior or inadequate. The situation can quickly escalate into an argument over who is right and who is wrong.

Instead, try to hear the comments as that person's style of showing concern and caring. If you can, remind yourself that this person's intent is to help, even though it may not feel that way to you. Acknowledge that intention as well as the energy your helper invested in producing the proposed solution. Your response could turn a prospective fight into a productive discussion. For example, consider the following possible responses Carol could make to her father:

Creates Conflict	*Prevents Conflict*
"That would never work. You don't understand my problem at all."	"I appreciate your suggestion. Because I'm trying to consider all the possibilities right now, maybe you can help me come up with some others."
"You always just take over and tell me what to do. Don't you think I ever have any good ideas?"	"I know you've had a lot of experience with this sort of thing, and I need practice in coming up with my own solutions. Could you help me consider some of the possibilities?"

Are You Giving Mixed Messages?

If you want to clearly communicate to your parents that you do not want advice unless you ask for it, make sure you are not unwittingly giving them the message that you really cannot manage without help. If you are still turning to them for frequent financial or emotional support, they may feel that you need direction and guidance as well.

Research shows that parents give more help and also more attention to their never-married and/or divorced adult children than they do the children who are currently married.[5] In general, unmarried adult children receive more financial assistance and more emotional support from their parents than do married children. These single adults may be at high risk of also receiving unwanted parental advice.

Gifts often have strings attached, especially when the favors are requested rather than spontaneously given. If you ask your parents to bail you out of financial emergencies or if you cry on their shoulders when emotional crises arise, they may feel this gives them the right or obligation to tell you how to live. Even if you are or have been married and you have children of your own, you may depend on your parents to help out with baby-sitting or to offer aid in financial emergencies like your children's medical or dental expenses. Although your parents may willingly give this assistance, they may see it as an indication that you are not a fully capable adult.

Adult children who live under the same roof as their parents are the most likely to get unwanted advice. Today divorced and never-married adult children are returning home to live with their parents in increasing numbers. According to Census Bureau figures released in 1989, 18 million single adults eighteen to thirty-four years old were living with parents. This is an increase of about one third since 1974.[6] While returning home as an adult may be necessary, or at least advantageous, it usually requires some major adjustments. Not only do you sacrifice privacy, you may find yourself losing autonomy as well. When your parents are providing your daily needs, it is hard not to slip back into the old parent-child role.

If you want to maintain or establish your independence, you must be willing to pay the cost. If you accept money, make it a loan, not a gift. Be businesslike; sign an agreement. If you move back home, set up a time limit for your stay. Make specific agreements with your parents before you move in concerning what you will contribute, what restrictions in your life-style they expect, and what process you and they will use to resolve grievances. Remember that it is their house, which gives them the right to set conditions, especially if they are paying the bills. That "free room and board" may exact a high price in terms of the autonomy you sacrifice.

If your parents are the ones you turn to when you are upset, worried, or depressed, be clear about what you want from them. If you just need someone to be there and listen, tell them that. You should be aware, however, that they may not be able or willing to accept this passive role. If that is the case, consider finding a friend you can discuss your problems with or joining a support group where members listen nonjudgmentally.

Are You Misreading Their Messages?

Because it can be difficult to establish your independence from your parents, you may be especially sensitive to comments they make. A friend may tell you that you could save money by shopping at a new discount store you have never tried; you hear useful information. But if a parent tells you the same thing, you hear a comment on your inability to manage money.

The more you focus on protecting yourself from their interference, the more likely you are to see them as controlling and manipulative. One young man commented, "My parents always tell me how bright and capable I am, but I see that as their way of telling me I should work harder."

In fact there is some evidence that young people tend to misperceive older people's motives such that younger people see older people as more dominant and less helpful than older people see themselves.[7] This misperception may lead to conflict when a parent's attempt to assist is seen as an act of management.

Furthermore, your image of your parents was probably set long ago, and you may find it as difficult to change that picture as they find it to modify their view of you. Even if they are actively trying not to give you unwanted advice and succeeding most of the time, you may notice only the few advice-giving comments that they do slip in.

Advice on Dealing With Advice

What if you have established yourself as an independent adult, have told your parents that you do not want so much advice, and have accepted their good intentions, but they still offer more opinions about your life than you can handle?

- *Experience your inner power.* If you are sure of yourself, of what you want, and where you are going, you can remain comfortable when others—even your parents—disagree with your approach. Advice often begins with the phrase, "If I were you . . ." The point is that they are not you and cannot know what is best for you. Remind yourself that while their advice may be what they would do in your shoes, you do not need to justify making your own choices.
- *Examine the possible usefulness of the advice.* Even the most opinionated person has worthwhile suggestions at times. If you can resist the temptation to ignore all their advice, you may find some of it helpful. Try seeing them as consultants whose opinions you will consider, rather than bosses you

must oppose. As one thirty-year-old woman said, "I think the older I get, the more respect I have for my parents and the more I appreciate their expression of concern for my well-being. In younger days, I saw them as prying and snooping into my business. Now I see that as concern for me."

- *Remind them that you do not want advice on some subjects.* Giving advice may be so automatic for your parents that they may not even realize they are doing it. You can casually remind them that they have given you these suggestions before, that you and they disagree on this subject, or that you are not asking for advice: "I know you think I should never wear black, you've told me that often." If they persist, "Well, you really should wear more colorful clothes so you don't look so pale," point out that you do not want to discuss this topic anymore. Tell them that you know they want the best for you and that you will let them know if you do need their help: "I know you are trying to help and that you want me to look my best, but I like to choose my own clothes and I like the way I look, so I'd rather you didn't comment on my clothes."

- *Do not accept unwanted advice.* If you agree with them, "You're probably right, I should live someplace cheaper," but admit that you have no plans to change, "but I just don't feel like moving right now," they will never let up. Acknowledge their concerns, but decline the advice: "I know you think I should move, but I'm not planning on it right now." If they keep at it, "You know you'd be much better off if you moved to a less expensive place, so why not at least start looking?" tell them that you do not want to talk about it anymore and that you would appreciate their not bringing the subject up again.

- *Do not argue.* Whatever reasons you come up with to reject their advice, they can find counter reasons. If you say, "I don't want to look for a better job right now because I think I have a good chance of getting promoted where I am if I stay another year," they may come back with, "Why wait around for a promotion? Go out and get a better offer, then you'll have something to bargain with." These conversations go nowhere you haven't been before and nowhere you want to go again. So avoid the temptation to try to convince them they are wrong. Many adults report that they simply listen, say little, and then do what they want to do in the matter.

* *Do not lose your temper.* Yelling at them about how much you hate all their advice or how they are always trying to take over and run your life will not help. They will feel misunderstood because, after all, they are only trying to help. And you feel guilty because they do mean well. If you need to, stop talking to them until you feel more in control.

* *Remove yourself if necessary.* If you are unable to stop the flow of advice and you find it hard to ignore, the best move may be to end the conversation. If it is a phone call, tell them you have to hang up; if you are with them, find a reason to leave the room for a while. You can do this without making a fuss or starting an argument. Eventually, if this happens often, they may begin to get the message.

What Can You Expect?

Realistically, you are more likely to learn to cope with your parents' advice than you are to teach them not to give it. At age forty-nine, Nancy does not enjoy her eighty-one-year-old mother's constant advice, but she has found ways not to make it her problem.

Nancy: Usually I Can Stay Cool.

I keep thinking that because I am forty-nine, Mother should realize that I can act on my own. But at eighty-one, Mother is a capable, intelligent woman who still seems compelled to share her wisdom with me. Mother suggests I should move closer. I should get a good job, as high paying as possible. I should double-check my will to be sure it is correct. I should see a physician. I should lose weight. I should exercise more. I should be more careful what I eat. I should be a better housekeeper. It goes on and on.

I used to make excuses, justify, argue, or feel guilty. But I have learned to ignore it, act like I think she is joking, thank her for her concern, change the subject, or just look at her, depending on my mental state at the moment. On rare occasions I lose it and thank her sarcastically, reminding her of my age and my feeling that

I am capable of making a decision on my own. Usually, though, I remain pretty cool.

I used to feel angry at the thought that she did not see me as competent, but I have come to realize that she is simply a person who thinks she always knows what is best. I know I am capable and I don't need to prove that to myself or to her. When I really get fed up, I just say, "Mother, I don't want to hear another word," and then I change the subject.

CHAPTER 7

How Can You Stop Feeling Guilty?

How many mothers does it take to change a light bulb?

None.

"Don't worry about me. I'll just sit here in the dark."

Messages designed to induce guilt seem to be a specialty of parents. Although mothers are famous for making such comments, fathers also use manipulative tactics at times to coerce their grown children.

Interestingly, most parents will say that they do not want their adult children to feel pressured to visit them, help them, or make choices they condone. Parents do want their grown children to be involved with them and to live "acceptable" life-styles, but they do not want their children to do this solely from a sense of obligation. Parents want grown children to *want* to behave in these desired ways. But adult children tend to have their own preferences, and parents do not like to leave the outcomes up to chance.

So parents use various subtle and not so subtle tactics to persuade their adult children to move in desired directions. The tactics involve maneuvers designed to create the appearance that the adult child is *choosing* to act in the desired manner. But when you are caught up in one of these parental gambits, you do not feel like you are choosing. You either do not feel free to make the choice you really want to make or you feel so confused that you no longer know what you want.

Confusing Choices

One especially frustrating type of manipulative interaction is a conversation in which parents do not directly say what they want but clearly expect you to know. When you get stuck in one of these, you seem to sink deeper and deeper no matter which way you turn.

For example, Judy and Paul recently visited Paul's mother, Alice, in Scottsdale, Arizona, where she spends several months every winter to escape the cold of Chicago. Because Alice, who is in her late seventies, complains frequently about tiring easily in the hot Arizona sun, Paul and Judy tried to accommodate her on their daily outings. But Alice did not make this easy. The following conversation, which took place during a walk through an outdoor shopping area, is one of many similar interactions that Judy and Paul found frustrating during the visit.

PAUL: "Shall we go back to the car or walk farther?"

ALICE: "Oh, we can go back if you want."

PAUL: "No, Mother, we're trying to find out what you want."

JUDY: "We don't know how tired you are."

ALICE: "How tired should I be?"

JUDY: "We don't know. That's why we're asking."

ALICE: "Well, we can go back if you want. You can always come here later without me."

PAUL: "No, Mother, you don't understand. It's not that we want to come without you. We're just trying to find out what you want to do."

ALICE: "Well, I thought you might want to see the other shops, but let's go back."

JUDY: "Let's go on if you want."

ALICE: "No, let's go back."

At this point, Paul and Judy feel guilty no matter what they do. They have no idea what Alice wants or what they did wrong, but it is quite clear to them that they did something wrong.

What Is the Payoff?

What does Alice want in this situation? Probably she is not sure herself whether she wants to walk on or turn back. But she does want her son and daughter-in-law to show her that they love her and want to meet her needs, which is what the conversation is actually about.

Alice seems to be saying, "If you really cared about me you would not have even suggested going back. Your asking about going back implies that you want to get rid of me so you can do what you want to do." Meanwhile, Paul and Judy, operating at an entirely different level, are saying, "Huh? We just wanted to know whether you are tired."

For various reasons Alice apparently feels uncomfortable or afraid of asking directly for what she wants. Instead, she hides her real message in a conversation about daily activities. This gives her the opportunity to try to get what she wants while preserving the option of denying that she is asking for anything more than a decision about a walk.

In this case Alice's maneuver did not get her what she wanted. In fact, unless Paul and Judy were very skilled in decoding hidden messages and responding to the real intent, her tactics were almost guaranteed to leave all three of them feeling frustrated. Probably Alice has engaged in interactions like this one with her son Paul many times over the years with similarly dissatisfying outcomes. Why does she keep doing it?

A Matter of Influence

Once children are grown, their parents' influence over them declines markedly. In fact our society's values hold that adult children should be independent and lead their own lives, free of their parents' demands. So parents are caught in a paradoxical situation. They want to be involved in their children's lives, but they do not want to seem to be making demands on their adult children.[1]

Because the grown children generally have less commitment to this involvement than the parents do, an imbalance exists in the relationship. The parents can ask for what they want, but the children can refuse or ignore their requests. Parents are not in a position to demand compliance unless they have some unusually strong financial or emotional control over a grown child. So some parents opt for the indirect approach.

Sometimes the manipulative games parents use are ones that have been in their family for generations. They learned them from their parents. Other strategies are approaches they have developed over a lifetime of discovering effective ways of influencing other people.

The more insecure and needy parents feel, the more likely they are to resort to manipulation and guilt to get what they want. These are tactics of desperation. Getting what they want is so important to these parents that they are willing to risk their children's respect and affection in order to exert control over their behavior.

Ten Toxic Tactics Parents Use

Many of the tactics are so universal that countless numbers of grown children recognize them instantly. The existence of jokes like the one at the beginning of this chapter is a clear indication of the prevalence of such manipulative parental comments. Although your parents may have their own unique ways of manipulating you and making you feel guilty, it is likely that you will recognize at least one of the ten frustrating strategies described below.

• *"After all I've done for you . . ."* Libby's mother had a very difficult time giving birth. In fact, she had suffered a late miscarriage with an earlier pregnancy from which she nearly died. Her doctor had warned her of the dangers of becoming pregnant again, but she and Libby's father very much wanted a child, so they went ahead. During the pregnancy Libby's mother was confined to bed much of the time. Libby's birth was complicated, requiring an emergency Caesarean section from which her mother recovered very slowly.

Libby has heard the story of her traumatic birth many

times, usually accompanied by comments such as, "After I went through all that pain and suffering for you, I don't think it's too much to expect you to consider my feelings once in a while." Or, "Sometimes I wonder why I went through all that for you. You don't seem to care about me most of the time."

Libby feels guilty when she hears this, and she also feels frustrated and angry. She says, "I can never satisfy her, no matter what I do. If I don't do everything exactly the way she wants me to, she starts telling me how ungrateful I am. Besides the difficult birth, she got up at night a lot with me when I was a baby because I was so small and needed to eat so often. Because I was an only child, she focused all her attention on me. She gave me all kinds of lessons, drove me and my friends around, made me special clothes and costumes and on and on. Now she wants me to repay her by living my life by her rules even though I'm grown up."

The "I sacrificed for you, now you owe me" theme takes many forms. You may hear about how you are wasting that "expensive education" your parents paid for or how ungrateful you are for moving "halfway across the country" when you know living so far away will make your parents miserable. It is not surprising if you feel guilty when you compare your contributions with theirs, but it is also not surprising if you feel upset that they believe you should somehow repay them in full.

• *"You're making me sick . . ."* Hal's mother worries so much about him that she "lies awake nights." Hal is an airline pilot, an occupation his mother finds extremely risky. She worries that his plane will be hijacked, that he'll have a mechanical failure that will cause a crash, that another plane will run into his plane, etc. Whenever she hears on the news about a plane crash or any problem involving a plane, she gets terrible headaches and is unable to sleep or eat. She wants Hall to change careers and has even offered to pay to send him to school to learn to do "something more sensible."

Although he regrets "causing my mother so much pain," Hal likes being a pilot and does not intend to change jobs. He also refuses to call his mother every time he completes a flight so that she can "stop worrying for a few hours at least." Still, he feels uncomfortable knowing that she is "worried sick" over him.

Parents sometimes collude in the "You're making me sick" strategy as a way of letting you know that you are causing misery without actually having to confront you directly with a request. For example, "Your mother would never mention it, but she was sick for two days after she found out that you weren't coming home for Thanksgiving." Or, "It will kill your father if you don't go into the business with him. He's worked all his life to build this up for you."

- *"How can I hold up my head? . . ."* Arthur's parents cannot accept his gay life-style. They are angry and upset that on visits home Arthur has let his old friends in town know that he is homosexual. His father complains that everyone is laughing behind his back, "knowing I have a fairy for a son." His mother thinks he is just trying to punish her by "making me look like a failure in front of my friends and family." They want Arthur to go to therapy, straighten up, and get married so that people can see that he is "normal underneath all this craziness."

Arthur is sad about their reaction but he has no intention of pretending he is not gay just so his parents can "keep up appearances." He feels guilty that he is not able to make them proud and that they feel disgraced by him, but he also feels that their demands for him to change are unfair.

Parents may feel similarly disgraced when their grown children marry outside their religion or race, or involve themselves in radical political movements, or choose a job or life-style that differs sharply from that of the parents. And somehow they believe that if they let you know just how humiliated they are by your behavior, you will change so that they can feel better.

- *"If you would just try . . ."* Karl's parents always knew he would make a wonderful doctor, and for a while he thought they were right. But he also loved music, and in his first year of medical school he dropped out to play with a group full time. In the five years since he left medical school Karl has not regretted his decision, but his father keeps suggesting that Karl could surely "make a go of it in medicine" if he would just "go back and really work at it." Karl's father reminds him that he is only looking out for Karl's best interests and that he is sure Karl would be happier in the long run if he "bit the bullet" and finished medical school.

Karl feels guilty that he has not met his parents' expectations. He is actually considering exploring the possibility of
returning to medical school while trying to keep up with his
music at the same time. He hates the thought that his father
sees him as having taken the lazy way out.

Parents who insist that your choices are actually due to
lack of effort create guilt by implying that you could make
everyone happy if you just tried a little harder. For example,
"If you would just try to get along with your brother, I know
you two could be better friends." Or, "If you tried, I'm sure
you could get a job around here so we could see you more."
These comments leave you feeling self-indulgent and inconsiderate for making your own decisions.

• *"I'll manage, don't worry about me . . ."* Diana and her
husband Hugh are in their late forties. Now that their
children are off at college, they would have time to do some
of the things they put off during busy family years. But
Hugh's widowed mother, Eunice, who is in her seventies has
recently come to live with them. Eunice is quite capable of
caring for herself, but she did not want to live alone after her
husband died, so she moved in with Hugh and Diana.
Whenever Hugh and Diana plan to go out without Eunice,
she always says something like, "Don't worry about me. I'll
get along fine by myself." But when they get home she has
either developed some mysterious illness or burned herself
on the stove or lost her glasses or had to call the police
because she heard strange noises.

Obviously the message here is "Do worry about me and
take care of me or you'll regret it later." Diana and Hugh do
not go out very often, and when they do they always feel
guilty afterward.

Parents may use this strategy to coerce their grown
children to come home for the holidays: "Don't worry about
us, we'll find something to do by ourselves. I'm sure you'll
have more fun with your friends." When you hear this you
are likely to think to yourself, "If I spend the holiday with
my friends, I'll probably feel too guilty to enjoy it anyway so
I might as well go home." Unfortunately, when you succumb
to this manipulation, you probably will not enjoy the
holidays no matter where you go.

- *"No one else can take your place . . ."* Dora lives on one side of a large midwestern city. Her widowed mother lives on the other side. Dora works full-time and has a family of her own, but she still finds time to drive across town to take her mother to doctor's appointments, grocery shopping, and to run errands because her mother no longer feels comfortable driving. Because Dora finds the frequent trips across town are interfering with her job and family life, she has investigated and offered to pay for alternatives such as the senior citizen van or taxis. But her mother complains that she "hates to rely on strangers who don't know how I like things done." She continually reminds Dora, "You're the only one who really understands me. I just can't deal with drivers and people like that. It just makes me too nervous." So Dora keeps driving her mother around.

  The message of this maneuver is that you have to personally solve all your parents' problems. When you comply, you may get a lot of praise for being such a wonderful son or daughter, but you will probably feel resentful at being unable to escape their demands.

- *"We didn't want to bother you . . ."* Martin's parents live about 50 miles away. He visits them about every six weeks, which is all he can manage because he travels so much for his job. His parents think he should come more often, especially now that they are getting older. Martin has told them that if they ask he will certainly adjust his schedule to be with them any time they need him for a specific problem or emergency. But somehow his parents seem to feel that Martin should know when they need him and show up without their request.

  He says, "Last February, Mom was in the hospital for five days and I didn't know about it until afterward. Then, of course, they both let me know how much it would have meant to her to have had me visit and how she kept hoping I'd call. I told them that I didn't know she was sick and asked them why they didn't call me. They said, 'We didn't want to bother you.' "

  This strategy is a more indirect method of enlisting your involvement in your parents' lives at the level that they think is appropriate. If you are not showing what they feel is the

proper devotion, they manage to suffer in some way from
your inattention and then let you know about it later.

- *"Why can't you be as nice as . . ."* Harriet's mother's best
friend has "the best daughter in the world" who visits every
week, takes her shopping and out to lunch, and is always
there for every holiday. Harriet makes a poor showing in
comparison, and her mother makes sure she knows it. "Of
course, my mom's friend's daughter doesn't work and her
children are all in school. I have a job and young children,
but my mom never seems to consider that. She also tells me
how she always spent so much time with her mother. But her
mother lived only a few blocks away. I live thirty minutes
away from Mom, which is too far to go even on my lunch
hour. What really gets me is that my brother Marvin who
lives only sixty miles from here hardly ever visits Mom but
he'll occasionally do something like send her flowers for
Valentine's Day. Then she goes on and on about how he is so
good to her. I'm the one who spends time with her, takes her
places, and helps her when she has a problem, but she thinks
he's the one who really cares."

    Unfavorable comparisons like this leave you feeling both
guilty and unappreciated. No matter what you do, you can
never measure up to the fantasy daughter or son that this sort
of parent wants you to be. Trying harder just seems to make
you feel more frustrated as the standard of comparison rises
along with your efforts.

- *"If you care about me, you'll do it my way . . ."* Noah's
parents were divorced a few years ago when Noah was in his
early thirties and they were in their fifties. Noah's son will
soon be celebrating his bar mitzvah, and Noah wants both his
parents to be there. But Noah's mother says, "If your father
comes, I won't be there. I will never forgive him for going
off with that woman, and I don't see how you can either. If
you want me there, you'll have to leave him out."

    Noah feels stuck. He cares about both his parents, but now
whatever he does will seem to imply that he cares only about
one of them. This sort of bullying threat can be very difficult
to respond to in a way that does not leave you feeling guilty.

- *"You'll be sorry when I'm gone . . ."* Rita's father has high
blood pressure and suffered a mild heart attack a few years
ago. Now he continually reminds Rita that he "won't be

around forever" and in fact "may not be here tomorrow or next month or next year." He tells her how this year may be their last opportunity to be together on Christmas, Thanksgiving, his birthday, her birthday, summer vacation, and on and on. Rita does not want to spend all her vacations visiting her parents, but if she does not go she worries that "something may happen to Dad, and I'll hate myself forever." So she either goes or she feels guilty.

This is perhaps the most powerful guilt-inducing strategy parents can use. If your parents remind you that they will not always be around, you are likely to think of some person you know who had a parent die suddenly and who has some regrets about not having done more for that parent. And of course you do know that your parents will die someday. Because you do not want to end up feeling guilty later, you succumb to the pressure now.

Breaking Free From the Guilt Games

Because these parental guilt-inducing tactics are so powerful, you will have to work hard to avoid being manipulated. But these strategies can control you forever if you let them, so the effort required to free yourself is definitely worthwhile. Here are some suggestions for changing the way you think, feel, and react when your parents try to manipulate your behavior through guilt.

- *Stop trying to be perfect*. Perfection is a myth. It is unrealistic to expect it of yourself. You are bound to disappoint your parents sometimes, and you need to accept this. You cannot meet all their expectations or all their needs anymore than they can meet all of yours. You do not need to constantly prove yourself by trying to meet their standards, nor do you have to compete with others for their favor. You can drive yourself crazy trying to conform to some vision of what an ideal son or daughter should be.

Harriet, whose mother compares her unfavorably to her brother and to a friend's daughter, needs to remove herself from the competition. First she must carefully consider how *she* feels about her relationship with her mother. Harriet's decisions about how much time to spend with her mother and what she will or will not do with her or for her can be based only on her own feelings and her assessment of what is reasonable for her.

Once she feels okay about what she is doing, she will be able to escape the competitive game her mother sets up. She can simply say, "That's great that your friend's daughter spends so much time with her. She must really enjoy that." Or, "It was very thoughtful of Marvin to send you those flowers. I'm sure you're happy to know he is thinking of you."

- *Make your own choices*. Choice includes responsibility. You must be willing to admit that you have wishes and desires that may not fit what your parents want. While it is important to acknowledge their wishes, you need to remind them that this is your life and you have to make your own choices and decisions. A certain amount of selfishness is necessary in order to move on with your life. You are not rejecting your parents by wanting to be autonomous and independent. It is normal and legitimate to disagree with them and to be different.

  Making choices that your parents do not approve of may feel risky. You will have to take responsibility for the outcome of your choices. If you are not happy with your life, you will not be able to blame parental manipulations for your dissatisfaction. Nevertheless, the freedom you will feel when you realize you are not obligated to follow their wishes is well worth the risk.

  Karl, whose parents want him to be a doctor instead of a musician, can let his parents know that although he understands what they want, he does not want to make a change right now. He might say, "I know you want what is best for me, and I know you think that would be medical school, but I have to do what seems right for me. I don't think it would be a good decision for me to go to medical school just to please you. If I'm going to spend that much time, energy, and money learning something, I think it should be something I have a strong commitment to and I just don't feel that way about medical school right now. I know music is a risky field to be in, and I'm willing to take responsibility for my choice. If I find I can't succeed at it, I'll do something else, but I won't expect you to support me."

• *Do not respond to intimidation.* Do not give in to tears, yelling, or martyr games. If you do, it increases the likelihood that they will continue to use these tactics. Make sure you have made up your mind about what you want or plan to do before you tell them something you think they will dislike. Then stick to your plans, regardless of their reaction. Be calm but firm. If this seems cruel, remind yourself that you are actually working to improve your relationship with your parents. Giving in to intimidation leaves you feeling resentful at having been manipulated.

Diana and Hugh, who are afraid to go out and leave Hugh's mother, Eunice, are letting her intimidate them. The next time she tells them, "Don't worry about me, I'll be fine," they need to say something like, "But we do worry because it seems that every time we leave you alone something bad happens. Because we still want to be able to go out occasionally, we will arrange for someone to stay here with you just in case any problem comes up while we are gone." If Eunice insists that she can manage and prefers to stay alone, they should take her at her word and let her handle whatever comes up. They have a right to have some time alone together without feeling guilty.

• *Realize you are not controlling their lives.* The old childhood saying, "Step on a crack, break your mother's back," seems to stick with many people for life. But you do not actually have the power to make your parents sick or miserable, nor can you keep them happy all the time. No matter what they say, they are responsible for their own feelings and reactions just as you are responsible for yours. You are not required to spend the rest of your life making up to them for your past mistakes or inconsiderate actions. The past is over. Guilt will not change it. If you have wronged them, apologize, offer compensation if it is due, and move on with your life.

Hal, the pilot whose mother worries so much, is right in refusing to take responsibility for his mother's pain. Her worrying is her problem, and it is very unlikely that he could solve it even if he tried. If he were to give up flying in response to her demands, she would probably worry just as much about him in some other way. What if he had a car accident or got mugged or had a heart attack? Hal needs to keep reminding himself that he is not responsible for her worry.

- *Set clear limits*. Say no clearly when you mean it. If you do not plan to visit them next summer, it is much better to tell them clearly that you are not coming even though you know they will be upset, rather than to try to avoid the unpleasantness by pretending you are unsure. If you say "maybe" or "It might work out," you are likely to hear "You promised" or "You said you were coming" later on when the visit does not take place. It is best to agree only to requests you can meet with good humor. If you acquiesce grudgingly to a request that feels unreasonable or seems to be more than you can manage, you will feel angry and resentful. It is better to explain that you have other plans, needs, or desires and then make alternative suggestions.

  Dora, who gives in to her mother's demands to drive across town to take her wherever she needs to go, needs to be more clear about her own needs. Rather than simply suggesting other transportation, she could say something like, "Mother, I can come over only once a week to drive you somewhere. Let's sit down and figure out which are the most important places for me to take you and which you could get to in a taxi or the senior van. If you would like, I'll help you write out instructions to give the drivers so that you can be sure you are being clear about where you want to go."

  When her mother resists, Dora must remain firm to her once-a-week trip. If her mother misses a few appointments, Dora must let her take responsibility for that: "I'm sorry to hear you couldn't get to your hair appointment. I guess the senior van really sticks to that rule that you have to call twenty-four hours in advance unless you have an emergency. At least now you know, so next time you can be sure to call far enough ahead."

- *Accept their difficulties and losses*. You cannot rescue your parents from the problems in their lives. Even though it may be very difficult to face, you must realize that your parents will change as they age. Feeling sorry for them does not help. You cannot spare them from the pains, illnesses, and losses that come with age.

  Your parents may feel frustrated at some changes and difficulties in their lives, and they may be looking for someone to blame. They may imply that somehow if you cared more, their lives would be different. But no matter how much you care, you cannot fix everything for them.

Rita, whose father "may not be here tomorrow," is letting her sympathy and fear for his future dominate her life. Both Rita and her father need to accept the uncertainty of his medical condition. Probably she will want to spend some holidays and vacation time with him, but she needs to realize that she is not somehow keeping him alive by being there. It is certainly possible that he will die when she is not around, but if that happens it will not be her fault.

If Rita can accept this uncertainty now, she will be more likely to be able to respond positively to his pleas. She could say, "I know you won't always be around, and I feel very sad about that. But if I put my whole life on hold until after you die, I may find myself waiting for you to die, which would make me feel even worse. I want to look forward to visiting you and enjoy our being together, but that's hard if I feel I have to come whether or not it is convenient for me."

Preventing Future Guilt

You may feel guilt over past incidents in which you truly believe you treated your parents unfairly or hurt them through your own insensitivity. As long as your parents are still around, you have the opportunity to rectify such situations by apologizing to them. Once you have done so, you need to let yourself off the hook by giving up your guilt. You cannot change the past, and feeling guilty creates a barrier to improving your relationship with them in the present.

If you do not resolve old problems with your parents or say what you want to say to them before they die, you may feel guilty for a long time. Rita is actually more fortunate than many grown children because her father's illness gives her the opportunity to ask herself what she would regret not having done or said once her father dies. Theoretically all adults could ask themselves this question while their parents are still living, but most do not, probably because it is an uncomfortable matter to contemplate.

Nevertheless, there is no time like today for taking action. You might want to try imagining that one or both of your parents has just died. Then ask yourself what you regret. Now consider what you can do today to prevent that future guilt.

This does not mean that you should sacrifice your life in the present to avoid future guilt. Rather, it is a reminder to stop and think about what you truly want to tell them and do for them.

What If It Is Too Late to Talk?

Some adults berate themselves after a parent dies. They look back and see themselves as having neglected or injured their parents. They wish they could somehow revise the past.

- "My mother wanted me to call more often, but I was always too busy. Now I wish I had taken the time. What would a few phone calls have mattered out of my life compared to what they would have meant to her."
- "I saw my dad only twice after he had his stroke. I was planning on going down for his birthday, but he had another stroke and died right before then. I wish I had gone more often before that."
- "My father and I had a huge fight and didn't speak to each other for seven years. Later we worked it out, but he died only a year after that. Now I really regret that we lost all that time that we could have had together."
- "My mother wanted me to take a trip with her down South where she grew up, but I never wanted to go, so I kept making excuses. After she was gone I wished I had gone on that trip with her. She gave up a lot for me. I could have done that for her."

These grown children are looking for forgiveness. But how can they get it once their parents are gone? Blaming and punishing themselves now over what they did or did not do in the past will not help. Instead they will have to forgive themselves so that they can let go of their guilt.

One way to do this is to use a technique called "imagined interaction." It works just like conversations you sometimes have in your mind when you imagine yourself asking your boss for a raise or confronting a friend about a problem between you. In these conversations you play both parts as a sort of rehearsal for the real conversation. You can use a similar process to have an imagined conversation with a deceased parent.[2]

To do this, find a place where you can be relaxed and free of distractions. Close your eyes and imagine your parent sitting nearby. Try to see your parent clearly, dressed as you remember him or her. Then talk to your parent in your mind. Say what you want to say and let your parent answer. If you can imagine your parent forgiving you, accept that forgiveness and let go of your guilt. If you cannot imagine your parent forgiving you, express your regret at the difficulties between you, but point out that that you are now ready to accept the situation without guilt.

You may find that you need more than one imagined interaction to let go of your guilt. Have as many internal conversations as you find useful, but beware of letting these turn into continuations of old arguments. Remember that your goal here is to express caring and resolve guilt. You must let the old struggles go so that you can get on with your life free of the burden of guilt.

PART THREE

Sticky Situations

CHAPTER 8

How You Can Change Family Gatherings and Holidays

"I would like everyone to drop their facades. Our family holidays never turn out to be much fun, so why do we go through these phony rituals? I wish that somehow these gatherings could be more meaningful. I wish everyone could be adults. Unfortunately, the holidays seem to throw us back into our old roles as children, Mom, and Dad."

(Cheryl, age 28)

Uncomfortable feelings of pretending, mechanically going through the motions, or stepping back into old roles are not uncommon at family holiday gatherings. The experience may be especially difficult because of a common illusion, sometimes called "the Walton-Family syndrome," which implies that most families share warm, wonderful holidays with no arguments or hurt feelings to spoil the fun.

Picture-Perfect Is Only in Pictures

In real-life, many adults do enjoy holidays with their parents, but many others report that they would like to change what goes on at their family holiday gatherings. Examples of changes some say they would like to make in getting together with their parents at family celebrations disclose a variety of dissatisfactions:

- "I would like both of my parents to enjoy a holiday with all of us. My mother gets angry and has hurt feelings at least

113

once per holiday. My father spends a lot of time outdoors while the family is indoors. My parents also say hurtful things to each other at least once a holiday."

- "My mother expects my wife and me to be at her house every holiday. This has caused many problems in pleasing both sides of the family."

- "I would like to see my parents relax a little more. At Christmas everything has to be done in a certain way. With twelve grandchildren, that's a little difficult. I wish they could just roll with the waves instead of tensing up when things don't go well."

- "I would like everyone's voice to be lowered to a pleasant listening level. I would like us to be able to do something fun together and get along. I would like my dad to quit hiding out in the garage."

- "I wish my mother would be kinder to everyone and not let the holidays get her so excited. I would like to be able to help her in fixing meals and other holiday preparations so she doesn't have to act as though she has to run the whole show."

- "I feel as though I have to perform the ideal homemaker role for my mother by preparing a big meal, being on top of everything, being superorganized, having a perfectly clean house, and so on. I wish holidays could be more relaxed and easygoing."

- "My parents concern themselves too much with the disagreements and confrontations between their children. When all of my brothers and sisters get together, there is always some kind of trouble. My parents worry too much about this and feel the sibling squabbles are their fault."

- "I wish my parents wouldn't bring up mistakes I have made and discuss them with other family members like I wasn't even in the room."

Why Is It So Hard to Have Fun?

As these comments indicate, people want and expect family celebrations to be enjoyable, relaxing times. They also want to share these special occasions with their parents without arguing, feeling upset, or slipping into difficult old patterns. But as the comments disclose, reality often differs from wishes. Instead of picture-perfect gatherings, people often find difficult holidays where parents fight with each other and get upset if everything does not go a certain way, and where they themselves get caught up in old family games and conflicts.

Where does the problem lie? Part of the difficulty is caused by unrealistic expectations of family life. Popular culture portrays holidays as especially fine family times, so our images of perfection tend to center on these times. Somehow we expect, or at least hope, that this time reality will rise to the occasion. If it does not, we focus on the problems and overlook the good parts.

Another complicating factor is that the dynamics of the family itself sometimes work against enjoyable gatherings when adult children and their parents get together. In particular, problems arise when families hang on to old roles, myths, and rituals that some members find distressing.

Old Roles: "Play It Again, Don."

While you may not want to play your old familiar part in the family one more time, somehow you find yourself stuck with the role at family gatherings. Maybe you are the peacemaker who resolves family quarrels, or the rebel who starts the fights, or maybe, like Don, you are the klutz.

Don: I Hate Being the Clumsy One.

I truly am a different person when I go back to spend vacations or holidays with my family. It's like high school all over again. Then I was a gawky teenager who broke dishes, spilled food, and always seemed to say the wrong thing. My clumsiness became a family joke. Now I'm a thirty-six-year-old dentist with a successful practice where I perform delicate procedures every day. But when I'm with the family, I revert back into "bumbling Don."

I'm not sure how it happens. I always tell myself this time is going to be different. But somehow I end up tripping over the dog and spilling a glass of wine on the carpet or asking my sister about her boyfriend right after they just broke up. As soon as I get there my mother starts warning me what not to talk about and telling me where to sit so I'll be less likely to damage anything. This just makes me angry and determined to show her she's wrong about me. But eventually I end up proving her right.

Why does Don continue to play his old role in the family drama, despite his resolve not to do so? In families, as in organizations, people take on different parts, depending on their personal characteristics and on the needs of the unit. While an organization may have officers, salespeople, production workers, and record keepers, roles in a family are not so easily defined. Nevertheless, over the years family members tend to "specialize" in particular ways when they are together as a group. One may be the organizer who makes sure plans are made and details are covered, another the clown who keeps everyone laughing, and another the caretaker who looks after anyone who is upset or ill.

Because such specialization helps the family operate as an efficient system, it can be very difficult for any individual member to shed an accustomed role. For example, if Don's mother is the one who makes most of the plans and arrangements for holiday celebrations, she may feel obligated to do that even at a time when she is in poor health. She may resist giving up the role because she feels no one else could handle the job, or she may prefer to give it up but find other family members feel unable to take it on. Because change is disruptive to a system, the inclination is for everyone to stay with their assigned parts if at all possible.

While some family members may be quite satisfied with their parts, others may feel stuck in roles that never felt comfortable or that no longer fit. For example, one thirty-five-year-old woman who is the youngest in a large family is frustrated that her seventy-year-old parents still introduce her as their baby and refuse to ask her for help when they are ill. Although she is a capable, independent adult in her own community, as soon as she goes back home for a visit she finds herself trying to prove she is grown up.

Similarly, Don, in the example above, is stuck in his role of the family klutz. His parents and siblings expect this behavior and somehow Don ends up meeting their expectations. Don does not enjoy playing this part, but he does not know how to escape it. Consequently, he tries to avoid family gatherings.

Myths: "We're One Big Happy Family."

Family myths are shared beliefs, stories, or legends that describe the way one specific family functions. Although the myths often do not reflect reality, family members generally overlook the inaccuracies. In fact, family myths seem to be unconsciously accepted without clear awareness that they exist. Family members act as if the myths were true, ignoring evidence that conflicts.

One common family myth is the myth of harmony. It paints a beautiful picture of the family's present and past togetherness, declares that everyone in the family is happy, and says the family has no problems.[1] Other myths maintain that family members share the same views and will never disagree on important topics, or that family members will always support one another to outsiders, regardless of what goes on within the family.

Because a family myth is a shared group image, it serves to unify the family and to protect it against internal conflict or external attack. Like unwritten family rules, myths survive through unspoken agreement among family members. Questioning a family myth is taboo because of the risk of upsetting the family system.

But as an adult you may begin to feel uncomfortable with a family myth. Perhaps your life has changed significantly or you have been away from your parents and siblings so much that you no longer feel the same unquestioning loyalty to that old view of reality. Or perhaps the family beliefs have begun to feel confining to you. If the rest of the family still goes along with the old idea of "This is the way we are," you, like Carla, may feel that you are stuck playing a disturbing game.

Carla: Why Are They Pretending?

When I was growing up my mother always talked about what a happy family we were. And because we didn't argue, maybe we did seem happy, but I don't think we really were. Mom usually had things her way, and Dad stayed busy and away from home a lot. Mom has this way of assuming that what she wants will make everyone happy, and somehow we all just went along. Mostly we just kept our feelings to ourselves. Probably my sister and I both suspected Mom and Dad weren't very happy together, but we never talked about that.

Even now they will not talk about any family problems. I'm tired of pretending to be a happy family just because we are all afraid to confront Mom. But my sister says she doesn't see a problem, and Dad acts like he has no idea what I'm talking about if I mention the way Mom controls everything. Meanwhile Mom keeps going on about what a happy family we are and how nice it is that we don't fight like so many families do. I feel like a total fake when I'm with them. It really drives me crazy.

Because Carla seems to be the only member of her family who wants to discard the happy-family myth, she probably will not be successful in initiating change in the way the rest of the family sees the situation. In fact, if we asked each of the others to describe their feelings, we might find that they actually do see the family as happy and do not feel that they are pretending. While Carla's feeling that their interactions are not genuine remains a problem for her, it is probably one that she will have to solve without their help.

Rituals: "We Always . . ."

The pull to gather and reinforce family ties by engaging in a special family celebration is strong, even if you typically find some aspects of the gathering stressful. Participation in family rituals reinforces feelings of family solidarity and of your own special place in the family. The continuation of traditions across generations provides a sense of family history and roots that we often miss in everyday life.

Rituals fill a human need to have a sense of belonging, an enduring sense of being linked to others through shared traditions and meaning.[2] At holiday time or for special occasions, most adults will go to considerable trouble to gather with members of their larger family to celebrate in the old familiar ways. Airlines report that the busiest travel days of the year are the day before Thanksgiving and the day after New Year's; highway travel is also especially heavy at those times.

Yet once you arrive at the family celebration, especially if it is at your parents' home, you may find some of the family rituals feel more like tyranny than festivity. Your parents want you there and they say they want you to have a good time, but they seem to want you to do everything their way, the old way. You may have never particularly enjoyed the old way, or you may feel you have outgrown it, or you may find that your spouse, lover, or children have other ideas about the way holidays should go. But your parents may refuse to change even the smallest detail of the usual celebration.

Gary, for example, complains, "I wish that food didn't have to be so important. We all eat too much at holiday time. I love to eat, but I am a food abuser. I have tried and tried to talk to my mother about this, but she'll never listen.

Probably Gary's mother would say that the holiday would not feel like a celebration to her without all the usual food. For her, the preparation and serving of the traditional food may be the core of the family holidays, which she carries on as a continuation of special times she remembers fondly from her own childhood and young-adult years. Furthermore, she very likely wants her own children to continue serving and eating the traditional holiday food as a way of carrying on the family legacy.

Unfortunately, rituals can lose much of their positive function for family members if there is no flexibility in the way they are carried on year after year. When a family does not adapt rituals to fit new stages in the family's development, the rituals may become empty and hollow. The players may continue to act out their parts, but without the same sense of meaning. This is especially true when parents insist on maintaining child-centered holiday customs after their children are grown or demand that adult children participate in a specific pattern of ceremonies established by the parents.[3]

Ann, a young woman in her late twenties, looks forward to the Christmas holidays as a break from her hectic life-style combining a demanding career and care of her young child. But her parents insist that the entire family take the children to see Santa, which means standing in line for hours, then have an elaborate Christmas Eve dinner, then attend late-night Christmas Eve services, and then get up early Christmas morning to open presents and prepare another big meal. "I end up exhausted and grouchy," she complains. "I wish we could cut back on some of it, but they say, 'We always did this, and it wouldn't be Christmas without it.' "

If you cannot stand to repeat the same holiday rituals year after year, but you still want or feel obligated to spend holidays with your parents, your best bet is to work for gradual change. Ann, for example, could start by deciding that she and her young daughter will stay at home while the others attend the Christmas Eve service. This would give them a little time alone to rest and gather energy for the next day's festivities.

Even if your parents are quite rigid in insisting on the familiar patterns, you can take steps to add new elements to make the experience more enjoyable for yourself. If Ann feels that she simply cannot cope with her parents' reaction to her skipping any of the traditional activities, she could arrange to arrive a day early to spread out the activities or have some time to prepare before the hectic celebrations begin.

Five Survival Steps for Family Gatherings

If you are willing to plan ahead and expend some extra effort, you can create a context for yourself that makes holidays with your parents more enjoyable. The key is to take time before the gathering to step back and think about what you want and what you can change.

• *Examine your motives.* Ask yourself whether you are planning to spend the holidays with your parents because you truly want to share that time with them or whether you are doing it from a sense of obligation or guilt. If you are not sure about your motives, apply the "blizzard test." Imagine that a major snowstorm forces you to cancel your plans to be with your parents for the holiday. Are you disappointed or relieved? If you feel a quick sense of freedom, you will know your plans were prompted by feelings of what you "should" do.

Of course, you may have many reasons why you choose to spend holidays with your parents even when you would ideally rather be somewhere else. You may not want them to be alone, or you may want your children to have the experience of continuity that comes with family celebrations, or you may feel that the guilt you would suffer over staying away would be worse than the discomfort of being there.

The point is to be honest with yourself and to be clear that you are making a choice. If you are choosing a family holiday even though you wish you could skip it, you must believe the reward is worth the price in some way. Ken, who has a rather difficult relationship with his mother has thought about this quite a bit.

Ken: I Want to Be with Her.

I like to spend Christmas with my mother, although I wish we could spend Christmas together in a more pleasant, enjoyable way. It's not just a matter of being a good son. I truly, actually want to be with her, even though she drives me crazy. I'm willing to put up with that for a couple of days because she's my mother, because I get something out of being with her.

Part of it is going back and getting in touch with roots, with family. Sometimes it's kind of nice to go through the memories. At Christmas it's nice to be with family, even though I know it's going to be unpleasant with some built-in problems.

I also have the sense more and more of feeling sorry for her being alone. This is something I can give her. There's a certain sense of obligation. I would like to do something nice for her.

• *Modify your expectations.* Now that you know why you are going, be realistic about what you expect. Remember that while fictional families may have flawless gatherings, real families have their ups and downs. If your mother always gets upset and your father usually escapes to the garage, this year will probably be that way, too. If your parents, like Ann's, typically insist that everything be done according to tradition, this year is unlikely to be an exception. But if you are realistically expecting your own family's behavior rather than counting on some miraculous transformation to the family you have always wanted to have, you will save yourself from feeling frustrated and disappointed. This does not mean you should expect to have a miserable time. In fact, you will probably enjoy yourself more because you will be expecting the usual difficulties as part of the territory, which will leave you free to focus on the pleasant aspects.

• *Know what you want to change*. Remember that you can change yourself more easily than you can change them, and if you change the way you think about and react to their behavior, it may not matter whether or not they change. Also, because you cannot change everything at once, it is important to be aware of what specific aspects you most want to modify. Begin with a list of complaints. To illustrate, consider the grown children who have described their frustrations in this chapter. Don might say, "My parents treat me like a clumsy jerk." Carla might say, "I'm sick of pretending we're a happy family." Gary might say, "My mother is always making me overeat." Ann might say, "My parents insist we do everything their way."

Now turn your complains into positive statements about something you want to change about yourself. For example, Don could say, "I want to feel more capable and composed when I am with my parents." Carla could say, "I want to feel comfortable and natural with my family." Gary could say, "I want to eat moderately at family gatherings." Ann could say, "I want to feel relaxed and rested on family holidays."

Now that you have your desired changes phrased in terms of yourself, you can make a plan for what you will do to achieve them. The beauty of this approach is that you are in charge. Rather than wishing, hoping, and complaining, you can act.

• *Plan to take care of yourself*. Your plan, like your changes must focus on yourself. Although it will take some practice, you *can* behave differently. The trick is to take responsibility for yourself, plan ahead, and stick to your convictions even if others do not approve. Decide what you can do to change the situation for yourself. Then, rather than discussing it or asking permission, simply act.

If Ann decides that skipping the Christmas Eve church service would give her some of the relaxed time she needs to enjoy the rest of the holiday, she needs to stick to that resolve even if her parents are upset. She should avoid arguing with them about it or blaming them for harried holidays in the past. Rather, she should quietly insist on doing what she thinks is best for herself and her young daughter and encourage her parents to enjoy the service without her. If they say they will not go without her, she needs to let them make their own choice and remind herself not to feel guilty. Regardless of what they may say, Ann is not ruining their holiday. While they may see her action as spoiling their plans, they do not *have* to see it that way. To stick to her plan, Ann must be willing to let her parents take responsibility for their own choices.

Don might decide that if he stayed at a motel rather than at his parents' home, he could feel more self-composed. Being able to periodically get away from the atmosphere in which he feels like a klutz may allow him to collect himself and avoid the downward spiral of mishaps he usually falls into. He does not need to explain why he is choosing to stay in a motel or tell them what he is hoping to change. He may decide to limit the amount of time he spends at his parents home to short intervals, at least until he begins to feel more comfortable. He might also decide to take the family out for a meal, in order to create a situation in which he feels more in charge and is less likely to fall into his old role of clumsiness. Although Don's parents may resist these changes, they will probably adjust fairly soon. And for Don, coping with their initial opposition is a far better long-term solution than simply staying away.

• *Add something of your own.* Another way of putting your desired changes into practice is to contribute new traditions and build new memories to replace aspects of family gatherings you find undesirable. As an adult you have your own specialties, strengths, and talents. You have had experiences that may be quite different from what your life was like when you were growing up. By finding ways to build your own unique contributions into family gatherings and holidays, you remind your parents and yourself of your separate identity.

Carla, for instance, might decide to bring along a gift of a new game she has enjoyed playing with friends, or a videotape she thinks her parents would enjoy. By involving the whole family in a new activity for at least one evening, Carla may find that she can enjoy being with them without feeling the usual pressure to pretend. Or she could take the lead in establishing a new tradition that focuses at least briefly on genuine feeling: such as having each family member describe the accomplishment he or she has been most proud of in the last year, or having each one express his or her wishes for changes in the world in the upcoming year.

Gary could try getting his family involved in some physical activity to replace, or at least compensate for, some of the eating. A family walk, sledding trip, or basketball game could become a new tradition. Even though some family members may choose not to participate, Gary would be changing the focus of activity for himself and some others. By bringing in a new activity to replace one that he wants to change, Gary would be approaching the situation in a positive manner that maximizes his chances of success. Rather than putting his energy into futile attempts to convince his mother to make less food, he would be establishing a new tradition that helps him cope more healthily with the overabundance he wants to resist.

Difficult Holiday Choices: The Tug-of-War

Some grown children have a different holiday problem. They want to be in two places at once. Grown children who are married or involved in a serious relationship may feel torn when a major holiday approaches bringing with it the difficult decision as to whose family to spend it with. Single adult children may have a similar problem if their parents are divorced. Feeling wanted can be heartwarming, but when two separate parents or sets of parents are each pulling you in their direction, tension is the more likely result. You want to be fair, you want to keep everyone happy, and you want to enjoy the holiday yourself. But if you are like many adults who juggle competing parental invitations, your own pleasure becomes your last priority.

Mary Jane and Rick have eaten two Christmas dinners every year for five years now and at this point they are not sure they can face a duel celebration again this year. The tradition began the first year they were married. Mary Jane's parents, who live 70 miles away in one direction, and Rick's parents, who live 60 miles in the opposite direction, each wanted the couple to spend Christmas Day at their house. Because this was impossible, Rick's parents offered to have their main celebration and big dinner on Christmas Eve, which would enable Mary Jane and Rick to be part of both family celebrations.

"It seemed like a good solution at the time," says Mary Jane, "and we actually enjoyed having two holiday meals and celebrations. But three years ago when our daughter was born, we should have made some changes. It's exhausting to dress up a baby, load up all her stuff and presents and food for the dinner, drive sixty miles, open presents, have dinner, reload the car and drive home late and then turn around and do it all over again the next day." The problem is that both sets of parents insist that it just would not be Christmas without Rick and Mary Jane and the baby, and Rick and Mary Jane do want to be with their parents at Christmas.

"It's not possible to have them all come here, even if we did have room," Rick says. "My parents have my aunt and uncle and my grandmother there and sometimes my sister from California. Mary Jane's parents have her brother and his family who live only about twenty miles from them and then her mom's sister and some cousins. So it seems like we're stuck with this running back and forth, but we sure don't look forward to it."

Rick and Mary Jane may be tired, but at least they do not feel guilty. They are keeping both families happy. Other grown children find themselves expected at two celebrations so far apart that they have to make a difficult choice each time a holiday comes along. Peggy, a thirty-year-old single daughter of divorced parents, is a good example. Peggy lives in Chicago, her father is remarried and lives in Maryland, her mother lives alone in California. "Maybe it's because I am single," Peggy says, "but they each assume I will go to one of them for Christmas, and they each spend months trying to maneuver things so I will go there. It's very hard because I sort of feel like I should spend it with Mom because she's alone, but Dad and his new wife really want me there, too, and I hate to hurt their feelings. Actually I enjoy being with either Mom or Dad except that I always feels guilty about not being with the other one."

The issue here is priorities. Not only are Rick, Mary Jane, and Peggy feeling the tension of being pulled in conflicting directions, they are so busy jumping around trying to keep everyone happy, that they have trouble enjoying the holiday celebrations. They must decide what aspects of various holidays are more important so they can make clearer choices.

Setting Personal Priorities

When you are in the habit of planning your holidays around parental expectations, it is not easy to imagine changing that.

And when you do contemplate a change, the negative outcomes that would result seem to outweigh any possible benefits. If Rick and Mary Jane would decide to skip one of the Christmas celebrations this year, one set of parents would be disappointed and might feel the couple was favoring the other set of parents. And either Rick or Mary Jane would feel a sense of loss from missing out on their parental Christmas celebration. And they would have to find a new tradition to replace the celebration they decided to skip.

To help themselves take a broader view of the situation, Mary Jane and Rick could make a list of what they would ideally like to get from their Christmas celebration. Perhaps their list would include such items as "relaxed time with each other," "an opportunity for our daughter to explore her gifts in her own way," and "time with parents without so much rush, fuss, and confusion." After looking at this list, they might decide to try skipping both family celebrations for one year to give themselves a chance to establish some traditions of their own or to share some holiday time with friends in town. Of course, their parents would most likely protest, but Rick and Mary Jane would have to remain firm in their resolve to try out this change.

Once the pattern is broken, Rick and Mary Jane will have a basis for comparison, which will make it easier for them to decide what they want in the future. They can see whether the negatives they feared were really as much of a problem as they expected, and whether they actually felt being less rushed was worth what they gave up.

Although it would not be easy for Rick and Mary Jane to say no to both sets of parents, it is important that they assert their own rights to have preferences about the way they spend their holidays, especially because they have a young child. Once their parents no longer automatically expect them to show up as scheduled each year, they can begin to negotiate with each set of parents for future celebrations that might work better.

CHAPTER 9

How You Can Have Visits and Phone Calls Your Way

"I went to a professional conference in San Antonio, where my parents live, and I decided to stay with them because I hadn't seen them for a while. I should have known better, but I always seem to forget how they are when I haven't seen them for a while. I was really excited about the conference, finding it stimulating and new, but then I'd come home at night and have only them to share it with. The contrast was amazing. I'd walk in feeling like an adult and in a few minutes I'd feel like a child again. If I tried to talk about the conference, my mother would find some way to turn the conversation around to her life or her friends. My father worried about me getting attacked coming home after dark. They don't see me as an adult. They don't want to know who I am now. They just want me to be their little girl like I used to be."

(Andrea, age 32)

Even when they live far apart, parents and grown children generally stay in fairly close contact through visits and phone calls, but the contact is not always comfortable. When you live far enough away that you see your parents only a few times a year or even less often, you tend to lose touch with one another's day-to-day activities. Even though phone calls may keep each of you up-to-date on the other, you do not usually see one another in new roles and contexts. So your perceptions remain somewhat static, and when you are together you may continue to react to one another in the old familiar ways.

This is usually more of a problem for grown children than

for their parents, because you are likely to be changing more than they are, especially in ways you would like them to recognize. When you return home and, like Andrea, feel that they still see you as a child, you are upset. The contrast between your life away from your parents, where people treat you as a capable, interesting adult, and your time with them, where they treat you as if you had not changed in ten years, can be hard to take.

When You Go Home From Far Away

Going home can be a push-pull sort of situation. You want to see them, but you know you will find some aspects of the visit uncomfortable. You look forward to it, yet you dread it at the same time. You promise yourself that you will be different this time, that you will not get upset so easily. You hope this time will be the ideal happy visit you want, but you fear the usual problems will come up. When you get there, you are likely to come up against the familiar difficulties once more.

- *You feel like a child again.* It is easy to revert back to old patterns when you go home for a visit, especially if your parents still live in the house where you grew up. Somehow it is like a time warp. Henry, who is twenty-eight, married and the father of a child of his own, says that before he goes to visit he always thinks that this time his parents will see him as the adult he is and will treat him the way his friends and co-workers do. But somehow when he gets there, he is unable to feel like an adult for long. He complains: "My mother treats me like a child, fussing over me, telling me what to eat, asking me if I'm too warm or too cold, reminding me to take a raincoat when I go out. It's like when I was in kindergarten and she pinned my gloves to my jacket so I wouldn't lose them."

  Henry does not feel his father sees him as grown-up either. He says, "When I'm there he seems to need to remind me of how to drive and the best route to get everywhere. He also reminds me not to spill food on the couch, as if I were fifteen again. In fact, I usually begin to feel and act like I did at fifteen—moody, awkward, and sullen."

  Henry also says he has a tendency to overeat when he is

visiting at home, another old behavior he hates to get into, because he has worked hard to break the habit. "But my mother keeps telling me I should eat more and asking 'don't I want another helping,'" he complains. "It would be hard to be hungry enough to eat enough where my mother would feel like you couldn't still eat more."

• *They Live in Your Past.* Although your parents may forget a lot about what you have told them about your life lately, they seem to remember vividly every dumb, "cute" thing you did as a child. And they love to remind you of these childish incidents, which does not help at all in your struggle to be more adult with them. According to Marge, her parents' favorite openings when she is visiting seem to be, "It seems like only yesterday when you were _____ ," "Do you remember the time you _____," and "You were so cute when _____ ." Inevitably the openings lead into an old story she has heard many times before, "Like the time my dog followed me to school when I was in first grade and waited outside for me all day, and the teacher told me to send her home, but I couldn't get her to go, so I cried."

Or your parents bring up old mistakes or accomplishments to measure against your present life. For instance, "You always did have trouble with math. No wonder you can't balance your checkbook." Or "You were always such a good athlete. How could you let yourself get so overweight and out of shape?"

They Want You to Impress Their Friends. Even though your parents may be dissatisfied with your accomplishments, they certainly do not want their friends to know that. When other people are around, you may not even recognize yourself as the person they are describing. Carl was recently amazed to hear his father telling some friends how proud he is that Carl has been made sales manager when, "At home he's always reminding me that I'll never get anywhere in that two-bit firm."

Carl complains that he feels like a possession his father is using to impress his friends. "Last summer he told me not to say anything in front of one of his friends about a job I had applied for but didn't get. Dad said that his friend's children are very successful, and he doesn't want to give him anything to gloat about. I was really angry, and I told him that what his friends think is no concern of mine."

* *They Have Rules*. While you may not expect to be a guest in your parents' home, you would like a little more freedom in your daily life while you are there. Instead, they expect you to fit into their schedule—get up early, eat early, go to bed early. They feel perfectly free to tell you where to sit, what to watch or not to watch on television. They remind you not to mess up the living room and to hang up your coat when you come in. They insist you spend time with various friends of theirs as well as relatives who are "dying to see you."

They expect you to be available for a list of activities they have planned, but they will not let you use their car to go anywhere by yourself. In fact, they do not want you to do anything by yourself. If you go in your room and close the door for more than 15 minutes, they come knocking to see "if anything is wrong," or if you "need anything."

Why Do They Still Treat You This Way?

Why is it so hard for your parents to realize you have changed and to treat you as the adult you are? Part of the problem is that they have a long history of seeing you behave in immature ways. Because people are generally resistant to changing their views of others, it is not easy for them to transform their impressions of you even when they have evidence that you have changed. They have a hard time reconciling their strong recollections of you as the teenager whose room always looked like a cyclone had hit, or who never refilled the gas tank in the family car, with the responsible, organized adult you are today.

You may think that all they need to do is realize you have grown up and are now much different from the person you once were. You may expect them to forget their old perceptions of you and see you as you see yourself today. But making this shift is actually more difficult than you may realize.

Social psychologists have accumulated an extensive body of research that explains how people go about organizing and reorganizing their impressions of other people. They have discovered that people use some predictable processes to combine different kinds of information to form an overall impression of another person and to reconcile inconsistent information about them. In general, the early information we get about a person has the strongest influence on the way we view that person. New information may be added to our initial impression; may be discounted, especially if it does not fit our initial impression; or may be reevaluated to make it fit our original view.[1]

If you think about it, you may recall some occasions when you had a hard time changing your impressions of someone else. To illustrate, suppose you go back to your fifteen-year high-school reunion and discover that the class "goof-off" is now a wealthy investment banker. What do you say to yourself to reconcile your former views of him with his present success? Do you say you always knew investment bankers were not worth the money they make and he probably only got where he is because of his father's connections? Or do you revise your opinion of him, tell yourself he was always smart but probably just going through an irresponsible phase in high school, and that he has clearly settled down and become a hard worker?

You may find your original view of your classmate as a "goof-off" stays with you, despite his obvious success. You might even remember after discussing the situation with others at the reunion that your irresponsible former classmate had actually begun to settle down during your last year of high school—a change which had clearly not induced you to alter your perceptions of him. In fact, all you had remembered about him before talking to other classmates at the reunion was his fooling around. And you still may find yourself looking for explanations for his success that attribute the cause to lucky or easy circumstances rather than to his ability and hard work.

Research has found that once we decide a person either has or does not have the ability and/or inclination to do well at a task, we then interpret that person's performance to fit our impressions of the person. For example, in several experiments, people watched others perform a series of 30 difficult intelligence-test-type items. Every test-taker answered 15 of the 30 items correctly, but some started out with mostly correct answers and then got worse, while others started out missing most of the items but improved. The observers guessed that the people who started out well but declined were smarter and had more correct answers than the people who started out poorly but improved.[2] Apparently the observers decided who was smart and who was not after watching only some of the trials. Then they stuck to these impressions, even though the test-takers' later performance did not confirm their initial views.

Similarly, parents who have a long-standing view of a child as irresponsible may overlook that grown child's responsible behavior, but notice the few irresponsible lapses because that is the sort of behavior they expect. Also, they may interpret your behavior as irresponsible when it is merely different from their own. So, for example, when you visit them and stay up late, sleep late, and skip breakfast, they may see that as evidence that you are immature and irresponsible, because it is not the way they think adults should behave. Even though you remind them that this is your vacation, that at home you are up and at work early every day, they seem to ignore that and stick to their original beliefs.

Why Do You Care So Much?

For most people, their parents' views and treatment of them have a strong effect on the way they feel about themselves. As humans we are social beings who develop our sense of self during childhood as we learn to see ourselves through others' eyes.[3] Our parents are especially important figures in this process. If, while we are growing up, they see us as capable, we are more likely to see ourselves that way. Even as adults most people's self-esteem is at least partially a function of the extent to which their parents see them as successful.

You may be feeling just fine about yourself, your life-style, your job, and your relationships until you go home for a visit. Suddenly your views of yourself are challenged. You are accustomed to having the people around you treat you as a capable adult, which fits the way you see yourself. But at your parents' house this self-image is threatened when your parents act as if they see you as a child. You feel conflict between who you usually are and who they see you as being, and even worse, you may feel yourself slipping into behaving in ways that fit their image. So you find yourself feeling worse about yourself than you did when you arrived, which naturally creates a desire in you to leave and go back to your own life where you feel like the person you want to be.

When They Visit You

You can go through the same feelings when they visit you, especially if they stay with you for an extended visit. Thirty-four-year-old Lois dreads her mother's annual two-week summer visit. Lois finds her mother's visits confusing and upsetting. While her mother maintains that their relationship is one of friendship, in which they spend time together because it is mutually enjoyable to do so, Lois sees it differently. She says: "My mother makes me turn into this other person when she visits for two weeks. My husband says I do, too. I hate it. She knows what buttons to push, and she uses all of them. Although she claims her children are really more 'friends' than children, all her children feel this is not true. No friend of mine would act the way she does on a visit, or if they did we wouldn't be friends any more."

Lois's experience with her mother's visits is not unusual. Lois feels that her mother violates all the codes of conduct that usually operate between friends, so she sees the visits as an obligation rather than a pleasure. Her mother apparently enjoys their time together and no doubt looks forward to the visits.

Lois says that her mother takes over her household and treats her like a child. "She cleans out my refrigerator and throws away whatever she decides is too old. She rearranges the kitchen cabinets so the arrangement will be 'more convenient.' Once she even decided to hand wash my underwear and hang it outside to dry on a little line she rigged up while I was at work. She makes lists of foods I should be buying and casseroles I could make and freeze in batches so we wouldn't eat so much take-out food. She acts like I have no idea how to take care of myself."

Lois has tried to arrange with her mother to stay for a shorter period of time than two weeks. "I think we could stay on better terms and maybe even enjoy each other's company if she stayed for only a week," Lois says. "There are a few things we like to do together that can keep us going about that long, plus I'm always more able to stay calm the first few days she is here." But Lois's mother insists that a one-week visit is not worth the price of a plane ticket. She is "deeply hurt" that Lois would even suggest shortening her visit.

With some parents, even a short visit can seem unbearable because they are so critical and demanding. Forty-five-year-old Joyce recalls a recent four-day visit from her father, which left both her and her husband feeling like they could not take another day. Joyce's father arrived in town unannounced at seven o'clock Friday morning, saying he was going to stay only overnight. He stayed until Monday evening, with no respect for Joyce's and her husband's life-style or previously scheduled activities. Joyce says: "He was demanding that we respect *his* schedule. He's up very early, and we like to sleep in on weekends. He 'had to go out for breakfast' because he couldn't wait, although I had provided food in the kitchen and pointed it all out. He indicated that I was lazy by sleeping in. I attended a baby shower that Sunday afternoon, and he was offended that I wouldn't stay home with him. He was angry that we wouldn't attend his church Sunday morning, and on and on."

Steps Toward Adult-to-Adult Contact

Lois seems to be looking for a better way to spend time with her mother, as does Joyce with her father, but they apparently believe that they cannot change the way the visits go. Joyce and Lois might be surprised to know that they are the ones with the most power to change their situations. Because she enjoys their time together less than her mother does, Lois probably has less investment than her mother does in their spending time together. Certainly this is true for Joyce and her father.

In any relationship between two people, the one who has the least stake in interaction between them can generally control the frequency and type of their contact. The other person, however, recognizing his or her lack of control, may success-fully even out the situation through manipulative ploys or insisting on commitments for specific dates and times of future visits.

Between adult children and their parents, it is more often the parents who want more contact than the grown children do. This means that the grown children are more likely to have the power, which means the ability to change the frequency and quality of the contacts between them. Yet many feel that their parents run things most of the time.

If you, like Lois and Joyce, feel that it is time to start having some contact with your parents on your terms rather than theirs, you can begin with some specific steps:

* *Choose the dates and length of visit you want.* Tell them what will work for you, rather than accepting their decrees. Let them know you are happy to have them come for a week (or whatever length of time works best for you), but that a longer visit is simply not a possibility this year. Also, let them know that you must work out with them in advance which dates would be best for them to visit. If they complain that you sound like you do not even want them to come, repeat that you do want them to come, but you want them to come for the sort of visit that fits your life as well as theirs.

Some parents, like Lois's mother, may find any limits inappropriate and very upsetting. Lois's mother probably believes that in order to have the sort of relationship with her daughter that she deserves, a certain amount of contact through visits and phone calls is necessary. She also probably feels that her status as a mother is threatened if she does not have the frequency and length of contact she and her friends consider the rightful due of a mother of a grown child.

The key here is to realize that you are an adult with rights and preferences that count as much as theirs do. You are not being cruel by insisting that you have a vote. Certainly you have a right to expect them to check with you before they show up for a visit so that you can choose times when you do not have other commitments.

Advance planning and limits can also be to their benefit. If a shorter visit between Lois and her mother turns out to be more pleasant, Lois is doing her mother a favor as well as herself by insisting on it. If Joyce's father plans his visits with her in advance, she is more likely to have her time free to spend with him when he is there.

The same holds true when you visit them. Some parents seem to focus more on the length of your visit than on its quality. As one man protested, "Usually they complain that we did not stay long enough, even though waking hours may pass with no interactions and everyone bored."

Even though they may "look forward to it all year," you

do not have to spend your entire vacation with your parents. If you want to visit them for a few days and then take a side trip somewhere else without them, there's no reason to feel guilty.

Just be clear from the beginning about your plans, so there is no misunderstanding later. Leading them on about how long you will stay may be easier than being honest, but it is unfair and also costs you much of the respect you are trying to gain from them.

• *Help them see you as an adult.* When they visit you, give them as many opportunities as possible to see you in your adult roles in everyday life. Take them to work with you, to community or church meetings, to meet your friends. Don't worry about entertaining them once you get there; just let them observe you in these unfamiliar contexts. Seeing you in adult, responsible roles, where you are respected and seen as capable by others, will do more to update their impressions of you than anything you can say to them.

When you visit them, try for adult compromises and avoid childish resistance. If you end up screaming at them that they are treating you like a child, you will only be confirming their view of you as immature. Instead, explain to them what is really important to you—like perhaps needing some quiet time alone and having a chance to visit with an old friend by yourself. Let them know that you would like to fit in with some, but probably not all, of their plans. Find out what is most important to them. Then you can make plans and set priorities together as adults.

Be sure to stick to the commitments you make and expect them to stick to theirs. If you say you will do something, but just do not get around to it, you will be showing them that you are not a trustworthy adult and they will very likely go back to demanding that you do what they want. If you let them back out of their agreements with manipulative tactics, they will not take your preferences seriously the next time you come.

When they bring up the past, ask them to recall how long it has been since you behaved in those ways. If Henry's father, who reminds him not to spill food on the couch, actually realized that it has been at least ten years since Henry had done that, he might be willing to agree not to mention it again unless Henry does spill something. Avoid arguing when you do this. Simply remind them to notice that you have changed.

When you visit them, do your share of the work. If you expect them to wait on you or clean up after you, it will be hard to insist they treat you as an adult.

• *Find new ways to be together.* When you visit them, you can join in some of their activities; when they visit you, they can join in some of yours. You each see the other in new contexts this way as well as possibly developing new interests. One young woman went with her mother to an aquatics exercise class and found it so enjoyable that she signed up for one in her own community after she went home. A couple in their sixties got so involved in their son's compost project that they decided to start one for their own garden back home.

Consider a joint vacation rather than a visit at either your house or theirs. Take a trip, rent a mountain cabin or a beach cottage, go fishing or camping, or whatever you can all agree is worth a try. If you can find new activities you all enjoy, it can give your relationship new life.

Problems When They Live Nearby

Significant numbers of adults live close enough to their parents to see them every day. A 1984 study found that 66 percent of parents aged sixty-five and older lived within 30 minutes of at least one of their adult children. About half of those saw a child every day or two.[4]

No doubt many adult children who live close to their parents enjoy seeing them this often, but others find themselves having more contact than they want or not enjoying the contact they have with parents. When distance is not a factor, it can be more difficult to set limits on the frequency and type of interaction you will have with them. Adults who find difficulties in having their parents live close by mention several common complaints:

• *They expect too much.* Kay's mother, who lives only a few miles away, calls her every night, often drops by unannounced, and expects to spend every Sunday with Kay and her family. "It's not that I don't want to be with Mother or talk to her," says Kay. "It's just that I don't have much free time." Kay works full-time and has two children in elementary school who are in various activities that take some of her evening and weekend time. She and her husband take care of the house and yard on weekends and do miscellaneous errands. "Mother never worked so she just doesn't understand what my life is like," Kay says. "She always seems to walk in when I'm in a rush and everything is a mess. She thinks I'm disorganized. She offers to help, but then she takes over and tells me how to do it better, which I hate. I wish I could see her and talk to her only when I want to."

- *They complain constantly.* When you live nearby, you're likely to be the one they call when they are miserable, which may seem to be most of the time. You hear about all their symptoms and aches and pains, and you get the distinct feeling they expect you to drop everything to come over and do something to help—even though there is nothing you can do. They call you after a shopping trip to let you know how expensive everything is, how crummy the service is, and how you should stay away from this or that store, which used to be good but has definitely gone downhill. They watch the news on television and call to tell you how worried they are and what a miserable state the world is in.

They tell you they want to go for a drive in the country to see the fall foliage, but when you go, they complain that it is too hot, too cold, too dusty, or too far to be enjoyable. Or they go with you to a restaurant that they agreed would be a good choice, but make negative comments through the whole meal about the service, the food, and the atmosphere. Somehow they seem to expect the whole world to accommodate their needs and they want you to make sure they get this special treatment.

- *They interfere in raising your children.* When your parents are part of your children's lives on a regular basis, it can be particularly hard to convince them not to criticize or undermine your efforts and quite frustrating to put up with their interference. As one man whose mother lives four blocks away complains, "My mother treats me like a child where my own children are concerned. She is very quick to judge and lets me know that she does not think I know what I am doing. She really believes that she was a perfect parent and she compares everyone to herself."

A woman who wishes her father would respect the decisions she and her husband make about their daughter says: "In his eyes she is perfect and can do no wrong. We feel that at three she needs guidelines and consistency. In his heart he knows that, but as Grandpa he can't stand it if she's unhappy even for a moment. For example, we don't allow our daughter to put her feet on the table during meals. One day she kept doing just that. When we told her not to, Dad laughed and said, 'But she's just a baby.'"

- *They are nosy about details of your life.* If your parents are often at your house or apartment, they may feel quite free to poke around, ask questions, and comment on every aspect of your life. One young woman complains that her father continually "inspects" her car. She says, "He points out every dent or scratch, wanting to know what happened. He wants to know why I let my friends smoke in the car. He is always complaining that my husband doesn't fix the car when he said he would."

Another woman says her mother looks through her groceries, commenting on what is healthy or unhealthy or what is too expensive. She says, "Her nosiness really irritates me. Last week she asked me why I had bought two boxes of cookies and then said, 'You must be really stressed out to be eating so many sweets.'"

The Value of Boundaries

Poet Robert Frost once wrote, "Good fences make good neighbors." This is also true for adults and their parents. Some boundaries must be respected by both generations if relationships are to be enjoyable, especially between grown children and parents who live close by and are together often. If you have no boundaries, you may be stepping on one another's toes practically every time you get together.

Issues around space, time, and authority are crucial ones that keep coming up in families. It is important that you periodically renegotiate and reach agreements with parents on these topics. If you have been simply drifting along with no clear

boundaries, a talk about what each of you would like from the
other one can improve the present and prevent future conflicts.
In fact, even though the problems may all seem to be their
overstepping bounds, they might also like some changes. Some
topics to consider include:

- *Space*. When they are at your house or apartment, are there
  areas you would like to have accepted as off limits? Perhaps
  you would prefer they would stay out of closets, kitchen
  cabinets, or the refrigerator unless they need to get something, and you might especially like them to refrain from
  commenting on or rearranging these areas. What about your
  car or your garage? They may have similar areas they would
  rather you would leave alone at their house. For example,
  they may not want your inspection or comments about how
  well they are keeping up the house and yard.
- *Time*. Do you want them to come only when invited, or only
  when they call first, or anytime they want? What about
  phone calls? Who calls, how often, and will the other
  person's feelings be hurt if you say you are too busy to talk?
  How much time does each of you want to spend together on
  a regular basis? Can you find a compromise that each of you
  can accept? Do you expect them to baby-sit? If so, how often
  are they willing to do it, and what can you do in exchange?
  If they have more free time than you do, can you agree on
  some ways to spend time together while also accomplishing
  some of the tasks you need to get done? If your time together
  is limited, do you want to ask them to try to focus on the
  enjoyable aspects rather than complaining?
- *Authority*. Do you want your parents to get your permission
  before giving your children treats or gifts? How much and
  what sort of discipline is acceptable for them to use with your
  children? Do you expect them to follow your rules with your
  children, or are they in charge when the children are with
  them? Can they speak for you around town, volunteer your
  time for causes, or ask their friends to help you find a better
  job? Or are you strictly in charge of your own life? Similarly,
  do they want you asking the family doctor about their health
  or making arrangements for having their snow shoveled
  without asking them?

Approach the discussion as a tool for building a better relationship, not an opportunity to get grudges off your chest. Talk about what you would ideally like, ask them what they would like, and try to reach an agreement together. For example, you might say, "I like talking with you on the phone, but I just don't have time to talk every night. Also, it works better for me to call you because I can pick a time when I have time to talk. How would it seem to you if I called three or four times a week?"

If they insist that they do not want any changes and refuse to consider your preferences, you can calmly tell them what your boundaries are and then proceed to implement them. For example, if they continue to call every night, simply say, "I'm sorry, I'm busy right now. I'll call you on Wednesday." This will be difficult at first, but it gets easier. You may find, as one woman did, that when she told her father specifically when and how often each week she could talk with him or spend time with him, he became much less demanding of her time.

CHAPTER 10

How to Stay Out of Their Relationship and Keep Them Out of Yours

"My parents do not communicate at all well with each other. They are in constant adversarial battles. Even when they basically agree, they argue. It is often hard for me to start a conversation with them when they are together for fear of starting an argument."

(Jean, age 29)

Living in the middle of a battle zone is tricky and unpleasant. If your parents quarrel between themselves, you may dislike being around the two of them together. Jean goes on to describe her parents' exasperating pattern.

Jean: Who Cares What Day It Was?
My parents always seem to be trying to prove each other wrong. Even about the simplest things that don't make a bit of difference. My mom will start to tell a story. She'll say something like, "Last Tuesday we were downtown to look for a new lamp and—" Then my dad breaks in, "No dear, it was Wednesday." Then she goes on, "No, it was Tuesday. I remember it was the day after Sara told me about that big sale at Sears." Then Dad will say, "Well, then she must have told you on Tuesday because it was Wednesday that we were downtown." Then Mom will say, "She couldn't have told me on Tuesday because that's her day to volunteer at the hospital. She told me on Monday and we went downtown on Tuesday." Then Dad will say, "I don't care what day Sara works at the hospital. I know when we were downtown and it was Wednesday."

About this time I am fed up and I'll say, "Who cares what day it was? Why don't you just tell me what happened, Mom?" Then Dad will yell at me, "Why are you always trying to start trouble?" And Mom will say, "Never mind! Forget it! It wasn't important anyway." And I'm just sitting there wishing I was somewhere else and not knowing how to get myself out of this mess.

No wonder Jean wishes she could somehow disappear from the scene. She does not want to listen to any more arguments, nor does she care who is right in this dispute. Most of all, she does not want to be in the middle of her parents' feud, which seems to be spreading to draw her in.

If your parents continually bicker over everything from the time of day to how to spend their money, you probably share Jean's frustration. Because you love them both, you hate to hear them attack each other. Even worse, you may find yourself in the middle, with one parent trying to enlist your support against the other.

Pulled in Both Directions

If you do not want to take sides between your parents, you may find yourself in a stressful situation. When you feel pulled between them, it seems as if anything you say will make matters worse. Yet you may be under intense pressure to say something.

They may put you on the spot when they are in the middle of a fight, or each parent may corner you separately to tell you his or her side of the story. You find yourself listening to your mother's endless tales of your father's stinginess, rudeness, and inconsiderate behavior. Next, your father describes in intermi-nable detail your mother's constant whining complaints. They each tell you they are fed up, they have put up with it too long, they cannot take it anymore.

Yet when you confront them with the problem, you may find them very resistant to changing that pattern. One woman told her seventy-year-old parents that she was tired of being in the middle of their "stuff" every time they visited. She pointed out to them how they would each get her alone to share their struggles and concerns about the other one. She was amazed and dismayed when they completely denied any problem and told her she was overreacting.

Getting Sucked In

Even though you may think you should stay neutral and let them solve their own problems, it is not easy. One way a problem arises is that your own opinions about the situation get in the way. Thirty-four-year-old Amelia, for example, has been angry for a long time about the way her father expects her mother to cater to him and upset that her mother goes along. She says, "Mom, to some degree, does not have a life of her own. Her only reason for living is to wait on other people, particularly my father. I've been trying to tell her for years that she was not put on this earth to be a maid, especially to a grown man with no physical or mental handicaps that would prevent him from throwing his own trash away."

Amelia had tried for years to get her mother to come for a visit by herself so that they could have some time together without her father dominating everything. It seemed to be a perfectly logical suggestion because her father works while her mother does not, so her mother could stay a couple of weeks if she came alone. But whenever Amelia brought up the idea, her mother would say, "No, I can't come. Your father needs me here to look after things." Finally last year Amelia asked her mother to come out for the week that her own children would be out of school for spring break and somehow her mother agreed.

"It turned out to be a big mistake," Amelia says now. "Almost as soon as she got here my father started calling to complain about how he couldn't find anything and he couldn't sleep and he wasn't feeling well. My mother felt so guilty she couldn't enjoy herself. I got upset and began to point out to her how much she always let him push her around. She broke down and agreed with me, told me that she had been unhappy for a long time but didn't know what to do about it."

Now Amelia finds herself in a situation where she seems to be her mother's sole emotional support. Her mother has confided that she has thought of separation or divorce, but she is afraid of living alone and managing her own life. She has never worked nor managed financial affairs.

Amelia has suggested that her mother talk to a lawyer, a counselor, or the minister of her church. Her mother says that maybe she will, but so far she has not done so. She seems to prefer to confide in Amelia, who is now hearing much more about her parents' marriage than she ever wanted to know.

"I feel stuck," Amelia says. "It's harder than ever for me to relate to my father now that I know all this. I can see why my mother would want to leave him, but I don't think she ever will. Somehow they need to work all this out, and I need to get out of the middle of it, but I don't know how."

Stepping Back

Amelia has gradually taken on the job of being her mother's confidante and protector. Now she needs to remove herself from that role. It will not be a simple task, but it is possible. Three important questions she can ask herself will help her discover how she got into this mess and what feelings or beliefs are keeping her there. Her answers will help her reevaluate her attitudes so that she can operate within limits rather than letting her parents' problems engulf her.

• *Do I feel responsible for the unhappiness of one or both of my parents?* If Amelia believes that her mother stayed with her father because of her, she may feel responsible for her mother's suffering. In fact, her mother may well have told Amelia, "I only stayed with him all those years because I thought it would be better for you." Even if that is so, Amelia must realize that it was her mother's choice, not her own that kept her there.

Parents may also blame their children for breaking up their marriage. One thirty-one-year-old woman recalls with horror one night when she was sixteen and her mother yelled at her angrily, "I'm not sure I would have divorced your father if *you* hadn't encouraged me."

No matter what your parents say, you are not responsible for their marriage or divorce. They are adults and have been since you were born. They are now and have always been free to make their own choices. Even though they may have considered the welfare of you their child when they made choices, they were still the ones doing the choosing. It is unfair for them to now blame you for the outcome of their choices.

• *Do I see the problems as one parent's fault?* Any situation involving three people has a natural tendency to evolve into two parts: Two people align into a powerful coalition, and one less powerful individual remains. The two can then use their combined weight to influence the one.[1] In a family, a husband and wife generally pair up to control a child. Sometimes a child and one parent may oppose the other parent as when a father and a son agree on the acceptable level of risk of an activity that the mother sees as too dangerous. Such shifts in the pairs who agree are not a problem as long as they are temporary.

But when a child and one parent continually pair up against the other parent, problems arise, especially if this same coalition pattern stays in effect over a period of years and if the focus is on changing the behavior of the other parent. The outside parent feels rejected, the bond between the parents weakens, and the child has increasing difficulty having a close relationship with both parents. It becomes easier and easier to see one parent as the "good parent" and the other as the "bad parent."

This can lead to a situation like Amelia's where a grown child blames one parent for the plight of the other. But because the situation is never that clear-cut, blaming one parent is harmful and unfair. Everything Amelia's mother says about her relationship with Amelia's father represents only one point of view. Clearly Amelia's father has a much different point of view. Even though Amelia's own observations over the years have seemed to support her mother's perspective, Amelia must realize that she knows only part of the story. She was not there at the beginning of their relationship and she has seen only selected aspects of it over the years. Furthermore, she is hardly an objective observer.

If you find yourself lining up on the side of one parent against the other, remind yourself that when a couple has difficulties, neither one is 100 percent responsible. Moreover, each of them must recognize and accept his or her personal responsibility for the problem in order to improve the situation. When you support one parent against the other you are helping that parent solidify an oppositional stance that will work against their resolving their difficulties.

• *Do I think I can solve my parents' problems?* Amelia must examine her feelings about the part she plays or should play in her parents' lives. She is already finding that trying to rescue her mother is difficult and burdensome. Her mother is becoming increasingly dependent on Amelia but seems to be making no progress on improving her situation. As Amelia feels herself getting in deeper and deeper, she becomes more frustrated and overwhelmed.

Amelia is discovering what other grown children have found in similar situations: You cannot solve your parents' problems. You may be able to help them by suggesting counseling, legal and financial advisors, or solutions to specific problems. You can even make the first appointment for them and take them to it if they seem to need that much help. But they must be the ones to actually take action to improve their situation. If one parent wants to initiate change but is afraid or lacks experience, you can help by offering support and encouragement. But be careful not to take over for that parent. Confine your assistance to helping them find ways to help themselves.

Although it may seem tempting to try, you cannot effectively mediate between your parents. No trained therapist would attempt to step in as his or her own parents' marriage counselor. A grown child's personal involvement in the family will overshadow the objectivity needed for mediation. If one parent asks you to intercede on his or her behalf with the other, refuse to take on that role. If you become the go-between, your relationship with each of them is jeopardized, with very little likelihood that their relationship will be improved. Again, suggest alternatives such as a family counselor or a religious advisor. Even if a parent insists you are the only one he or she can talk to or the only one who understands, remain firm in your resolve to stay out of the middle.

If They Are Divorced

It is not necessarily any easier to stay out of your parents' relationship when they are divorced, even if they have been divorced for a long time. They may each still complain to you about the other, imply that you are disloyal if you spend time with the other parent or accept the other parent's new partner, or try to use you to manipulate the other parent. For example, twenty-nine-year-old Sally finds communication with her divorced parents a continual struggle.

Sally: I Wish They Would Quit Using What I Say to One Against the Other.

My parents have been divorced for five years now. Many communication problems stem from that. I have to watch what I say to Mom so she won't reword everything I say so it gets back to Dad all wrong. Mom likes to make a big deal out of everything, and she will keep adding to something you've told her until it's all blown out of proportion.

The communication in our family was always very bad. Dad never talked about much. He never said how he felt about anything until after the divorce. I think he was lonely then, so when we visited him he talked to us. Mom lived through some hellish years with Dad because he would never share his feelings with her. Mom also lied about a lot. I think because her life was so boring she started blowing little stories up to something great and exciting which led to lying to herself. Now I think she believes her own lies.

I wish they would quit using what we say to one against the other. I seem to be the one who must help them communicate, and many times my thoughts and feelings are miscommunicated between them. Then one or the other will call and think I'm taking sides.

I don't feel like I can trust Mom with anything I tell her. She'll use anything she can to start trouble. She even used my three-year-old daughter to get back at my stepmother. My three-year-old told my stepmother that she "stoled" Grandpa from Grandma. Mom denied teaching her that and said she must have picked it up somewhere.

Divorcing Yourself

If your divorced parents are managing to keep you in the middle of their "stuff," you will need to find ways to remove yourself. Ideally you will stay on good terms with each of them and keep your opinions about their decisions to yourself.

Sally would do best to refuse to have *any* discussion about one of her parents with the other. Not surprisingly, helping them communicate is not working out well for her or for them. Her energy would be better spent trying to have the relationship she wants with each of them as separate individuals, rather than trying to referee between them.

She should also let her parents know her limits and what she finds objectionable. Certainly using a three-year-old child to get back at an ex-spouse is unacceptable. Sally could tell her mother how she feels about this and insist that if her mother wants to spend time with the grandchildren, she must not discuss their grandfather with them.

Sally should particularly resist any attempts by her parents to make her choose between them. If her mother threatens to stay home from a family gathering if her dad and stepmother are invited, Sally can say, "I hope you change your mind. We'll miss you if you don't come." If her father accuses her of visiting her mother more than she visits him, she can say, "I don't keep score about who I visit. If you want to see me more, let's talk about how we can do that."

You do not have to justify your relationship with one parent to the other, nor are you required to parcel out your time and energy equally between them. Just as they had the right to divorce each other even though you may have preferred that they stay together, you have the right to choose how you will interact with each of them.

When They Step Into Your Relationships

Just as their relationships are their business, yours are your business. But many parents do not see it that way, even though their children are grown-up. They seem to feel that without their intervention you may pair up with someone who is all wrong for you, will make you miserable, or, even worse, will make them miserable.

Many parents seem to feel perfectly comfortable setting up rules for the type of person their children can become seriously involved with or marry. One young man's mother repeatedly reminded him that he must marry a Jewish girl because he owed it to the family to do so. A young woman from a Protestant family found that her parents were seriously upset when she began dating an Italian Catholic. They were convinced that his family was in the Mafia. Another woman, who was seeing a divorced man, could not get her mother to even meet the man. Her mother kept crying, "I never thought my daughter would go out with a married man."

Certainly it is easier for parents to accept someone of similar background as a partner for their grown child. Similarity in race, religion, education, and family fit parents' expectations of the person their child will marry. They also want someone who seems to be a good prospect for a successful partner. Someone who has been divorced, fired from a job, or treated for emotional problems may seem to be cause for alarm.

Other reasons for rejecting an adult child's choice may seem less rational. Arlene, a tall, pretty young woman who likes to dress up, became engaged to a man three inches shorter than she who wore cowboy boots and studied agriculture education. Arlene's mother found the choice unbearable, crying to the rest of the family that "he is just a little cowboy and not the quality Arlene needs."

Whatever their reasons, they are most likely acting from what seem to them to be vital concerns. They may believe deeply that it is unthinkable to marry outside your religion or race or that marrying someone who is divorced or comes from a much different background is extremely risky. They may truly have your best interests at heart. Or they may at least be operating from what they have always assumed are their legitimate rights as parents.

Even so, you are not under any obligation to acquiesce. It is possible to acknowledge their position without accepting it as a guiding principle for your life.

How to Make Your Own Choice Even When They Disapprove

The days of arranged marriages are long gone in our society. You know you are free to choose, yet you may not feel free in the face of parental rules and disapproval. Even worse, if you find yourself choosing a partner your parents find unacceptable, you may not be sure whether you are making this choice in part to demonstrate your independence. One young woman who was dating a man of whom her parents disapproved, continued seeing him but kept this a secret from her parents. They found out she was still seeing him and were even more upset. "Then," she says, "I just about married the guy, probably for spite, I do not know for sure."

To preserve your freedom of choice and avoid reacting angrily or defiantly when they pass judgment on your relationships, remind yourself that you are an adult. While you will most likely want your parents to know and like the person who is most special in your life, their acceptance and approval of that person is not a requirement.

Ideally you are entitled to expect their acceptance of the person you choose, or at least their acknowledgment that you have the right to choose. So present or describe this person to them as someone who is special to you and who you want them to meet, not as someone who is on trial for their approval. You can let them know that it is very important to you that they like this person without giving them the power to control your choice.

If your parents object to your relationship because you do not choose a partner who fits a category they have deemed essential, you can let them know you hear their objections without jumping into a battle to justify your position. Michael, the man whose mother wanted him to marry a Jewish girl, describes how he learned to deflect her attacks.

Michael: I Decided Just to Acknowledge What She Was Saying.

Before I got married we'd have constant conversations where she would ask, "Have you dated any Jewish girls lately?" and I'd usually say "No," and she'd say "Why not?" I'd say something like, "There aren't many Jewish girls around here." And then she'd say, "Well, I really want you to marry someone who's Jewish." And we'd get into a big argument because I'd say something like, "Look, I'm going to marry who I want to marry whether you like it or not." And she'd say, "But, I'm your mother." And I'd say, "Well, that's true, but—" And she'd say, "You have to do this." And I'd say, "No. I don't have to do this."

I didn't see any way out of it for a long time. It was sort

of like fighting this constant war. I didn't see any way to change it, and I felt that somehow if I let her win battles, then she was winning the war, and I wasn't about to let her do that. We'd been having this war for a long time.

Then what I finally realized was that I didn't have to participate in those conversations. What I decided to do was change the way I reacted to her. Instead of arguing with her and putting energy into confronting her, I decided just to acknowledge what she was saying. So when she started the conversation, I said, "Well, it's really important to you that I marry a Jewish girl." And she said, "Yes, it is." And I'd say, "Yes, I can really see that." And then she said, "Yes, it really is important to me." And I'd repeat, "Yes, I can see it is really important to you." And that would go on for thirty seconds or so, and that was the end of the conversation.

Once I stopped putting energy in, she stopped. I guess what I realized was that she wanted her concerns to be heard, and once they were heard, then she felt differently about it. I suppose another possibility is that she was so surprised at my reacting totally differently that she reacted totally differently.

As it turned out, Michael did not marry a Jewish girl, but by the time he got married, his mother had realized that who he chose to marry was not an item open to negotiation from his point of view. Although he acknowledged her wishes, he was not willing to give them priority over his own choice.

At this point Michael's mother may still not admit that his right to choose his own partner should legitimately come before her preferences regarding the type of person he selects. But she does seem to recognize that he is not willing to debate the issue any further with her.

When They Will Not Accept Your Choice

Many grown children complain that even after they have married or made a clear commitment to someone they love, their parents continually remind them of that person's faults and defects. Somehow these parents seem to believe that if they keep criticizing long enough their children will admit that they chose the wrong person. Caroline has put up with this treatment for twenty years.

Caroline: She Thought I Could Do Better.

I got married very young. I was only nineteen. My mother thought it was a big mistake, and she still thinks so even though Jay and I have been married twenty years. She said he wanted to marry me only because our family had more money than his and because we were more respected in town than his family. She said I could do better and that I would regret it if I married him and that even if we ended up poor, she'd never help us.

But we've never needed her help. In fact, it's the other way around. Jay is really good at fixing things around the house, and ever since my dad died, Mom calls Jay when she needs something done. He always helps her out even though she doesn't give him much credit for it and even though she treats him like a second-class citizen.

Mom talks a lot about my cousin Trudy, who married a doctor. Trudy has such a lovely house and fancy clothes and trips to Europe and on and on. Mom tells me how sad she is about the sacrifices I've had to make because I married Jay, which she says was definitely a step down for me.

I used to argue with her and try to tell her what a great person Jay is and how he's easygoing and loving, which is what I care about, not about his background. But it's useless. She'll never change. So I just ignore her.

Parents like Caroline's mother who feel that their grown children have chosen ill-advisedly often find it very difficult to see beyond their own opinions. No matter how much evidence you provide to demonstrate that your spouse or lover is not using you or mistreating you and that you are actually happy with this person, these parents predict doom for the future. "You'll regret it." "I'm only telling you for your own good." "Don't come crying back to me when things go wrong."

Caroline is probably correct in deciding that her mother will not change her opinion of Jay after all these years. Her decision to ignore her mother's critical comments seems to be a solution that works for her, even though she would prefer that her mother recognize that her marriage to Jay is a good one.

Yet, Caroline and Jay might also decide that they do not want to spend time with Caroline's mother as long as she treats Jay like a second-class citizen. They have a right to expect respect rather than verbal abuse from her. Caroline seems to see only two possible responses: argue with her mother or ignore her. A third alternative is to tell her mother that she is quite aware of her mother's feelings in this matter, but that she will no longer tolerate her mother's criticism and discounting of Jay. Caroline should be clear about what is specifically unacceptable and what the consequences will be if her mother continues to insult Jay as she has done for the past twenty years.

Although this may seem harsh, it is probably the way Caroline would have responded years ago to anyone but a parent who had treated her husband this way. Being your parent does not mean someone can be rude and disrespectful to someone you love without experiencing any consequences from you in return. By telling her mother what she finds unacceptable, Caroline is giving her mother the opportunity to choose for herself how she wants her interactions with Caroline and Jay to go in the future.

Problems of Rivalry

Other parents have trouble accepting any partner their grown child selects. These parents feel that they should always come first with their children, even when those children are grown and have their own intimate relationships with friends, spouses, or lovers. They are appalled at the idea that you could feel closer to someone "outside the family" than you do to them or at the thought that you might tell this person "family secrets." They may become upset if you discuss important decisions in your life with your partner instead of with them, or angry if you no longer take their advice as much as you formerly did.

Some parents react this way because their rigid ideas of who is "family" and who is not do not allow for the inclusion of additions to the inner family circle. Others want to influence the major decisions in their adult children's lives—such as where you live, what job you have and how you spend your money—without outside interference. In cases like these you will probably do best to adopt Michael's technique of acknowledging their desires without going along with their demands.

But some parents who seem to want to come between you and any partner you select are worried mostly about what place they can continue to have in your life when you are attached to someone else. In particular, a parent with whom you have had an especially close relationship may fear the loss of this special closeness. In such a situation an open discussion with your parent can help each of you understand the other's feelings and work toward a happy compromise.

When twenty-three-year-old Miriam moved in with her boyfriend, Ethan, her mother began acting very strangely. "She was always trying to find ways to see me alone, which seemed odd because she had acted like she liked Ethan up until then," Miriam said. "And she kept starting sentences with, 'Now don't tell Ethan I said this, but—'"

Miriam felt as if she was being pulled in two directions at once. After she talked to her mother several times about the situation, Miriam began to realize that her mother felt excluded now that she was living with Ethan. Miriam and her mother had been unusually close since her mother and father's divorce ten years before. Now her mother feared they would never again have that special time together, "just the two of them."

Miriam was able to understand the sense of loss her mother felt and to discuss her own feelings openly. She explained that her commitment to Ethan meant that she did not want to have conversations with her mother that she had to keep secret from him. Rather, she would like to include him in these family matters. At the same time, Miriam did want to continue to spend some time alone with her mother, sharing some of their special favorite activities.

Miriam did not try to convince her mother that nothing had changed, because she knew that this change in her life would affect her mother. Rather she acknowledged her mother's feelings of loss and was as honest and also as reassuring as she could be about the future.

In this case, Miriam's willingness to understand her mother's point of view has saved them from a potentially painful time. It is never easy for a close established twosome like Miriam and her mother to adjust to the changes that come when one of them brings in an important third person. But now that Miriam realizes that her mother's main concern is to stay close rather than to disrupt her relationship with Ethan, she can respond reassuringly to her mother's distress. If Miriam and her mother keep talking about how they are feeling and make a special effort to have regular enjoyable time together, they can continue to make this transition in their relationship a positive one.

CHAPTER 11

What If They Need Your Help?

"I would do it lots differently if I had it to do over again. I would know what my limits were. The thing about her illness and illnesses like that is that they are gradual. You find yourself saying, 'Well, I can do this one more thing.' You take it on bit by bit and one morning you wake up and you're a nurse. You're taking care of someone who cannot do anything alone."

(Maxine, age 35)

We have a strong belief in our society that grown children should take care of their parents if their parents need help. And most adults live up to this principle, regardless of the burden it may become. In contrast to the prevailing myth that Americans are quick to abandon their parents to nursing homes, approximately 80 percent of the older people who need care get that care from family members. Nursing homes are a last resort. Only 5 percent of people over sixty-five are in a nursing home at any one time.

Today most communities have organizations and agencies that help older people and their families when care is needed. But many adults who face the situation still have severe difficulties. Taking care of a parent is not simply a practical problem, it is an emotional issue. How or if you will provide care to your parents involves your feelings, their feelings, and the relationship you have had with them up to now.

What Adult Children Expect to Do for Their Parents

Most adults say that they want and expect to help their parents when and if that help is needed. Even grown children who report frequent conflict and dissatisfaction in their relationships with their parents plan to take care of their parents if that becomes necessary. For example, one forty-nine-year-old woman who described her eighty-one-year-old mother as a "nosy busybody who is very manipulative and controlling," went on to say, "I do feel that I owe Mother a great deal. She has always been available to me when I needed help, so I can do nothing less for her."

We asked people, "What (if anything) do you feel you owe your parents now or in the future? What would you be willing to do for them?"[1] Many placed no limits on what they would do or expect of themselves. These grown children spoke of being willing to do anything their parents need or to help in any way they can, some from choice, others from duty:

- "I owe my parents everything, especially my mom. She shaped me into the person I am. She encouraged me and stood by me through everything. I would be willing to do anything for my mom. I would even give my life for her. I feel I owe her that much."
- "I feel I owe them a great deal but not that I'm expected to pay them. I've always told them the same thing I'm sure thousands of people tell their parents—'I'll never put you in a rest home.' I would be willing to take my parents into my home when and if they are unable to care for themselves."
- "I would do whatever I could—not because I 'owe' them anything, but because they are persons I love and respect."
- "All children owe their parents in some respect. Some feelings of obligation come because one wants to reciprocate the love that he or she was given over the years. Other feelings come from duty, what is expected, and the feelings of guilt associated with not being dutiful. My love for my mother is genuine, and I would support or do for her now and in the future whatever is in my power. For my father, I would feel obligated to do for him what will be necessary because he is my father."

• "I owe my mom respect because she did what she believed in, provided me with physical necessities, and took care of me (although in the role of a martyr). I am willing to do anything I need to do that is possible for me to take care of her if she needs it. I would and could establish living quarters for her in my home if the need arose."

• "I feel that my mom has helped me out so many times and in so many ways that I will do anything I can for her. If that means keeping her with me or honoring her choice to live where she wants to, then so be it. I will allow her to make whatever choices she is able to make when the time comes—I hope!"

"I do feel a sense of duty to care for them when they are older, and I do not believe I would resent it. They cared for me as a child, and I feel a sense of responsibility to care for them when they are elderly. For my mother, it would be out of love and concern. For my father, it would be out of love and pity."

"I 'owe' my parents unconditional love. Whatever my parents need, if I can supply it or get it for them, I will do that for them because they do that for me all the time. If they should become ill or in need of nursing, I will help them, not really because I 'owe' it to them but because I love them."

Other adults gave more qualified responses. They are willing to help their parents if needed, but recognize some limits in the level or type of help they feel able to give:

"I owe it to them to be available to assist them in any way they would want, should they become infirmed or incapacitated. They would do that for me. Their needs, however, would have to be balanced against the needs of my children and the capacity of my sibling to help out as well."

"I feel like I owe them to be as concerned and caring for them if and when they are unable to care for themselves properly as they have been for me the past thirty-three years. This is difficult because I would not want to completely give up my life to be their nurse and I know they wouldn't want this either. But I would do what I could within reasonable bounds to see after their comfort and best interests."

"While I tell myself I don't owe her anything, on the other

hand I still feel that I am responsible for her life and happiness. I would not be able to care for Mom in my own home because she weighs two hundred fifty to three hundred pounds and I weigh one hundred ten pounds and it would not be physically possible. I hope I would be able to help financially and would always try to visit many times a week."

- "Mom did everything she could as well as she was able. I owe her the same. I help her financially as I can, buy things for her, and took her on a trip this summer. I would prefer *not* to live with her. The two-week trip was just past the limit of our togetherness."

- "I feel they have given me life, and so I feel I owe them gratitude for my life, but it is *my* life, not theirs. Therefore, if in my life I am able to show a respect and gratitude for them, I will, but it must be in a balance with my own life. Their lives and my life are equally valid, but one to the exclusion of the other has consequences that must be foreseen."

Because of the strong traditional values about family responsibility for taking care of aging parents in our society, it can be very difficult to set any limits on what you will do for them. Even if you are quite sure that having a parent live with you would be more than you could handle, you may feel very guilty at the thought of not doing so. One thirty-four-year-old woman explained the dilemma:

"Although I feel that caring for my mother is my responsibility, I am afraid that I will not be capable of caring for her when the time comes. I am not talking about being *unable* to care for her. I am sure that physically and financially it will be a possibility. I am talking about being incapable of dealing with the intrusion into my life of another person; incapable of dealing with the added responsibility; incapable of dealing with the clash of personalities; incapable of dealing with the clash between my identity as an adult in the outside world and my identity as a child at home. I see a general consensus in society that says, 'Of course you should want to take care of your mother. After all, she took care of you for all those years. She suffered for you. You owe it to her.' But personally, I feel confused about what I should do and afraid of what I will do.'

Parent Care: Expectations Become Reality

Millions of Americans are living up to the traditional expectations today. As our society ages, more and more adults find themselves taking care of aging parents who suffer from various chronic or acute illnesses or who are simply unable to do as much as they formerly could. In the past twenty years the population of people aged sixty-five and older in the United States has grown twice as fast as the general population. And the fastest growing age group is the "old-old" aged eighty-five and older, who are the most likely to need help.[2]

About 7 million American households contain someone who has provided unpaid assistance in daily living activities to an older person within the past 12 months, according to a 1989 survey conducted for the American Association of Retired Persons. The majority of caregivers are women who have been providing care for an average of 12 hours a week for 2 years.[3] Adult daughters are on the front line for helping aging parents who need help with the actual tasks of day-to-day living, such as household chores, shopping, and personal care. Sons are more likely to help with home repairs or finances.

But caring for parents can exact high costs, which may include emotional and physical exhaustion, interference with work and family life, anger, frustration, isolation, health problems, and financial strain. Women especially tend to suffer from feelings of stress, burden, and guilt when taking care of parents.

If you found your parent difficult before, caregiving is likely to be even more trying. You may find yourself in a situation where you are breaking your neck to keep your parent comfortable, but both you and your parent are increasingly unhappy. You may be exhausted from keeping up with the demands of caregiving on top of the rest of your life, yet your parent may criticize and complain frequently. You feel as if you have given up much of your life, but that nothing you can do is enough.

Getting Stuck: Maxine's Story

Consider Maxine, the thirty-five-year-old woman whose words appear at the beginning of this chapter. Her story is an example of how dreadful caregiving can be when guilt and obligation are the primary motivators. Maxine took care of her mother for eight years, during which her own life became gradually more and more miserable. Maxine was young and single when her widowed mother's rheumatoid arthritis got so bad that she could barely walk anymore. Although Maxine lived in another state, her mother expected her to move back home and take care of her, so Maxine did.

Maxine remembers that earlier, when the arthritis had begun to seriously affect her mother's hands, the doctor had recommended surgery and some joint replacements in her hands. But her mother decided not to do it and eventually lost all use of her hands. That meant that when her hips and feet started to go, she was almost completely disabled. When Maxine first moved back, her mother could still go to the bathroom on her own and fix an occasional meal, but she shortly gave that up and stopped walking.

Because they could not both live on her mother's limited income, Maxine held a full-time teaching job in addition to taking care of her mother. Because her mother would not tolerate any help from anyone else, Maxine did it all. She gave her mother breakfast in the morning before she left for work and fixed her lunch and left it by the bed. She hurried home to bathe and toilet her and fix her dinner. Looking back, Maxine recognizes that her mother's demands were outrageous, but at the time it all just seemed to be part of what she was expected to do:

"It was real clear what my role was. I was the caregiver. I would make her a sandwich for lunch before I left for work and leave it beside her bed. We tried Meals on Wheels for a while, but she didn't like that too much. A few times my boyfriend made her sandwiches, but she wouldn't eat them because she said, 'Men aren't supposed to do things like that.' I would come home from work and the sandwiches would be sitting right there, not eaten. They weren't nearly as good as the ones I made.

"She had the amazing ability to hold her bladder all day long until I got home. I think now that the reason she did that was so I would be sure to come straight home from work knowing she had to pee.

"She was a very interesting manipulator. She would shower

me with praise and thanks and love whenever I was doing exactly what she wanted me to, but it was a very different story if it wasn't exactly what she wanted me to do. She could change just like that."

Maxine can see now how easily her mother controlled her through guilt and how her own expectations of herself contributed to the problem. But at the time, she had no idea how to set any limits or that she even had the right to do so:

"I was raised with an attitude that my purpose was to please. There was no place for me to have my own reality or my own feelings. My mother always told me that I was very selfish. She made lots of declarations that I believed then but that seem ridiculous to me now.

"Every time I would go off for something for myself, something terrible would happen to her. One year it was my birthday, and I had a birthday party and was gone all day long at a picnic at a state park. When I got back, she said she couldn't turn her head.

"Once I was gone all day on a Sunday, and when I got back, she told me her hip was broken. But she wouldn't let me take her to the doctor. Every time I moved her for any reason, she would scream. That lasted for four months, and I never could get her to a doctor.

"If you had told me at the very beginning that someday I'd be taking care of this woman with a broken hip who wouldn't let me take her to the doctor and I would put up with that, I would have said, 'Forget it!' But that was just one more step in a long string of things that happened."

Living With Your Choices: Guilt Versus Obligation

Maxine lived through eight years of a choice she made without ever realizing she had a choice. Today when people talk to her about what they are going to do if Mom or Dad have to come live with them, she says:

"The advice I give people is, 'Know your limits before you start.' Say to yourself, 'Can I deal with having her live with me? Can I deal with someone who is incontinent? Can I handle feeding somebody three meals a day? Can I handle being on call twenty-four hours a day? Can I handle being on call every other day?' What are your limits? Because I didn't know what mine were. I just kept saying, 'Okay, I can do that.'

"People would come up to me and say, 'You're such a good daughter for taking care of your mom.' And I just wanted to scream at them, 'I hate it! And I want her to die.' But I felt so guilty for thinking that.

"I felt so trapped and I didn't know how to get out of it. I just didn't know what to do and it was miserable. It never occurred to me that I could say, 'I'm sorry, I just can't do all this.' I didn't know how to set any limits."

For many, parent care seems to be a no-win situation. They feel terrible doing it, but they feel even worse at the thought of not doing it. Often adult children who finally place a parent in an institution feel just as much burden from guilt as they did earlier from providing care.

Unfortunately, Maxine was so young when her mother needed care that she jumped into taking care of her mother without having had the benefit of time to consider what she was and was not willing to do. Even more unfortunately, as the comments earlier in this chapter show, many people do not think in those terms even if they do have time to look ahead.

Thinking about this issue is uncomfortable for most people. It brings up feelings of loss as well as confusion, obligation, and guilt. Most of us know very little about the problems of old age—another uncomfortable topic. So the tendency is to hope rather than plan. You hope you can do what they need or that maybe they will never need your help. You hope you will get along better with them if they are sick or disabled and need your help.

Rather than hoping, planning ahead is the best way to do as much as you can for your parents in their later years without falling into a trap like Maxine did. If you simply drift into caregiving one step at a time, you may find yourself over-whelmed without any good ideas of how to reduce your burden.

Plan Together as a Family

Family meetings are a good way to explore your parents' needs and involve the whole family in making decisions. Possible participants include you, your parents, your spouse, and your brothers or sisters and their spouses. Ideally you will do this before a crisis arises, but if not, you should still do it once your parents need help. Your parents should be at the meeting, unless that is impossible. Even if they are quite sick or confused, their input is important. After all it is their life.

Despite some popular media references to "parenting your parent," grown children and their parents do not reverse roles when a parent becomes sick or disabled. Even though your parents may need a lot of help, they are not children. They have a right to make their own choices and decisions so long as they can manage the life-style they choose with the resources they have available. Of course, if the life-style they choose is moving into your house and having you take care of them, you have something to say about that, too.

One purpose of the family meeting is to get as much information as possible from your parents about their preferences and resources. Find out as much as you can about your parents' medical insurance and benefits available through veteran or retirement programs. Talk to them about their preferences in case of serious illness. Do they have living wills? How do they feel about life-support systems? What sort of living arrangements would they want if they could not stay where they are because of illness or disability?

They may resist this discussion, and you obviously cannot force them to participate. But you may be surprised at their willingness to talk about issues that would have been taboo a few years ago. Problems associated with aging and families have been so widely publicized in recent years that many parents of grown children have given considerable thought to what they would and would not want their children to do for them.

If you parents need help now, help them make a complete list of what they need and how often they need it. Make another list of possible sources of help including community services, family, friends, neighbors, or church groups. Then the whole family should work together to come up with an action plan that details how everyone can help. Usually one adult child takes on the primary responsibility for helping a parent. If you are that person, you should still expect help from your siblings, even if they live far away. They can help financially or by taking over for a week or so when you want a vacation. It is important that each family member make a commitment to help right from the start.

If you think your family will have trouble discussing this topic without arguments, you may want to invite a professional mediator. Social workers, clergy, mental health professionals, or hospital discharge planners are possible choices. A mediator can help family members move beyond emotions to find common interests, identify new options, set criteria for choices, and make agreements.

Be Realistic

Even though you may feel that you somehow want to pay your parents back for all they have done for you, it is unlikely that you can do so. Grown children who are already taking care of parents say they have a hard time deciding how much they should do and how to divide their time and energy between their parent, other family, career, and their own well-being. If you believe you should do whatever is possible, you may find yourself giving extensive personal care such as bathing, feeding, and dressing day after day without a break. You may give up your job or cut back on the time you work so that you can have more time for caregiving. You may have virtually no time to yourself, no social activities, and very little sleep. And, strangely enough, you still may feel that you are not doing enough!

Unless you are already in that position, this may sound unbelievable. But hundreds of thousands of adult children—primarily women—in America are living this life today.[4] Unless you are sure you can and are willing to do all this and more, be careful about the promises you make to yourself and especially to your parents.

It may be very tempting to tell your parents you will never put them in a nursing home or that they will always have a place to live with you. But you cannot foresee the future to know whether you can keep this promise. When the time comes, you may not be physically, emotionally, or financially able to care for a parent who needs round-the-clock nursing care including lifting or who is in the late stages of Alzheimer's disease. What if you are seventy by the time your ninety-year-old parent needs help?

So be careful what guarantees you give. The most honest assurances you can give will probably be that you will try to do your best for them when the time comes, that you will not make decisions for them unless they cannot make their wishes known, and that you will make every effort to accommodate their preferences.

Understand Your Motives

It will be easier to avoid making promises you cannot keep or getting entangled in a caregiving nightmare if you understand your motives for helping your parent. Offering to provide care because of feelings of guilt, obligation, or a need for appreciation can lead to trouble.

This is no time to live in a fantasy world of finally becoming the loved and appreciated child you always wanted to be. If you have felt unloved, it is unlikely that you will get that love now by taking care of them. Although you might reasonably expect appreciation, a parent who has not shown this in the past is unlikely to give it for the care you provide. With a parent who treats you that way, it is more likely that you will somehow fail to measure up once again.

If you feel that you must always put your parent's needs before your own, or you expect yourself to be perfect and do it all, or you think that you must somehow relieve all their suffering, you will probably feel guilty no matter what you do for them. Even worse, your parent may take advantage of your guilt to coerce you into doing more than you want to do. Many of the manipulative ploys described in Chapter 7 are especially common in situations where a parent depends on a grown child for help.

It is important that you feel you are making a conscious choice to take care of your parent, rather than having been trapped into doing it. Whether the reason you choose to provide care is that it makes you feel better about yourself to do so, or that you truly enjoy doing it, or that you want your parent to have the best care, the key is that you *want* to do it. The next important step is to decide how much and what types of care you want to give.

Take Care of Yourself

Although you may sincerely want to provide for your parent's every need, it is unlikely you can do so. If you burn yourself out doing more than you can manage, your parent may end up much worse off. To avoid this, you need to: get help rather than doing everything alone; take advantage of community services available to your parent; and set and stick to realistic limits on what you can do.

Even though your parent may tell you, as Maxine's mother did, that you are the only one who can do what is needed, this is not so. Other family members, friends, and neighbors can all help, even if only to stay with your parent for an hour to give you a break. You should not feel reluctant to ask other family members to help out and to be specific about what they can do. If your parent objects, explain that you cannot do everything and you must have some time to yourself. If friends or neighbors ask you to let them know what they can do to help, have some specific suggestions. For example: "Thanks for asking. I'd love to have you visit with Mother for an hour on Saturday so I can do some errands."

Surprisingly, many community services that are available to older people and their families are not used as much as the professionals who develop them expect them to be. In fact, the American Association of Retired Persons National Caregivers Survey found that the vast majority of family members caring for an older person did not use services such as respite care or home health aides to give themselves some relief from caregiving tasks.[5] Professionals who operate such programs say that families often will not use the services until a desperate crisis arises, even if the services are free or very inexpensive. These experts suggest that families have been conditioned by society to carry on without outside help unless they can no longer do so and that many older people refuse to accept care from strangers.

All of this comes back to Maxine's advice: Know your limits. Beyond that, you need to be firm. If you defer to all your parent's requests, no matter how unreasonable, you impose burdens on yourself that lead to feelings of anger and resentment as well as exhaustion. When Helen's mother wanted her not only to do her shopping but to go to several different stores to get the best buys, Helen drew the line. "I did it a few times," she said, "but it took way too much time and didn't really save that much money. I told Mom that I would pay the difference instead, but that wasn't good enough. She accused me of throwing money away just because I was lazy. And this was when I had a full-time job plus my own household and hers to take care of! So I just told her that as long as I was doing the shopping it would have to be my way and if she wanted to find someone else to do it, that would be fine with me."

If Helen's response sounds insensitive to you, remind yourself that Helen, like all adult children, has a right and a need to take care of herself. To give her mother loving care, Helen must set some boundaries and pay attention to her own needs.

Encourage Their Independence

Another way to avoid getting overwhelmed with caregiving tasks is to help your parents find new ways to do tasks for themselves, rather than taking over for them. Even though the natural response is to make your parent's life easier by taking over chores they find difficult, it is better to support their independence by helping them find ways to modify the environment or reorganize tasks so that they can continue to take care of themselves. Not only will this preserve your freedom, it will preserve theirs also. When older people curtail their activities in response to aches and pains, their joints and muscles begin to freeze up, making activity even more difficult. Staying active and completing as many of their own daily tasks and activities as possible is important for their physical and mental health.

Although allowing or encouraging people who are sick or disabled to test their limits in caring for themselves may seem cruel, they can often do more than they realize and will benefit from the sense of accomplishment. To avoid creating dependency, you will probably need to let them take some risks. Remember, you cannot shelter them from the losses of old age any more than they could shelter you from the pains of growing up. You can help them by finding or making adaptive devices and aids such as grab bars for the bathtub, stairlifts for people who cannot climb stairs, jar and bottle openers to use with one hand, magnifiers for reading, or devices for picking up objects without bending over. Consult an occupational therapist, home health nurse, or hospital social worker for sources of such products.

Some parents, especially recently widowed parents, want their children to rescue them. They will resist learning to do tasks that their spouses formerly handled. Fathers may seem completely helpless at cooking or doing laundry, mothers may be unable to manage finances or home and car maintenance. Rather than accepting their helplessness, find ways to help them learn to do these chores themselves or help them arrange to have the jobs done by others.

Fortunately, most parents do not want to be dependent on their children and will welcome finding ways to keep on "doing for themselves." They may seem resistant initially because they are afraid of failure or intimidated by new devices or ways of managing tasks. At this crucial point they need encouragement and reassurance, not help. Research has shown that older people who feel a sense of control and responsibility in their lives are not only happier, they are healthier.[6] So think carefully if you hear yourself saying, "Let me do that for you," or "Be careful not to overdo."

Look for the Silver Lining

Considerable evidence indicates that people who are able to see difficult circumstances as positive challenges feel better in stressful situations than people who focus mainly on the negative aspects.[7] Adults who find satisfaction in caring for their parents can cope more easily with the burden of caregiving. Many grown children do find specific benefits come from taking care of parents.

Some adult children find satisfaction or meaning in carrying on a family tradition of caring for elders, or in reciprocating for care that their parents have given them.[8] They tell themselves, "My mother took care of her mother, and I'm glad I can do as much for her." Or "After all my parents have done for me, I feel proud that I have been able to make their later years more happy and comfortable."

Another source of positive aspects of providing care for parents is the sense of accomplishment you can derive from doing what you set out to do. It can also be a unifying experience for family members who work together to find the best solutions to difficult problems. People say, "I feel pleased that I have found a way to keep my father at home even though it takes a lot of my time and energy." Or, "We are doing our best for Dad as a family, and it has brought us closer together."

Some adults find benefits in being so much a part of their parents' lives, in sharing this difficult time, and in discovering their own inner resources. They say, "I am happy to to be able to be with my mother so much. I know she won't be around much longer, and I will miss her terribly." Or, "I am a more compassionate empathetic person now that I am taking care of my parents."

If you find it hard to see any benefits, remind yourself that you are looking for these positives in a situation in which you have *chosen* to be involved. As long as you have decided to take care of your parents, you may as well enjoy it as much as you can.

Accept Your Own Limits

Whatever you choose to do for your parents, remind yourself that your performance does not have to measure up to some outside standard. You know yourself, your situation, your parent, and your relationship with that parent, so you are the one who should decide what you can do to help. Regardless of what you think society expects, what your family expects, or what your parent expects, there are no right answers. You are not required to prove that you care about your parents by sacrificing your own life for them.

After sacrificing her life for eight years, Maxine was finally able, with the help of a counselor, to move her mother into a nursing home. Her mother died a year later. After her mother's death, Maxine talked to a priest about her feelings of confusion and guilt about her relationship with her mother during those years. To her surprise, he said: "You know, I don't think we have any obligation to take care of our parents. They're supposed to take care of their kids, not the other way around. If you want to do that, it's fine, but I don't think it's an obligation."

PART FOUR

Comparisons and Change

CHAPTER 12

Is Your Family Exceptionally Difficult?

A mother gives her son two ties for Christmas—one striped, one polka-dotted.

A week later, the son arrives at the mother's house for dinner. He's wearing the striped tie.

MOTHER TO SON: "What's the matter? You don't like the other tie?"

Why do we find this funny? Possibly because it is such a familiar example of how impossible our interactions with parents can seem. And also because we feel better knowing other people have the same problems.

As we move through life, we tend to look around for targets of comparison to help ourselves evaluate our own situations and actions in relation to some standard. Psychologists have discovered that people make both upward comparisons, in which they compare themselves to those who are better off, and downward comparisons, in which they compare themselves to those who are worse off. Making a downward comparison can help you feel better because you are not as badly off as everyone, but it can also show you that it is possible for you to get worse. Making an upward comparison can give you information and inspiration for improving your circumstances, but it can also make you feel worse because you are not as well off as others.

The Problems of High Expectations

Pictures in your head of perfection can create disappointment when real life fails to measure up. So we look for social

175

support to help us accept the reality of conflict in family life, which is contrary to our expectation of harmony. We laugh at books like Dan Greenburg's *How to Be a Jewish Mother*,[1] and we share our own "Can you believe this . . ." stories with our friends.

If popular culture reflects experience, we must assume that conflict and misunderstanding are not usual in family life. Furthermore, studies of communication in close relationships have repeatedly shown that family harmony is *not* the usual state of affairs.[2] Yet somehow we hold an ideal that says families should be free of such controversy.

You probably have a picture in your head of what you, your parents, and your siblings could be like and should be like as a family. Most people do. And you may see your family as being far removed from this ideal and unlikely to ever reach it. Debbie's description of her family is a classic example.

Debbie: Mom was One Hundred Pounds Overweight and Dad Was Drunk.

My parents never were your "average American family." My mother talks about twenty different things at once, doesn't trust a soul, is very outgoing, very nervous, closed-minded, worries constantly, has a very hot temper, is always right, doesn't drink or smoke, loves material things and food, and is very conscious of what people say about her and her family. My father is very intelligent and quiet-spoken, but when he does say something it sure has meaning. He's also nervous, a former heavy drinker, hates to spend money, is trustworthy, and trusts others.

Mostly what I remember from when I was young is my parents' constant fighting. Dad would come home with a few drinks under his belt, and with Mom and her temper, she wouldn't give Dad a chance. Here Mom was one-hundred pounds overweight, and Dad was drunk, so I tried to patch up their fights but wasn't usually too successful.

All through high school I would fight with Mom constantly, and Dad would be on my side 75 percent of the time. The other 25 percent he would be on Mom's side because Dad didn't want the fight to continue and Mom was always right and would not change her stand. Mom and I did get along well at times, but there was no happy medium.

Now my Dad has emphysema, has quit drinking, and he and Mom get along better. Mom and I don't yell at each other much, mainly because I'm not with her that often anymore. But our family times together are never what I truly want or hope for. There's too much conflict, mostly because of Mom. I wish it could be different, but I know she'll never change.

While Debbie's parents may be difficult, they certainly are not unique. Yet Debbie feels cheated somehow, like she has missed out on her American birthright. The happy family is the American way. Politicians, physicians, psychologists, social workers, counselors, educators, and other respected professionals hold the family sacred. They worry about the decline of family life in modern times; they describe children whose parents are divorced as victims of broken homes. Naturally, we assume that the families they admire so much must be very special.

As a society, we expect the family to be our backbone. It is the conveyer of values, the guardian of its members, the glue that holds us together. But as individuals we really do not know what to expect from the family.

It is not surprising that many adults believe that their parents and their families are impossibly difficult. Consider where we get our images of happy versus unhappy families, our view of what is optimal, our ideal. We rely on the images we develop as we grow up, images of "good" families, "bad" families, and our family. Then we supplement these images with material from popular psychology that finds the roots of many individual problems in a dysfunctional family background.

Images of Happy Families and Miserable Families

Our images tend to be snapshots that capture what we see as the essence of the family experience. As we grow up, we find several sources of families to observe.

• *Fictional families*. Some of us grew up with *The Brady Bunch*, others with *Ozzie and Harriet* or *Leave It To Beaver*.

Although problems arose for these families, the Brady parents or the Nelson parents or the Cleaver parents were always understanding, accepting, and supportive. They might make mistakes—even to the point of falsely accusing a child—but they always apologized later and made amends. And none of them ever made nasty cracks like, "How do you ever expect to amount to anything when you're so lazy?" Certainly they never stomped off in anger, bemoaning the fact that they had ever become parents in the first place. In real life, however, 70 percent of the 10,000 parents who responded to advice columnist Ann Landers's question asking readers, "If you had it all to do over again, would you have children?" said they would not.[3] Apparently these parents' experiences with their children were somewhat less than perfect.

Childhood reading was another source of ideal families. Did the parents of Dick, Jane, and Baby Sally ever do more than shake a finger in dismay to show displeasure? Did the Bobbsey Twins' parents ever fight?

Of course, fiction also showed us the depths to which families can sink, although an evil stepparent was often the one directly responsible for the misery as in *Hansel and Gretel* or *Cinderella*. Adult fiction showed us more realistic family misery. From Shakespeare to contemporary drama, family conflict has been a universal theme. Films and stage plays are powerful media for illustrating the fights and broken ties between adults and their parents. For example, consider a bitter interaction between Biff and his father, Willy, in Arthur Miller's play, *Death of a Salesman*. After years of shared pretense, Biff finally refuses to fabricate any more stories of success or to make believe that everything will be wonderful tomorrow. He says he is going away, but his father cannot accept that decision.

Their conversation descends into recriminations and angry words. Willy, as father, tells Biff he's done himself in and ruined his life by himself no matter what, Willy seems to be saying, don't blame *me*. Willy's parental message is that since Biff didn't do everything his father wanted, Biff had spoiled his chances permanently.

These miserable families usually seem too extreme to disconfirm our belief in family harmony as the norm. Rather, they serve as warnings of the ordeals to which conflict can lead.

• *Our friends' families.* While some of our childhood friends' families were clearly worse than ours, others seemed unquestionably better. It was this second group that aroused our envy and also gave us hope for a better day to come. When I was about ten, my best friends across the street were the children of the minister of one of the largest churches in town. To me they seemed a model family: The parents never fought, they took their kids camping every summer, they had family outings and church activities. My parents were loving, but hot-tempered; their arguments were noisily obtrusive. They hated camping, my father never went to church, and our family outings consisted of a yearly picnic at a nearby lake.

I remember asking my mother why our family could not be more like my friends' family. She replied with some comment to the effect that things are not always as desirable as they seem. In retrospect I agree. My friends had many rules and expectations to live up to as the minister's kids; their roles in the family and in the community were defined for them by their parents. Conversely, in my family we had freedom to be, to try, and to make mistakes. Is the moral of this story that my family's way is the better way? No. The point is that most family situations have both pros and cons. No one has it all. But somehow we take the agreeable aspects for granted and focus on the problems of disagreement.

Expanding the Images

So we have two types of pictures in our heads as we evaluate our family's functioning: good and bad. The negative looks like the horrible examples of abusive or neglectful families we have seen and heard about. The positive is a kind of fantasy-world family like the Cosbys, where problems always work out, and anger quickly turns to laughter

For most of us, neither picture fits our reality. We know our family is not the worst, although we probably do see some of the bad habits of these problem families in our own. But we also feel a long way from the ideal. Only 11 percent of 4,700 readers of *USA Weekend* who responded to a recent survey said that their own families resembled TV families in being able to solve family problems in 22 minutes.[4] Nevertheless, this model is not easy to give up.

If we turn to popular books and articles about family interaction, we find they tend to focus on the negative, telling us what is problem behavior in a family. Today we have plenty of sources that describe dysfunctional families. Most have been written by psychologists or other mental health professionals, with principles and examples derived from their clinical practices. The writers tell us that codependency and addiction are intergenerational family diseases and warn that we may be perpetuating destructive family patterns. They suggest that dysfunctional families devour or destroy their individual members in order to keep the family system alive.

Because we hear so much about dysfunctional families, we might assume that a clear picture also exists of what a functional family is like. Unfortunately, however, we have less information available that tells us realistically how a healthy, effective family functions. When we look for answers that have some scientific validity, we find that the value of specific family characteristics is hard to determine.

How Do Experts Recognize a "Healthy" Family?

Family functioning is a difficult topic to study. To illustrate, suppose a researcher, Dr. Kops, has an idea of a characteristic that might distinguish between healthy and unhealthy families. If Dr. Kops believes that families who show this characteristic are healthier than those who do not have it, how could she test her theory? She could find families that meet some objective criteria of healthiness versus unhealthiness and determine whether her characteristic is significantly more evident in the healthy than the unhealthy families. Or she could take a sample of families, some of whom show her characteristic and some who do not, and ask expert clinicians who are unaware of the characteristic she is studying to independently rate each family's health. Then she could check to see whether significantly more of the families rated as healthy have the characteristic.

The obvious problem with both approaches, and similarly with research of healthy family functioning, is that it presumes that an objective standard exists for assessing families. Actually we do not have such a yardstick. Values, cultural norms, religious beliefs, and personal experiences all affect people's judgments of what a family should be. For example, a dominant value in our society is that a family should provide an environment that promotes the optimal development of each individual family member. But some religious or ethnic subgroups in our society value family cohesion, unity, and loyalty above the self-expression of individual members.[5]

Another problem is determining how a family actually *is* functioning. Some researchers bring families into a laboratory so they can observe and record family members' interaction as they work together on an assigned task. Others find families who will allow themselves to be videotaped at home as they go about their daily routines. Clearly both methods introduce at least some artificiality into the family dynamics. And both must rely on ratings or judgments by clinicians or other experts to evaluate the family behavior recorded.

Another way to access family functioning is to have family members describe their family's operation through interviews, questionnaires, or tasks such as drawing diagrams that depict the way various members interact. Of course, these reports are subjective; each family member has his or her own perceptions of how the family works. The "reality" of the family's functioning is actually impossible to determine; major disagreements between family members as to how the family operates are common. For example, Chris enjoys gatherings with his parents, brother, and sisters. He particularly likes the joking around and teasing that goes on· among them all, because it gives him a feeling of closeness. Conversely, his brother Ed says that he feels tense and uncomfortable when the family is together because some of them always seem to be picking on others.

Is this an unhealthily argumentative family, or one in which members enjoy one another's different views? Some experts in family studies suggest that it is both, because for practical purposes the way an individual perceives the reality of his or her family functioning *is* that person's reality.

What Do You Want to Change?

Clearly, it is not simple to determine how much you could reduce your dissatisfaction when your family's interactions by changing your own thoughts and feelings about what is going on, even if the family does not change at all. It does seem likely, though, that if Ed could find a way to experience the family interaction the way his brother Chris does, nothing else would have to change for him to feel much better. That is not to say that this change would be easy for Ed, but it does have the advantage of being much more under his control than is changing the behavior of other family members.

Some people believe that it is impossible to improve communication with parents who seem to have no interest in changing. Certainly a situation in which everyone in the family decides to work together to change their communication is ideal. They might go so far as to attend a class or workshop together or visit a family therapist. Or they might each read this book and then get together to discuss ways they could change. This, however, is not the norm. Usually one person wants change more than others in the relationship.

In Ed's case, he is the one who is unhappy. You might argue that others in the family are also unhappy but are unwilling to admit or confront the problems, so they pretend everything is fine. Unfortunately, this argument takes us right back to our impossible search for "reality." So Ed can only take them at their word if they say they do not see a problem.

Nevertheless, there is much Ed can do all by himself. First, he can change his picture. This may seem like giving up, but actually he is giving himself a chance to succeed by changing expectations that may be a major cause of his unhappiness. As long as he expects his family to fit his picture of an ideal family in which members do not remark on one another's weak spots, he will probably be continually disappointed. But if he can stop expecting them to meet this standard, he will probably notice other, more pleasing aspects of their behavior. As a result, he will probably change the way he reacts to them, which will change the way they react to him, which will change everything.

Next, Ed can take a problem-solving approach to his

family's interactions, rather than avoiding or lamenting the circumstances he dislikes. Too often we throw up our hands in despair, believing that a situation can never meet our standard of perfection, so we may as well give up. Much in life may be difficult, but who can say what is impossible? Families certainly have the potential to change and grow. Although changing your family's communication may be extremely difficult, it is possible. The key is to see it as a gradual process, rather than an overnight revolution.

Improving Family Communication

To begin, it is helpful to get away from an either-or, all-or-nothing way of looking at your family. Rather than thinking of your family as healthy or unhealthy, functional or dysfunctional, a more useful approach is to think of a continuum of family functioning, from less effective to more effective.

In fact, very few characteristics of people fit easily into a yes-no type system of classification. With some categories such as male-female or alive-dead, most people clearly fit one division or the other, but even with these some gray areas occur. Think about trying to classify people as happy-unhappy, smart-dumb, or selfish-generous. Although some people may tend to be consistently at the high end or the low end of the scale on these qualities, most people fall somewhere in between and most also vary on those dimensions from time to time and situation to situation. Unfortunately, if you judge someone to be a selfish person based on one or two observations of that person's behavior, you may tend to overlook the person's unselfish behavior in other situations to keep your view consistent.

It can be just as problematic to negatively categorize your family. Families, like individuals, vary in their functioning across times and situations. Rather than deciding whether or not your family *is* dysfunctional, it is more useful to compare the specific contexts in which your family has difficulty and the ones that it handles easily. This gives you a way to move beyond making judgments to considering family functioning as a process that can be improved. But how do you know what you are striving for?

Despite the difficulties in assessing families, researchers and therapists generally agree that certain styles of family communication work better than others. They base their conclusions on the results of research using the techniques described in this chapter and on years of personal observations of families.

No family uses the best approach all the time, nor does any always use the worst. Your goal is to increase the amount of time you and your family spend interacting effectively and to decrease the amount of time you spend communicating in ways you find frustrating or upsetting. Specifically, five major dimensions stand out as areas for possible improvement.

Five Goals for Effective Family Functioning

Overall, the continuum of family communication is characterized by direct, open, flexible, clear exchanges at one end as opposed to closed, rigid, or manipulative interactions at the other. Specifically, families are functioning at the positive end of the continuum when they:

• *Work together to solve problems.* All families have problems, many of which have no obvious simple solutions. When a family is functioning effectively, members discuss problems openly, share their feelings, and come up with possible solutions to try out. Rather than blaming one another or hiding the details of their problems, they work together as a unit to resolve the issue. Their focus is on using their collective strengths to deal with the stresses that arise. Thus, they can emerge from a stressful time as a stronger, rather than a more fragmented, unit.[6]

While you cannot control the whole family, you can do your part to involve your parents in the downs as well as the ups of family life. June, for example, says, "I still try to include my mother in most good or bad news about my children, even though mother is ninety years old. My brother and sister believe it is best to keep bad news, such as the impending divorce of a granddaughter and her husband, from mother because she will feel bad and worry. But I disagree. Mother often talks about feeling useless, and I think asking her opinion and advice alleviates this. Shutting her out creates distance between us."

• *Communicate clearly and directly.* Ideally, family members say what they mean and identify who the message is for. For example, an adult daughter might say, "Mother, I am angry at you because you keep mentioning my weight." In that statement the daughter told her mother quite clearly how she felt (angry), and admitted she felt that anger directed at her mother because of what her mother had said. Family communication, however, is often characterized by comments where the message is much more confusing.

One group of family therapists who studied family communication for more than twenty years, developed a model known as the McMaster Model of Family Functioning[7], which defines three common styles of family communication that are less effective than the clear, direct approach illustrated above. For example, the adult daughter might say to her mother, "People make me angry when they mention my weight." In that case, her message is still clear (anger), but it is no longer direct. She is not directly confronting her mother or even admitting that the statement is directed at her mother.

On the other hand, the daughter might make a statement clearly intended for her mother but which masks the actual message. She could say, "Mother, you seem irritable today." This would convey her annoyance to her mother, but not explain why she is feeling upset.

The final and most difficult to interpret style uses statements that are both masked and indirect. For example, the daughter might say to her mother, "People's comments drive me crazy sometimes." In this case, the mother would probably not know whether her daughter's statement was intended for her, or what the purpose was.

The more masked and indirect messages family members give one another, the fewer clear and direct responses they will get, and the less effective the family communication will be. You can improve communication in your family by making your messages clear and direct.

Although speaking clearly and directly to your parents may seem risky, the results may surprise you. For example, twenty-six-year-old Amy says, "I had trouble communicating with my mom. She always said I could talk to her about anything, but I didn't think I could. The things I wanted to discuss I thought might offend her or hurt her. My older siblings had caused her enough pain; I never wanted to add to it. It wasn't until I was in a desperate situation that I realized I could talk to her. She was understanding and helpful and she didn't blame me. Since I got married, my mom and I have been able to communicate even more. It is wonderful."

- *Interact in a variety of styles.* At their best, families are flexible and versatile: They are able to express all sorts of feelings to one another: joy, sadness, love, anger, and so forth. They use a wide range of communication styles and patterns, alternating these to fit specific circumstances. Conversely, a family functioning less effectively may use the same rigid communication patterns across all situations. For example, certain members always side with certain other members, or speakers always follow a predictable arrangement of turn-taking during conversations.[8]

  Taking the first step toward more flexible communication with your parents is a risk because you have no idea how they will react. But, as Mark describes, the risk can pay off: "For years, my father and I interacted in only one of two ways, our three-minute bull sessions or discussing business matters. We would either talk for about three minutes about surface matters, jokes or such, or have a serious talk about some financial concern. Then Dad had a heart attack and I realized that I had others things I wanted to say to him. So I told him that, and I also told him that I love him. It was hard to say because he and I haven't talked that way. But he listened, and he said he would like to talk more, too. Now we talk more openly. I feel very lucky to have had this chance to know him better."

- *Avoid manipulative communication games.* Psychiatrist Eric Berne's popular book, *Games People Play*, describes the sorts of manipulative games people unconsciously play to get some sort of payoff.[9] For example, in the game called "If It Weren't For You," one person uses the other to justify inaction. In this game a son may complain to his father that the father's criticism has made him afraid to apply for competitive jobs. The payoff is that the son is able to avoid doing something he fears, perhaps something his father wants him to do, but does not take responsibility for his choice.

Berne describes many other games, such as "Look How Hard I've Tried" and "See What You Made Me Do." While it it unlikely that any family can avoid slipping into such interactions occasionally, the goal is to substitute genuine expressions of feelings for the pretense of communication games. Gail explains how she worked on this: "My father and I always used to dredge up old mistakes to make each other look dumb. I would remind him of the time he killed the dryer with a hammer, and he would recall the time I hit a teacher's car in the high-school parking lot when I was sixteen. Finally I got tired of it and simply stopped playing that game. When he brought up those times, I would say something like, 'That was a long time ago. Let's talk about what you are upset about right now.' After a while he stopped too."

- *Support one another's autonomy.* Ideally, family members are close but also respect one another's individuality. They accept differences and encourage the expression of diverse points of view. They try to understand rather than coerce. They do not attempt to control another by punishing behavior they dislike. Rather, they take responsibility for their own desires, express their concerns openly, and search for acceptable compromises. They trust family members and forgive them easily when misunderstandings occur.[10]

It can be difficult to find effective ways to remind parents to respect your individuality. Sometimes, though, a simple, direct approach can work well if you can say what you mean without blaming or criticizing. Forty-five-year-old Kurt remembers the time ten years ago when he finally found a way to end his mother's criticism of his beard: "My mother said for probably the hundredth time, 'I see you haven't shaved that damn beard off.' Instead of responding angrily as I usually did, I said jokingly, 'I keep it just to bug you! I know you've never liked the beard. Maybe it reminds you of hippies or that we are growing older.' Then I said, 'Seriously, I don't wear it just to bug you. Remember how my face used to break out when I shaved every day? The beard protects my face, plus it saves me a lot of trouble in the morning, *and* I realize you would prefer I shave the beard

off.' She said something like, 'Oh, I never thought of that.'
And that was the last time she mentioned the subject."

Expect to Solve Problems

The key is to expect conflicts and problems and to be
prepared to deal with them. If you went out in a boat assuming
that nothing would ever go wrong, you might find yourself in
deep water with no life preserver. But if you know you cannot
assume clear sailing all the time, you will go prepared. You
might even have someone give you a lesson in what to do if
your boat capsizes. Then if a storm suddenly comes up and
your boat overturns, you will cope as well as you can and learn
to do better next time.

Families who confront problems instead of avoiding them
learn to cope and move on. Family members who feel prepared
for difficulties that come up are less likely to see each problem
as a catastrophe. This brings us back to the issue of expectations. If you believe that your relationship with your parents
must always be harmonious, you will do everything you can to
avoid conflict with them rather than finding ways to work
through problems. If you feel continually frustrated that your
relationship with your parents does not measure up to some
mythical ideal, you will waste your energy bemoaning what
you wish you had instead of acting to improve what you do
have.

At age forty-four, Meg had only recently come to this
realization. She had a difficult relationship with her parents for
years. When she was in college, they objected to her choice of
a sociology major, refusing to pay her tuition if she stayed with
that choice. When she was divorced in her twenties, they
disapproved strongly and did everything they could to influence her to stay married. Later, her parents themselves
divorced, and Meg's father refused to speak to her for three
months because she would not intervene in her parents'
marriage problems.

Meg did not suffer in silence. She recalled: "For a long time
I complained about my parents to anyone who would listen
about how they controlled my life, how I wished they were
different, and how unlucky I was to have such irritating
parents." Finally, a good friend grew tired of Meg's complaints

and asked her if she really thought her parents were going to change. "I told her that I did not expect them to change, I just expected them to keep on ruining my life," Meg said. Meg's friend then asked her why each new incident with her parents was so upsetting to her if she expected that behavior all along. "That's when I realized that I had been expecting them to change," Meg said, "and each time we had a conflict it was a new insult."

So Meg changed her way of thinking about her parents. She explained: "I stopped expecting them to be someone they aren't. I decided to simply accept their pluses and minuses as parents and recognize my pluses and minuses as a daughter. I give them only as much of my time and myself as is in my best interests. This was very difficult at first, but after several years of practice, I have become more comfortable with it. I have worked through most of my past anger with them, which helps me set limits with them. I may not have the parents I always wished I had, but I get along a lot better with the ones I do have."

CHAPTER 13

Are They Responsible For Your Behavior?

"My mother made me a homosexual."

"If I buy her the yarn, will she make me one, too?"
(Graffiti)

People tend to look to their past experiences to explain their behavior in the present, especially aspects they see as difficulties or shortcomings. Typically, parents get the major share of the blame for their grown children's undesirable personality traits and problem behaviors.

Clearly, adults who were physically, sexually, or emotionally abused by their parents during childhood must deal with the effects of that mistreatment in their adult lives. Similarly, adults who suffered severe neglect as children because their parents abused alcohol or drugs or had other major problems must find ways to cope with the consequences as adults.

Yet, popular psychology has encouraged us to look far beyond obvious parental mistreatment in our search for causes of present-day difficulties. Frequently adult children trace the origins of minor as well as major unwanted characteristics back to family habits or early interactions with parents.

Carrying on Undesirable Family Traits

Sometimes the objectionable trait is a peculiarity or matter of personal style that an individual feels was somehow inherited from a parent or was a family custom. For example, Elaine attributes her worrying to her mother's influence. She says:

"I'm a worrywart. I worry constantly. My doctor has told me I'm heading straight for an ulcer, but I can't help it. If I don't have something to worry about, I'll find something somewhere. I can't relax and take things as they come. I worry for weeks in advance. This I inherited from my mother. She has always been a worrier, too, and I guess it rubbed off on me."

Similarly, Scott assumes he inherited some difficulties: "My wife tells me that I've inherited my father's coldness and bullheadedness as well as my mother's constant worrying. I suppose she's right. When we argue, I've always been able to turn off my emotions. I rarely become angry. I just become distant whenever we disagree. And I do worry a lot about finances."

When a person sees a trait as a family predisposition or custom, it seems more acceptable and less under the control of the person exhibiting the behavior. Kelly, for example, may not like feeling nervous, but her explanation seems to imply it is inevitable for her. She says, "One thing I have inherited from my mother is my nervousness. I get nervous whenever I have to get up and talk. And when things start getting rough, it seems like my whole world is caving in and I just can't control myself. I let little things upset me too easily. This is how my mother is, and I think I learned it from her."

Similarly, Julie seems to see her lateness as a family habit she is unlikely to change: "My friends bug me about being poky. My whole family is slow, so that's why I'm that way. We were never on time for things when I was growing up at home—always late."

Responses to Difficult Parental Behavior

Others explain today's difficulties in terms of what their parents did or did not do and the reactions their parents' behavior created in them. James explains his reserved personal style this way: "I'm a pretty quiet person, which is often taken as snobbery. Actually it is a reflection of my father's domineering and very vocal habits. He barely lets a word in edgewise when he has something to say, and he's so domineering I was scared to say anything for fear it would be wrong. So I kept my mouth shut."

Similarly, Teri believes her parents prevented her from

learning how to handle common daily circumstances. She says: "I am considered intelligent but definitely lacking in common sense. I think this is because I was never given a chance to fend for myself in everyday situations. It annoys me when everyone tells me how scatterbrained I am, and then I do try to improve but it never does much good."

Such explanations serve to excuse and justify behaviors that people dislike in themselves, without seeming to call for any specific action to change. For example, Ron sees his undesirable attitudes about money as his father's fault. "I've been referred to as an 'Old Scrooge' at times for my miserly qualities. I really am a cheapskate, and I hate being that way. I blame my father. As I was growing up he never gave me any money. I could never do anything like roller-skate or go to the movies or even buy a stick of gum because I never had any money. I got a job after my sophomore year in high school, and they haven't paid for anything since. So I was forced into learning every technique of stretching a dollar from my parents."

Many people also blame their parents for more serious flaws, such as alcohol abuse, difficulty in forming close relationships, or fears that control their actions. Owen is lonely, and he blames his parents: "Displays of emotion in our family were practically nonexistent when I was young; little emotion was shown to either my sister or myself unless it was anger. The folks were sober and never argued or showed any affection toward each other in our presence. My parents were responsible for my biggest hang-up; I was never shown how to feel emotion or how to display it to other people. I was taught that rationality was more important than emotions. Now I have trouble establishing meaningful relationships with others. I find it difficult to give enough of myself to another to become a close friend of that person."

In fact, problems with physical or emotional intimacy are among the difficulties adults most frequently see as stemming from their parents' behavior. Monica blames her mother for her own sexual problems: "My mom always led us to believe that everything about sex was bad. Whenever my dad would kiss her, take her hand, or anything at all, she would come back with, 'Stop it.' My sexual hang-ups today come from what I learned from her." And Teresa blames her mother for her own inability to trust: "My mother always ran down our friends and aid we shouldn't get involved with anyone because they couldn't possibly really like us. After a while of having this pounded into you, you sort of develop an inferiority complex. Now it seems that I just can't get really close to anyone."

Mary Beth feels an insatiable need for physical affection; Karen hates to be touched. Both see their parents as responsible. Mary Beth says: "During my family life, physical relationships were never stressed. Of course, we hugged and kissed our parents at night, but this lasted only until they thought we were too old, probably until the age of eight. Today I blame this family life-style for many of my present actions. For example, I am starved for love and the physical actions that go with it. My relationships with men always break up because I want and need more affection than one person can possibly give me. I feel that the affection I was denied during my childhood has brought me where I am today."

Karen complains: "My father honestly thinks, even to this day, that the only way to make a child behave is to yell, insult, and hit. We never knew what would set him off. At the same time, he wanted our affection. I felt that hugs and kisses were expected of us, but it was very one-sided. I think we satisfied his needs more than he did ours. I think this is one of the reasons I dislike being touched by anyone—I feel that *I* am not being considered, I am just being used."

Wishing They Had Reacted Differently

No matter how our parents brought us up, it is easy to look back and wish some aspects had been different. For example, adults who have problems with alcohol or drug abuse, and whose parents also abused alcohol or drugs, are likely to blame their parents for passing on these unfortunate patterns. But grown children whose parents were seriously opposed to these substances may also blame their parents for their own abuse. Greg explains: "I have abused alcohol and drugs as a direct result of my parents' narrow-mindedness. They taught me that anyone who consumes any alcohol at all is evil. When I figured out they were wrong about that, I rebelled against all their ideas and became a profound drunk. I went on to use drugs for the same reasons. It took me a long time and some bad experiences

194   **Lynn Osterkamp, Ph.D.**

to realize that I was doing this out of a sense of rebellion, not because I enjoyed it."

Similarly, adults tend to feel that parental influence had a major effect on their level of accomplishment. Whether they wish they did not feel a need to work so hard or whether they wish they worked harder, they can see parents as the culprits. For example, Scott says: "I have this horrid drive to succeed even if it kills me! I have a fear of failure when I really should not. One of the reasons why I think that I'm this way is because my parents were always very appreciative and rewarding of good grades and hard work." On the other hand, Derek complains: "As a child I was very much on my own. I was the middle child of seven and my parents were just too busy to pay much attention. I was happy about this but it had some unfortunate consequences. I had a great social life but did terrible in school because I hated school and my parents didn't push me to do well. I could have done a lot better and been better off today if they had paid more attention."

Clearly these adults believe they would be living happier lives if they had grown up with parents who treated them differently. Whether or not this is true is something we cannot know, nor is it the issue here. An exploration of what happened in the past is only useful insofar as it helps us improve the present or the future. The challenge is to find ways of looking at your upbringing that moves you beyond blaming your parents or feeling stuck with unwanted behavior patterns.

Freedom Versus Blame

Viewing your adult self as the product of your childhood experiences can be a problem if you feel that you are stuck with the results. Feelings of helplessness and powerlessness generally accompany this outlook. For example, Andrew believes that his father's domineering insistence on always being right is responsible for his own lifelong feelings of insecurity and low self-worth. He says: "Today I am what I am—not totally mixed up and confused but a person with definite problems and handicaps. I am what my past and family life have contributed. I know I can never change the basic 'me.' It is strange how one can see a problem and yet one feels hopeless to eliminate it."

Considerable psychological research has shown that people

who believe they do not have control over their lives tend to have high levels of stress and low life-satisfaction. Thus people like Andrew who feel that they cannot undo damage from the past are less likely to be happy and more likely to report major problems in their lives. While blaming his father for his current difficulties offers Andrew the solace of absolving himself of responsibility for his problems, this approach also leaves him feeling like a helpless victim of his past.

The renowned psychologist Albert Ellis has explained how people's *ideas* about their parents' treatment of them are more damaging than the treatment itself. During years of clinical experience, Ellis found that no matter how difficult a person's past experiences have been, that person can change the impact of those experiences in the present by changing the way he or she thinks about what happened in the past. For example, Ellis discovered that in our society our ideas about the impact of being rejected by a parent are so strongly negative that we allow this childhood rejection to cripple us as adults. He points out that even though rejection may create many difficulties for a child, it continues to be a source of problems for the adult only if that adult still believes society's irrational ideas about the consequences of parental rejection. If that adult believes that children who were rejected by a parent will never feel secure as adults, or will be afraid to try certain tasks, or will be unable to deal with criticism, then he or she will remain disturbed.[1]

A Tradition of Looking for Causes

Why are our beliefs about the disastrous consequences of childhood experiences so strong? One major reason is that mental health professionals continue to point the finger at parents as the cause of their children's problems.

Throughout the twentieth century, psychologists have offered a variety of explanations and solutions for dysfunctional human behavior. Despite the differences among these approaches, one factor the majority have in common is a focus on children's interactions with their parents as a source of emotional or behavior problems.

To illustrate, in a study of 125 articles published in a variety of mental health journals between 1970 and 1982, Canadian psychologist Paula Caplan found that mothers were blamed for 72 different kinds of psychological disorders in their children. In these articles, mental health professionals not only held mothers responsible for their children's phobias, schizophrenia, hyperactivity, and other problems, they ignored evidence that challenges simplistic mother-blaming theories.[2]

Theories that have focused on the childhood roots of adult problems have also found ready acceptance in our popular culture over the years. Four theories in particular have contributed to blaming parents for their children's problems:

- *Psychoanalysis*. Sigmund Freud, the father of psychoanalysis, published his first book in 1895 and presented psychoanalysis to America as a scientific system in a 1909 lecture series at Clark University in Worcester, Massachusetts. His theory, which focused on abnormal behavior and the role of the unconscious, was a major departure from accepted explanations of behavior at that time.

  Freud based his theory on his own life experiences and on his interpretations of information his disturbed patients provided during the analytic process. He became convinced that adult personality patterns were established early in life and that his patients' neurotic disturbances originated in their childhood experiences.[3]

  Despite its questionable scientific validity, Freud's therapeutic approach, which consistently moved from effects to causes, tracing symptoms to traumatic childhood events, has been extremely influential in this country. Furthermore, certain of his central concepts, such as the effects of upsetting childhood experiences on adult personality have been widely accepted by the lay public.

- *Behaviorism*. A different approach that has also been a major system of explaining people's actions is behaviorism, which began with John B. Watson's 1913 paper advocating the study of behavior rather than feelings. Watson wrote both scholarly and popular books and articles explaining his method of studying behavior by reducing it to its simplest elements, stimulus and response. Watson's belief that early training accounts for adult performance led to an acceptance of the idea that a person's behavior, problem or otherwise, is shaped by the actions and reactions of others in his or her environment. Watson achieved a large following among the lay public largely because of his conviction that it was possible to train children to be whatever one wanted them to be.

Behaviorism achieved its widest popularity through the work of B. F. Skinner, who wrote scholarly and popular books and articles explaining the role of reinforcement in shaping behavior. The basic principle of his work is that people repeat behavior that their environment rewards. Skinner's 1948 novel, *Walden Two*, describes a community in which every aspect of life is programmed and controlled through positive reinforcement to produce an orderly society.[4]

Although criticized as atheoretical, behaviorists have accumulated a wealth of data to support their assumptions that human behavior can be controlled, modified, and shaped by others. Their techniques are widely used in teaching and working with children and adolescents who have behavior problems. Their ideas—that people behave as they do because of early training and environmental conditions—have become widely accepted in our culture.

Family Therapy. Coinciding with the postwar focus on the family in the late forties and early fifties, some researchers began to look at ways family functioning might explain children's emotional problems. The research led to theories that implicated dysfunctional family interactions in the development of such childhood emotional disturbances as schizophrenia. In 1956, Gregory Bateson published a now famous paper entitled, "Toward a Theory of Schizophrenia," which described the role of a form of habitual, destructive communication called double bind in creating schizophrenic behavior. The double-bind theory explained how parents who communicate a demand at one level but contradict that demand at another level elicit crazy responses from their children.

By the sixties and seventies, numerous research projects around the country were studying the relationship between emotional disorders in children and their family environment. Therapeutic approaches evolved in which entire family units were the focus of treatment when a child was identified with a problem.

One of the most popular approaches is that of Murray Bowen, which explores relationships for several generations back in the extended family in order to explain present emotional problems. Bowenian therapists conduct multigenerational family therapy to identify and change destructive patterns that have been passed down within the family.[5]

• *Codependency.* A relative newcomer, but rapidly achieving popularity, this approach originally referred to the problems of people married to alcoholics. It has grown into a major self-help movement that explains virtually any adult problem as an addiction developed in reaction to childhood experiences in a dysfunctional family. Recovery, it suggests, comes about through healing the wounded inner child.

Melody Beattie, who has written several popular books on the problem of codependency, explains that people develop codependent behaviors when they grow up with a needy or dependent parent or in a family that has unwritten rules against expressing feelings, talking about problems, communicating honestly, or spontaneously having fun. Even after the codependent person no longer lives with the problem person or in the unhealthy environment, he or she continues to seek and become involved in other unhealthy relationships.[6]

Blaming Versus Understanding

Each of the above approaches to explaining human behavior is just that—one of many possible explanations. Ultimately each explanation has two constructive goals: 1) to teach people ways of interacting that prevent problems from arising; and 2) to help people who already have problems to change their feelings and behavior in a positive direction. Unfortunately, however, as theories of human behavior become popularized, the original goals are often ignored. People tend to look at the explanations, say, "No wonder I am the way I am," and assume they are stuck with these problems that their parents caused.

The understanding that theories of human behavior offer is helpful only if people are willing to use it as a basis for change. If, instead of an explanation, the theory is used as an excuse, it will merely help people stay stuck where they are.

Excuses are appealing as justification for our faults and to explain behavior that puts us in a bad light. Psychologists C. R. Snyder, Raymond Higgins, and Rita Stucky, who conducted a comprehensive study of excuses, describe an excuse as an explanation that lessens the negative implications of one's performance to help one maintain a positive image. One large group of excuses are those that fall into the category of "I couldn't help it." Such excuses absolve us from responsibility for our undesirable actions by showing how we had no choice but to act as we did.[7]

Family therapists find that some adults who come to them with an apparent desire to change are actually more interested in complaining about how they have been done in by their parents than they are in changing themselves. Eileen Pender-gast of the Center for Family Learning in New Rochelle, New York, sees this as a waste of time for both the therapist and the client. She says: "I am less and less willing to waste my therapeutic hours on a quest that ends in righteous blaming of one's elders whose lives may have in fact been a good deal tougher than one's own. I have all kinds of time, however, for those hardy souls who really want to find out what makes the family tick and then want to try to apply what they have learned to their own lives. Alas! These folk are few and far between."[8]

Breaking Free of Blame

If you find yourself continually blaming your parents for problems in your adult life, how can you get out of that cycle? Several approaches are useful:

• *Consider your goals.* Ask yourself whether you actually want to change the behavior in question. Answer truthfully. If you do want to change, blaming your parents is not a useful strategy. If you want to get your anger out so you can move on, expressing the anger to a counselor or therapist can be helpful, so long as you truly are willing to move on. If your goal is to have your parents admit their mistakes and apologize, remember that blaming generally creates defensiveness rather than apologies. Furthermore, even if they do apologize, they cannot change the past.

At age thirty-eight, Gerald has just recently found this out.

Because of a problematic childhood during which he felt unloved, lonely, and depressed, Gerald has had, he says, "some deep-seated emotions of hurt and anger that seemed to need to be released" when his mother came to visit. In the past, Gerald would find that he would feel happy when his mother first came, but then he would get angry and express this anger to his mother, which did not create the type of visit he wanted to have with her. Lately he has begun to focus on expressing love instead of anger. He says, "I have been telling her that I love her without the anger and at times when I am happy. When I hug her and share love and happiness with her, I am much happier with my relationship with my mother."

• *Reframe the past.* Remember that there are many different ways to view any situation. If you think about your parents' difficult behavior differently, you may see some positives as well as negatives that have come from what you experienced. For example, growing up with a severe, demanding father is not easy, but some adults see this as the source of their success. Darren explains: "My father gave a lot of orders. He demanded a lot from me and expected me to handle a lot of responsibility. I have sometimes wondered if it was too much, but now he tells me he just wanted me to grow up. Now I can see he taught me a lot of valuable qualities. For example, I like things to be organized, and I do not like to procrastinate when I have something of importance that has to be done."

Similarly, Evelyn believes that she derived benefit from her father's early distrust. She says: "I have pretty high standards and high goals. I won't settle for second best if I can do better, and I always set my goals just a little higher than I think I'm capable of and then work hard and accomplish it. I respect myself and demand respect from others. My high standards are probably partially a product of my father's distrust. He didn't trust me and told me so quite often. So I always worked hard to gain his respect and trust. I kept trying to do good, which resulted in some self-pride and high standards."

Clearly Darren and Evelyn could see their fathers as having created anxiety, fear of failure, and low self-esteem rather than as having taught them to accept responsibility and set high standards. If you look for positives among the negatives, you may be surprised what you will find.

- *Forgive and forget.* Forgiveness is hard, because our view of the world as just and fair tells us that people should pay for what they do. If we forgive them, we let them off the hook. When you blame someone for something hurtful they have done to you, you feel righteous. If you see your parents as responsible for your problems, you probably feel they deserve the blame. And perhaps they do. But continuing to blame them hurts you more than it hurts them, because you are the one carrying around the resentment and anger that keeps you stuck in your old unhappiness.

Letting go of the blame, forgiving them for hurting you, leaves you free to heal yourself and begin to work on changing aspects of your behavior associated with those old patterns. Forgiving your parents also gives you an opportunity to develop a new, more satisfying relationship with them.

It is not necessary, nor in most cases advisable, to tell your parents you forgive them. What you do need to do is to look closely at what they have done that has hurt you. Rather than judging them, consider as well as you can what may have been going on in their lives. Recall the discussion in Chapter 5 about the value of seeing your parents' perspective and unfreezing old misunderstandings. Remind yourself that your parents are fallible human beings who make mistakes as we all do. Then decide whether you are willing to forgive them for the mistakes that have hurt you.

It is also useful to accept them as they are. If they are still behaving in a way that has hurt you in the past, you will feel better if you do not continue to blame them for this behavior. As Dana realized, they are probably not willfully hurting you, they are just stuck in their own problems.

Dana: They Just Aren't Demonstrative.

It took me a long time to forgive my parents for giving me so little physical affection. After I married into a family who hug and kiss whenever they get together, I felt even worse about my parents' distant behavior. I am more physically affectionate with my mother-in-law and father-in-law than I am with my own parents. I love the way my husband's family interacts and expresses affection, and I wish my parents were like them.

It was my mother-in-law who helped me understand my parents better. My mother's family is close but not demonstrative. My father rarely communicates with his family. Now I don't feel that my parents deliberately deny me their affection. They just aren't demonstrative. Instead they tend to compensate with gifts, sometimes expensive ones. Often my mother buys me things for no reason at all, other than she simply thinks I would enjoy the item. I used to refuse to accept some of her gifts, but now I see that this is her way of expressing affection, so I take what she gives and thank her. Overall, we get along much better now than we did in the past, probably because I have stopped expecting them to be different from who they are.

• *Release yourself.* Remember that you are an adult, free to make your own decisions and choices. Understanding and forgiving your parents does not mean you must continue to support them in behaviors that hurt you. Forgiveness is all you have available for the past, but the present is another story. If you are unhappy with the way you and your parents interact today, you can change the amount of time you spend with them and the types of situations in which you and they interact.

In most cases you will be able to break many of the old patterns and change your reactions to your parents using the suggestions in this book. Ideally you will reach a point where you can be with your parents being who you are and letting them be who they are without finding the differences upsetting. But in extreme cases this may not be possible.

Some grown children may choose to have very little or no contact with their parents. Jenny, who is thirty-seven, chooses to live 1,300 miles away from her parents and to see them only once every year or so for a brief visit. Jenny's parents are openly critical of her lesbian life-style, her friends, and the woman she has lived with for ten years. When Jenny came out to her family ten years ago, they were shocked and angry and felt uncomfortable being around her. At first she was hurt and stayed away. Then she tried to change their feelings, but without success. Eventually she told them she did not want to spend time with them when they continued to treat her as if something is wrong with her.

Jenny's parents are still part of her life, but only a small part. She says she wants them to be healthy, happy, and comfortable, but she doesn't want to be around them very much. For her, this choice is the best alternative she sees in a difficult situation.

The next chapter will look more closely at various options available to grown children. It will focus specifically on the process of choosing the type of relationship you want to have with your parents today.

CHAPTER 14

What Role Would You Like Your Parents to Play in Your Life Today?

"My parents have been and are an important part of my life. I love and respect them in spite of the problems. I am grateful that my children can know and relate to grandparents. I'm grateful for the connection with my own personal history. I want Mom to keep telling me and my children the important stories I need to know to carry on in the world I live in. I want to give them love and kindness and a sense that they are still an important part of our family—that they still belong."

(John, age 47)

John's parents are in their seventies and live nearby. He and his wife see his parents regularly once a week, usually for Saturday breakfast. John also tries to include his parents in gatherings and activities involving his grown children who also live in the area. He does not feel particularly emotionally close to his parents, because they do not like to discuss problems or personal matters. He also sees them as trying to control him and as expecting more time and attention from him than he feels able to provide.

Nevertheless, John accepts the relationship for what it has to offer and is not looking for more from his parents at this point. Over the years, he has come to terms with what he is willing to give to the relationship, what his parents are willing to give, and what the benefits are for each of them. As he says above, he wants them all to feel the family connection and to share a sense of personal history. He chooses to include them regularly in his family life and to ignore or overlook the difficulties.

The kind of relationship John has chosen to have with his parents is more superficial than many grown children would want. Some adults might say that John has decided to settle for too little. In John's place, they would miss the emotional support and closeness that they feel with their parents.

Conversely, other adults would say that from their point of view John is doing too much. Many grown children whose parents are difficult do not want the level of involvement with their parents that John chooses to have with his. In his place, they would feel that they need more distance from the long struggle with their parents in order to feel like capable adults.

Choosing What You Want

Social exchange theory tells us that people like a balance between costs and rewards in relationships. It is not surprising if you feel that way, even with your parents. If you feel that the costs of being with your parents are very high or if you seem to be always giving more than you get, you may decide to limit your interactions with them in certain ways. You do not have to go for the whole fairy-tale relationship. It may be enough just to find ways of getting along without fighting.

Some adults have close, intimate relationships with their parents, in which trust is absolute, secrets do not exist, and no effort to help the other is too great. Others, like John, have made choices to operate at a less intimate level.

If you think of the possible types of relationships you could have with your parents as a continuum with intimacy at one end and withdrawal at the other,

intimacy   withdrawal

_____

you can conceive of a limitless number of possibilities in between. Clearly intimacy and withdrawal are extremes. Most people's relationships with their parents do not fit the descriptions of either end point. Few adults share all their innermost thoughts and feelings with their parents, nor do many cut off all contact with them. Relationships between grown children and their parents can be placed along this continuum according to their level of commitment to intimacy, the types and frequency of interactions between them, the amount of support they offer and expect from one another, and the amount of desire they have for change.

The purpose of examining relationships between adults and their parents along this continuum is to clarify the many levels of choice that exist for these relationships. Although we have a tendency to view such a system as a yardstick that will measure the good or bad aspects of any given example, this continuum is not meant to be a grading system. In an ideal world, most, if not all, people would choose to have intimate, open relationships with their parents. But when you are choosing what you want for yourself, you must take into account your own personal situation and decide what will work best for you.

Typical Relationship Choices

If you take a look around at the ways your friends relate to their parents, you will find several common styles. Some feel very close to their parents, fully share the ups and downs of their lives, and have few problems beyond an occasional minor misunderstanding with their parents. These adult children are satisfied with their relationships with their parents. They are giving a lot and getting a lot in return. While this is the ideal, it is also the exception.

Other adults are actively involved in working to improve the connection between themselves and their parents. Many find the going very rough, but they keep trying to find ways to move beyond the difficulties. Their parents are a very important part of their lives, and they would like to feel emotionally closer to them. These grown children have some limits where their parents are concerned, both in what they will give and what they expect, but the limits usually are not firmly established.

Some adults have chosen to limit their relationships with their parents to certain specific types of interactions. Above all, they want to avoid arguments and anger between them. They have found ways to have peaceful contact with parents, and they accept the status quo. They have changed their expectations of their relationships with their parents such that they are no longer looking for emotional support or approval from them. Whether they live far from their parents or nearby, they limit the frequency and amount of contact with them to what has proven to be a manageable level. They are willing to give some support to their parents if the need arises, but only within certain limits.

A few adults are fed up with their parent or parents. They have decided the relationship is not worth the agony, so they have no contact with their parents. Although most of these grown children wish their situation with regard to their parents were different, they have found the personal cost of continuing to relate to their parents too high to tolerate. These adults have withdrawn from the relationship because they see no other choice. Yet they often retain at least a faint glimmer of hope for change in the future.

People's reasons for making the choices they do are complex and personal. Each person must consider his or her own background, current life circumstances, and hopes for the future when making decisions about how much energy to invest in improving a relationship with a parent. Listening to other people's thoughts about their choices regarding their parents can broaden your perspective and help you consider your own options.

In the rest of this chapter four grown children will discuss their goals and decisions regarding their relationships with their parents. The stories will depict various points along the continuum that illustrate the complexities of the choices grown children often find themselves facing.

Sam: Pursuing Intimacy While Maintaining Independence.
Sam is in his mid-thirties, and his parents are in their early sixties. When Sam was growing up, his father had a master plan for him. Sam followed it pretty much through college and law school, but then he married someone his father didn't particularly like and moved 600 miles away, which changed things considerably between them. Sam feels that his mother is very accepting of whatever he does but that his father is very controlling. During his adult years Sam has been striving for a balance between independence and intimacy with his parents.

"I do care very much for them. When they are coming out for a visit, I usually have a sense of looking forward to seeing them, of missing them. I don't get a sense that they expect a lot of support from me. They're tickled when I invite them to do something, almost always very pleased and willing to go along.

"My mother is a "live and let live" kind of person. Her interest is that I'm happy. She's an amazing person, very easy to be with. But my father focuses on doing rather than being. Doing is important. I did well in school, got in to law school, and did well there. In that sense I have accomplished a lot of things that make him proud. But he just can't stop teaching me. 'You ought to do this better, that better.' Little helpful hints.

"When I look back, I moved away to get away from that. I wasn't purposely trying to be away from him, but there was some subconscious need to do it. I had very little contact except Christmas for several years and would often go for months without calling. I would just call occasionally to say, 'Hi.' They didn't call me much, either, probably because they knew I was very busy and also because I didn't emote the opportunity. I didn't welcome it. I wasn't hostile, but I just wasn't interested.

"I do feel that I had cut myself off from him because I sensed the amount of control he wanted. I withdrew so I could minimize it. I was not very affectionate with him. The only way for me to protect myself was to withdraw so that I could maintain my own power.

"Then I went through a workshop where I dealt with my relationship with my father. I called them after and told them I loved them. I could not recall ever having told him I loved him. I still had considerable trepidation about his ability to manipulate. But I called and told him that I loved him and that I didn't remember having told him that before and that I was sorry about that. My father was real taken back, real choked up about it.

"There was a pretty stormy period after that. Because what he felt was that now he was finally going to have the relationship he wanted with me, that I was going to be close and appreciative and grateful. That wasn't the case. I was just letting him know that I loved him and that I appreciated his caring. He expected more. He has a real idealized idea of what a father-son relationship should be. He didn't have that kind of relationship with his father. It would be real buddy-buddy and supportive and accepting of everything he wanted. I'd call them all the time, I'd go there more, I would not resist his teachings and his wisdom. I do resist to my detriment a lot of things, but I was unwilling to surrender, and it was frustrating for him, and we got into some very vociferous arguments.

"What I was doing was beginning to share with him how I felt about him and me, and it was certainly not what he expected or wanted to hear. But my mother simply refused to accept these arguments between Dad and me. I think she knows my father well enough that she knew this would not get anywhere. Most of the arguments took place out here when they would visit. She would come in and say 'Stop this. I'm not staying here. We're leaving.' So we stopped. It was probably good because it was not a productive thing.

"The attempt to be honest and open with Dad didn't work. So I pulled back from that, and he was really frustrated. He would push and pull. I also think I wanted him to see that I was right. What I realized was that either I was never going to get it expressly or that it didn't matter.

"I suppose we'll keep on struggling, but it's different now and better because I know I want to be close to them and I'm willing to keep working on it. Last time they came to visit, he was going on and on. I had spent too much time with him, and I was irritated with the comments and topics of conversation and the judgment. It was just driving me crazy. All I could do was nothing. Just not be with him or not respond at all. So I just didn't respond. I let him talk, and I just listened. But it irritated the hell out of him that I didn't respond. Finally the day before they left, he was angry and he said, 'It seems like you are just tolerating me.' So I decided to give him a bit of information and I said, 'I just don't enjoy discussing those kinds of things.' And it just pissed him off. He didn't speak to me again. They flew home, and I took them to the airport, and he picked up his bag and walked off into the airport, and that was it.

"I guess the interesting part is, and maybe this is an important key, I never feel that I will lose him now or lose his support, never. I think at this point he believes that I will always love him. With that I can kind of let things happen and not freak out. In fact, what happened then was I gave him a hug and said 'I love you.' No response from him whatsoever, and

it was okay with me. All I wanted to do was reinforce that I did
love him.

"They're coming again in August. At first when I wrote to
them saying we wanted them to come, my Dad wrote back
saying they were not coming. He said, 'I refuse to be treated
the way you treat me.' My first response was to write back and
tell him that was crazy and why he was wrong. Then I thought
better of that, so I just said they were welcome if they wanted
to come. I said 'I'll miss you if you don't come.' That's why
that bottom line is still there. I still could say I wanted him to
come after he said that. And they are coming after all. I'm
looking forward to their visit. It will give my father and me
another chance to see how we can get along."

Jackie: Limiting Involvement to Preserve Peace.

Jackie is in her late forties, and her parents are in their
seventies. She lives about 1,300 miles away from them,
usually sees them once a year for a week or so, and talks to
them on the phone every two or three weeks. Jackie prefers this
limited contact because she finds her parents difficult to be
with. She says:

"I don't see them very often, but because they are my
parents, I like to keep some minimal contact with them. I used
to argue with them whenever I was with them. They always
have to be right, and they are very bossy and controlling. But
I have made a lot of changes in the way I am with them. Most
of the changes had to be in me. My parents aren't going to
change.

"I'd say I'm resigned to the situation between us now. I
don't expect my parents to really see me as a person anymore.
I don't feel like they know me all that well. They know some
of who I am, but in terms of really being able to take my
perspective or have any idea about how I see the world, I really
don't think they're very capable of doing that. I used to try.
Where I really feel unable to do it is with issues that are really
important to them, like my divorce. If I thought there was a
possibility they could understand how I feel about it—I'd like
them to, but I don't think there is that possibility, so it's okay.

"Ideally, I'd like them to know me better, but I don't think
that will happen. Approval is nice, but I have pretty much

given up on that, too. As the years go by and I don't see them very often, I feel less and less connected to them, and their approval makes less of a difference.

"They're my parents, and I care for them, but I feel that they're out there and I am here. I acknowledge their point of view but don't necessarily accept it. If I tried to be really connected with their lives, I'd start feeling a lot more emotionally battered. I don't see how I could be really connected with them without continually trying to change their minds about life. So I stay distant from them and relatively unconnected.

"The main thing is I have found a way to end the battles and keep peace between us. I don't ask for more, and I usually don't give more. Now and then when things seem to be going particularly well, I try to be a little more affectionate. Right now I know I haven't told them that I love them in a long time, and I might regret not doing that if they suddenly died."

Dick: Maintaining Contact with Few Expectations.

Dick is fifty, his father is eighty, and his mother is seventy-six. His parents are wealthy and have frequently used their money to manipulate Dick and his two brothers. The parents have given the three brothers very little over the years, because they believe that giving money makes people like alcoholics—they want more and more. Of the three brothers, only Dick is in his parents' good graces today. One brother no longer speaks to the parents at all, and the other has been cut out of the parents' will for two years but does not know this. Dick has chosen to keep communication open with his parents, but only on his terms.

"In my family you just didn't ask for anything and you never complained. This is kind of old-fashioned. My son was joking about that. He said, 'Grandma will say "It hasn't been a very good day, Grandpa died." ' Because they always kind of hide everything and everything is so perfect. That's about it. Dad's on oxygen, he's had a heart attack, but my mom just thinks everything is so pleasant. She waits on him hand and foot, but she never complains. The thing is never to complain and you never talk about your health problems in public. Really old-fashioned. You never discuss business and that type of thing. Lots of rules and regulations.

"I really needed money once after I was in an accident, but they didn't help me. My brother helped support me, which was really nice of him because he didn't have that much money. He was paying my health insurance and car payments to make sure I was okay. Other people had to come forward. I was pretty angry. They had so much money they wouldn't have missed it. I was angry. It's like a progression. You almost have to be angry. You have to go through that to get to the other side. I think I have forgiven them.

"They never said much about anything I accomplished—my degrees or career success. There was always an expectation. If you did something wrong they would tell you, but they never gave praise or rewards. I really had to learn that your rewards come from yourself. I always felt that my parents were never there for me. I always had to be on my own.

"My brother told them how he felt about growing up in the family and about a lot of the things they did, and they just totally freaked. They cut him out of their will, and they've never told him. My other brother cut himself off. He had a lot of anger.

"I was definitely a rebel, and I still am very rebellious. I broke all the rules, and that was very distressing to them. But I am like their pet. I am the only one left. I call them every weekend, every Saturday morning, and they look forward to that. They wait for me to call.

"I don't think they can change. They have tons of friends, but there's no closeness with them either. I always envy close families because I didn't have that. Close families protect one another, and they're loyal to one another, and they help one another and it looks very supportive to me.

"I feel like my parents could never understand that. They think they've done everything right. I did go through a very cruel phase where my mother would say, 'Oh, you're raising the children just like I raised you.' and I'd say, 'God, I hope not.' Very mean because I was really angry. Now at fifty I've really mellowed out and I want to make their last few years pleasant. And so I will not confront them.

"I always tell them that everything is wonderful because that's what they want to hear. I actually do play to them. My brother doesn't, so he's the one who's cut off. And maybe I won't get anything either. Who knows. It's really not the money. It's not that I'm sitting there counting it. I wouldn't be surprised if they gave it all to charity.

"I think they did the best they could. Now, if he leaves all his money to Harvard or an art museum I still think they've done the best they could. They thought theirs was the best way—'don't give money no matter what because people become dependent on it.'

"They're so hypersensitive. For me to start bringing things up at their age I think would be really cruel. I don't think they really understood. They've never once said they did anything wrong—ever. On the other hand, maybe they were right about the money. I did start a new business without their help, and I'm making more money than I ever made in my life. If they had helped me, maybe I wouldn't have worked that hard at it.

"I don't like to visit them very much. It's very hard to be around them because we're so different and they're judging. There are so many rules, and it's just a stressful situation. I don't put myself in it too often. The phone calls are nice—what have you been doing this week? They tell me what they've been doing. I enjoy the phone calls. I feel like I'm touching base with them. I think I'd miss it if something happened that I couldn't call them. That's about as close as we've been. The phone calls don't really change. That's how it's always been, and that's how it's comfortable for them and for me. That's how I'm used to relating to my parents."

Kristin: Withdrawing as a Last Resort.

Kristin is in her late thirties. Her mother died a year ago after a short illness. Her sixty-three-year-old father recently married a woman he had been having an affair with for several years before Kristin's mother died. At the time of Kristin's mother's death, her parents were separated but had no legal separation agreement. Now Kristin's father has taken all the assets he and Kristin's mother had accumulated, including the profits from the sale of the family home, for himself and his new wife. Kristin and her brothers are shocked and irate at his actions, because their mother had worked for many years in a high-paying job and had intended to have the estate she accumulated go to her children eventually. Ever since her father's lawyer notified Kristin and her brothers that they are not legally entitled to any of their mother's estate and will never get anything from it, Kristin has not spoken to her father. From her point of view, it is as if she no longer has a father.

"I'm still in shock about it. My mother died just a little over a year ago. I think in some ways he has been this neglectful person all our lives, but my mother was always there to cover up for him. When she died, unconsciously or subconsciously we expected him to jump in and take her place. Not only did he not do that but he has just done horribly cruel and insensitive things ever since. We got a double whammy. We lost our mother and at the same time had to realize that we have an insensitive uncaring father. I think for me it's too much to let it all in at one time.

"Things had been difficult between my parents for quite a while. A few years ago my father came to visit me in Chicago to tell me that he was leaving my mother for another woman. He spent a week with me, and in that week I had the father that I had always wanted. He was caring, he was open, he was empathic—it was amazing. I would walk down the street with him, and he would hold my hand or put his arm around me. We sat and talked for hours about what it was like for us to be in that home with my mother who was often a very difficult person. He talked about what it was like to be married to her. I talked about what it was like to have her as my mother. We really just opened up totally.

"They didn't separate for about another ten months. My mother didn't even know about the whole thing when he came to visit me. After his visit, I felt this deep connection with my father and wanted him to be happy. I wanted to find a way to maintain contact with him that wouldn't hurt my mother's feelings. I wanted private interactions with him, so I wrote letters to him where he worked. Well, he took the letters home and left them on the dining room table. He lied about that. He said he didn't do that and that my mother went snooping in his closet. I don't know which happened. My mother was devastated. Then my mother started to know about Margaret (the other woman) because my father was also leaving letters from Margaret on the dining room table.

"All the way along he wanted to be able to have it all. He

wanted to be able to stay married to my mother and maintain that life with his family, and he wanted to have Margaret on the side. He was manipulating his environment to try to figure out a way to have it all.

"He did some really cruel stuff to my mother in her last illness, but I have to try to separate that, because that's stuff between her and him. They had not had a good marriage, which was at least as much her fault as his, but I don't respect him for moving out. After all those years, you can stay a few more months. Two weeks before she died, he took her to a dinner where she was so sick and weak that he had to carry her and he laid her on the bed and left. And the next morning she was in a coma, and two weeks later she died.

"It's interesting because I was certainly hardened toward my mother. My last face-to-face conversation with my mother was the Christmas before she died. She was sobbing, and I just sat there and I couldn't go over and take her in my arms. I just couldn't do it. All I could say to her was, 'I don't hate you.' I couldn't say, 'I love you.' Literally as she was dying, I said, 'We love you.' Now I kind of say prayers to her sometimes. I say I'm sorry that she's gone and I miss her. I don't think I say, 'I love you.' I've healed a lot of my stuff with her. I don't feel angry with her anymore. I accept where I was with it. I just did the best that I could do.

"I usually saw her about once a year. But it had been bad between her and me for so many years. Then just when it started to improve, she died. I was feeling more compassion for her. I wrote her a note right before she died. I guess she and I did some of the work that we needed to do. My anger had dissipated. Even though I couldn't say, 'I love you,' I could be there.

"I think she knew that she and my father didn't have a good marriage and that she set it up that way. She really saw the role she played in that. I think she did a better job of forgiving him than I have.

"By the time she died, he had moved out. She wasn't ready to get a divorce yet, which was why nothing ever changed in terms of the property settlement. She wrote him a long letter saying he had to choose between her and Margaret, and he sent us a copy. We didn't know all the stuff he was doing to her, so we supported him. He set us up and we fell for it. We got sucked in, and it created a lot of pain for my mother.

"After my mother died, we kept hoping my father would be who we wanted him to be. I wanted him to hold me while I sobbed. Instead, he came to us two days after she died and said, 'I can get married now.' He denies that now. We were in all that grief and he couldn't even be there for us. Even at the hospital, I was sobbing because she was unconscious and I couldn't say good-bye to her, and he held me a minute, and the second I stopped sobbing, he pushed me away and said, 'Am I going to get blamed for this?' He was just so lost in his own stuff.

"Not long after my mother died he wrote us a letter saying, 'When I sell the house, I will give you your half.' Then somewhere, he changed his mind. We can't blame Margaret—he's responsible. Because if he had integrity, and if he wanted to give it to his children regardless of what she said, he would say, 'No, I can't do that.' And we made deal after deal with him. Like, we would loan him the money from our half now and when he died it would be ours. Now he's already married to her (with no prenuptial agreement). We wanted him to put it in writing that after he died it would be ours.

"We kept giving him the benefit of the doubt. We went to his attorney with him the day before the wedding because he had said he would sign something, but in the attorney's office he backed out. The attorney had it all right there and my dad refused to sign. He said, 'I just can't do this to Margaret.' He kept leading us on. He said, 'When we come back after the wedding and get settled, I will go to the attorney and make arrangements for you to get what's yours.' Plus he also told me, 'Margaret is only going to get my half of the estate.' So he lied to us, and we kept believing him.

"The money is gone. He sold the house and he took it. Every penny of it is gone. It's long gone. Margaret is supposed to get $100,000 from her ex-husband when he sells their house. So the deal we made with my dad was that he could take our money now and when she got her money, he could pay us back. When we would talk to him, he would sit there and say, 'Yeah, that's a good idea. I should look into that. I'll think about that.' But he never did any of it. He led us on for a year. Then he went back to his attorney and had him write this letter saying, 'Your father doesn't owe you anything and he's not going to give you anything.'

"For all practical purposes I've lost both parents. I don't see any point in doing anything. I'm sure there is a little hope down there somewhere, because hope springs eternal but I think that's part of the pain. Every time we get our hopes up, he slaps us in the face with something worse. The letter from the attorney was the last straw. Every time we asked him what he was going to do, he just avoided the question. He was too chicken.

"It seems like he didn't have a clue that everyone would be this upset. I can't even begin to imagine how his mind must work. I feel like he and I live on different planets. As far as I'm concerned, I am not going to continue to act as if nothing has happened. I'm not going to hug him and pretend this hasn't happened. He has pushed it too far. I wrote him a letter and told him how I feel about it all. And I said that as far as I am concerned he and I no longer have a relationship and I no longer have a father. I don't think he deserves to be a member of our family anymore. Relationships don't just happen. The rest of us support one another and make it clear that we care. I don't think my father deserves to be a part of that unit anymore. Because what he has done is just kicked us. Ultimately I don't want a relationship with someone like him."

Accept Your Own Decisions

You may feel that all the adult children who spoke in this chapter could have done more. Probably they could have, but they have every right to choose the point on the continuum that they feel best fits their situation with their parents. Kristin does not deserve any criticism for deciding to withdraw from her father, nor does Sam warrant praise for continuing to try to get closer to his father. They have each made the choice that works for them right now.

These four personal accounts focus on the difficult side of the choices adult children make. They are here to illustrate that adults and their parents often do not have particularly easy or close relationships. In past chapters the issue of choice has come up over and over again. Techniques and approaches to changing relationships are merely tools, not ends in themselves. It is important to choose the tools that are most likely to create the result you want. To do that, you need to know what you want. You also need to be willing to accept the legitimacy of your decisions.

There is no right and wrong about the sort of relationship you should have with your parents. Only you know your situation and your own feelings about it. Eventually you must decide what you want and are willing to do, as John, Sam, Jackie, Dick, and Kristin have done. Once you do decide, you do not have to defend your choice.

CHAPTER 15

How You Can Make Lasting Changes

"I have started setting limits with my mother. For example, my brother and I recently had a major falling out. When Mom called to 'hear my side of the story' and give her lecture on the situation, I was able to tell her that the problem was between my brother and me, that I understood her pain over it, but that I did not want to use her as a go-between. Before, it would have all ended up with a three-ring-circus family squabble, with our whole family taking sides and pressuring us to make peace. But this time they are leaving it up to us to work out."

(Cheryl, age 28)

Making change is a gradual process that requires patience and persistence. The patterns of communication between you and your parents have been firmly cemented over long years of practice. You cannot dislodge these habits overnight or by simply skimming through a book of advice. If you truly want change, the best way to bring it about is to make a specific plan, write down what you intend to do, and keep notes on your progress as you go along.

Actually this is easier than it sounds, once you get past your initial reluctance to commit yourself in writing. It is tempting to simply plan in your head with global statements like, "I'll try not to argue with my parents so much." But if you do that, you have no criteria to guide you as you evaluate your progress. A written plan is best because it forces you to be specific and make clear choices about what you want and what you will do.

Start Your Plan With a Wish List

Although it may seem strange or inappropriate to think of your relationship with your parents in terms of what you can get from it, to do so is a natural human tendency. In general, people do not continue to invest time and energy in a relationship that shows no promise of offering anything in return. Of course, in the case of parents, elements of duty enter in as discussed in Chapter 11. Many adults feel that they should and would do whatever they could to help their parents, regardless of how difficult their relationship has been. But the majority of adults who have living parents are not involved in a one-way association where they do all the giving. Usually grown children expect and receive certain rewards from their association with their parents.

While reading the earlier chapters in this book, you have probably given quite a bit of thought to what you would like to have more of in your relationship with your parents. Your list will probably include some of the following wishes:

• *Friendship and love.* This seems to be the number one item on grown children's wish lists regarding their parents. Those who have it consider themselves lucky. As one middle-aged woman expressed it: "At my age, there are few people left on this earth who unconditionally love me, think I'm great, and would do anything they could to support me if I needed that. Having people like that in your life is great, and it continues to be their most important role."

Those who are still waiting to get this from their parents often feel the lack sharply. As another middle-aged woman said: "I would like my parents to be my friends, to be people I can share my strengths as well as my weaknesses with. Most of the time I feel unconditional love from my dad, but I feel my mother has many strings to her love. I would like it if my mother and I could have a warm, understanding relationship. I would like to get along so we could share some rewarding time together. My mother is constantly giving me instructions, moralizing, and judging me. I would like her to be a warm, loving, accepting friend whom I could visit and feel comfortable being around."

- *Help or support*. Some adults say they need more support from their parents, which could be financial or other types of tangible help, to reach a goal or make it through a crisis, or emotional support, or backing for their choices. One thirty-one-year-old woman said, "I have always wanted Mom to be more of a mother to me. This is somewhat of an unmet need from my childhood, I think. Mom isn't very involved at all in my life." A man in his late twenties said, "I would like my parents to be more supportive financially because I am in school. I will not be able to work as much in the last two years of my program as I am now."

- *Acceptance and approval*. Grown children who feel that their parents do not treat them as adults because they do not accept their right to make their own choices in life will echo the wish of a man who wrote, "I would like my parents to support me in whatever decisions I make regarding my life." Most adults would ideally like more than acceptance, they would like approval. As one woman said, "It's hard for me to feel good about myself when my own parents don't approve of what I'm doing." These people wish they could tell their parents about their plans and activities and get a positive response.

- *Peaceful conversations*. Some grown children's first wish is to end the continual arguments and struggles they find themselves in whenever they talk with their parents. As one young man said, "I wish we could just sit around and talk without getting into a fight. I'd like us to enjoy being together instead of each trying to win over the other or convince one another that we're right."

- *Details of my family's past*. Some adults express a wish to have more "real" conversations with their parents about the past. You may feel you need more information and explanations of your shared past or of their past to understand your relationship with them, but they may be reluctant to discuss those topics. One forty-seven-year-old woman said, "I would like to be able to talk about things that have bothered me about my childhood and have Mom really listen and answer instead of sweeping it under the rug. I am old enough and far enough removed from the bad times that I am no longer bitter, but I still wonder why it was that way. She could help me with this." A forty-nine-year-old man said, "I would like to have my mother tell more about her life. She has had a stormy past even though she was somewhat spoiled as a child. I would like to focus on her sense of personal history."

- *Grandparents for our children.* Some adults have specific ideas of the sort of grandparents they would like their parents to be, but their parents are not fulfilling these desires. One woman in her early thirties said, "I hope my father will continue to be an important and positive influence in my daughter's life, but that he will start spoiling her a little less." Conversely, a woman in her forties said, "We do not have traditional family gatherings with my parents, which I would like for my children. But that doesn't seem possible at this time. I wish my parents could be loving grandparents to my children, accepting and somewhat indulgent."

Set Priorities and Goals

The next step is to go through your wish list and set priorities. What is your number one choice on the list—the one change you would most like to have or that you are most interested in working on between you and your parents? Label that wish Number 1. This Number 1 wish may not necessarily be your ultimate ideal wish for what you would change with your parents. It may be the one you feel most capable of getting or the one that you think would make the most immediate difference in your life.

For example, in the last chapter Jackie explained that while she would like to have approval, acceptance, and a closer relationship with her parents, she has decided not to actively pursue those desires. Instead, she has chosen maintaining peaceful but limited contact with her parents as her main priority. She made that choice because she felt that the possibility of getting what she really wanted from her parents was unlikely and because she felt she would have to sacrifice peace with them to pursue other goals. After years of ongoing battles with her parents, Jackie was happy to achieve peace.

Of course, Jackie could decide to work on some of her other wishes now that she has achieved her first priority. You also may want to set several priorities in your wish list. You can either decide now which two or three wishes you would like to work on after you work through the first, or go back to the list later to choose your next priority.

Right now, though, it is important to select one to begin with and to translate that one wish into specific goals. For example, a twenty-four-year-old man, Clay, whose relationship with his father had been difficult for several years, wanted to stop fighting with his father and enjoy spending time with him. He said, "My relationship with my father has been a major stress in my life. Dad lives only fifty miles away, but because every visit to his house seems to lead almost inevitably to some sort of disagreement or fight, I have distanced myself to the point where we rarely see each other."

Make a Plan and Stick to It

Now it is time to decide what changes you are willing to make in your own behavior to get what you want from your parents. For example, if your wish is to feel more acceptance and approval from your parents, you may decide to go through the "Six A's of Negotiating Approval" as described in Chapter 3. Or you may decide to stop responding in your usual way to the comments you hate, as suggested in Chapter 4. Or you may decide to simply sidestep their advice as discussed in Chapter 6.

You should choose the approach that feels the most comfortable to you in your situation and that you feel has the best chance of success with your parents. Select a plan that you are willing to commit yourself to following for at least two months without giving up, even if nothing seems to be changing. Altering old patterns takes time.

Clay, the young man who wanted to enjoy his father instead of fighting with him, decided to work on the situation between them by trying to see his father's perspective as discussed in Chapter 5. He wrote the following plan:

"For the next two months I will try to see my father's point of view and understand what is happening in his life. I will ask him questions, listen to him without judgment, and be sensitive to his feelings. When problems come up between us, I will try to see the situation from his perspective. I will also work on letting him know I appreciate him for the person he is."

Clay then kept weekly notes for himself on how the plan was working out. As you will see from his notes below, Clay found that by attempting to put himself in his father's place, he became more aware of some of the major sources of stress in his father's life, such as a collapsing second marriage, long, strenuous hours at work, and financial problems. This awareness changed Clay's reactions to his father, which led his father to respond differently to him. Gradually they became closer, as Clay describes.

Week #1—My dad has been bugging me, saying I don't care enough about our relationship. He always pressures me to spend time with him. I'm trying to ease this tension by taking a look at the situation in a new light. I think he thinks I take him for granted. I'm trying to get a different perspective and imagine how my father must be viewing my life. He probably sees my life as easy. I definitely see his life as troublesome. He is unhappily married to a second wife and has few friends. These may be two big keys as to why he puts so much pressure on me.

Week #2—My father has been very busy lately. I called him, and he was angry about something. Instead of getting down, I took a different perspective and acknowledged the fact that everybody has bad days, and he probably feels pressured from work and no sleep. I simply put myself in my father's shoes and imagined what he was feeling like since he's been on call for two days straight.

Week #3—I wrote him a letter today thanking him for having supported me through college and for helping me get started. Next week I am going to run in a 5K race with him that he's been wanting me to do with him for years, but I've never gotten around to it before.

Week #4—Things have improved 100 percent between my father and me. This morning I spoke with him on the phone and felt like we were finally relating to each other. Before, I had just assumed that he was my father and therefore should be nice to me. When he got angry at me it infuriated me. Now that I have opened my mind and put myself in his shoes, he has started doing the same for me. My willingness to hear his problems led to his increased interest and appreciation of mine. Now he asks me about things he used to see as unimportant. When there is a problem between us, we seem to talk about it in a more friendly way and listen more intently.

Week #5—My father is coming up here next week. We are going to the races and out to dinner. It should be a great day. I'm looking forward to spending some time with him. Trying to take his perspective has enabled me to focus in on his problems, such as his marriage, and realize that these have contributed a lot of stress to our relationship. I am extremely pleased and amazed that this really works so well.

Week #6—This weekend was the real test for me with regard to my new way of relating to my father. He came up Saturday for the races and we went out afterward and really had a great time together. We finally started talking about things that were relevant to our relationship, not simply money or other stale, meaningless topics. I can now honestly say that my father and I are friends. I feel at ease with him now. I am positive that taking his perspective played an important part in the healing process between us.

Week #7—My stepmother suddenly sees me as the source of all her problems with my father. It is unfair, but I am not going to let it bother me as long as my father and I get along. I have made every effort to get along with her, and now she sees me as the villain. I plan on having a talk with her, but my relationship with her is not a high priority. I am still really happy with the way my relationship with my father has changed. I was talking to a friend who is really stressed out about his parents and telling him about what has been going on between my dad and me. Just talking to him, I was able to reflect on how much my relationship with my father had changed. Also, my friend could not believe that my father had come up and we had actually enjoyed a weekend together.

Week #8—I spoke with my father on the phone this morning. He thanked me again for showing him a great time that weekend. He said, "I couldn't have asked for a better time." It's great to see my efforts working! Putting myself into my father's place has led to an increased interest and appreciation of him as a person. The channels of communication have opened and I can finally say that he is my friend as well as father.

When an Action Plan Seems Too Difficult

While there is no substitute for a good plan, sometimes you simply do not feel that you have the time or the energy for a formal plan. If that is how you feel right now, you can still take steps to improve your relationship with your parents by informally trying out some of the ideas discussed in the earlier chapters. Anything you do to reverse old argumentative patterns or find new ways of enjoying one another will make you feel better about being with them. For example, here are some changes other adults made to improve their interactions with their parents:

- "I have changed the way I discuss a problem I may have. When I speak to my parents now, I tell them first what I need from them, such as if I just need them to listen, or if I need some feedback, or if I need them to give me some options. By doing it this way, my parents know what I'm looking for and don't have to guess, and I get what I want more often."

- "My dad is retired from an airline and my parents can fly free on standby, so they often fly down to visit with little or no notice. This was a problem until my husband and I worked out an agreement with them that they are welcome anytime, but we will continue with our regular lives when they are here. We invite them to join our activities whenever possible. This has been successful for all of us, and we all feel happy and relieved to have a plan that works."

- "In the past few years my communication with my parents has improved. Two things have changed—I am not as confrontational, and I am learning to understand their views of reality, which were tempered by the times they have lived in. I have been listening and asking questions about their past. I recently talked to my father about his working experiences and found that he had to confront some of the same problems that I have faced. His solutions were different, but I found them interesting."

- "I have learned to be more assertive about what I believe and why I believe it. I have tried to see myself in an adult role in my relationship with my parents. I think it was *me* who had to be convinced that I am not a child anymore, not them."

- "I have learned not to take things so personally. Whenever they get short with me or angry, I generally attribute it to work or something unrelated to me. Some of their remarks I just shrug off or joke about. This seems to stop a lot of arguments."

- "My parents are not very direct about their wants and feelings. I have learned to ask them more questions to find out and get a better idea of how they feel about things going on in their lives. I have also begun telling them more often how I feel about things going on. Honesty is hard in this relationship but most beneficial and necessary. I think it has been very helpful for me to take the initiative in opening the lines of communication and keeping them open."

- "My dad and I are communicating a lot better. I brought about this change by apologizing to him for having so much anger toward him, which was really because I took my mother's side against him. I explained to him why I did and said the things I did when I was younger. We are beginning to get closer."

- "I used to feel guilty that I could never please my parents, but I have come to realize that this is their problem, not mine. I have begun to accept what they can offer without expecting more. I am still struggling. It doesn't make all the hurt go away, but it does help."

- "I am much more assertive with my mother, yet I am also very accepting of her. I try not to be judgmental, but I do speak my mind and let her know how I feel in a firm but tactful way. For example, when she is giving me a sermon after I have told her about a problem, I have told her that I would appreciate having some loving support from her rather than pat answers."

- "I try to participate in a hobby or sport with each of my parents. This is an enjoyable way to spend time together and helps us form new bonds."

Don't Give up on What You Want

No matter how bad things are between you and your parents, there is always a chance you can find a way to make it better.

If you do, the rewards are usually worth the effort. It may require putting aside a lot of old hurts and bad feelings, but the eventual satisfaction can be one of the most significant achievements of your life.

One of the most heartwarming stories of such accomplishment was told to me by a middle-aged woman, Loretta, who found a creative way to reconcile with her father after he had refused to speak to her for ten years. Because she was able to reach out without blame and to forgive the past, she had the opportunity to share her father's last years.

Loretta: There's Always That Draw.

My parents were divorced after I was grown and married. They had been married for thirty-six years, but they should have divorced many years before. My dad was always out carousing, and Mom was at home taking care of us kids. Daddy and I were very close when I was a kid. He played with me, taught me to ride horses. But as a teenager I felt very abandoned by my dad. When I got older he was there again. He was very supportive of me. He was always the type of person that would brag on you. He would always tell everybody that I cooked for harvest hands when I was ten years old.

He and Mom got their divorce and went their separate ways, but Mom waited and waited for him to straighten up and come back. She waited for seven years. Daddy didn't really change. He mellowed out and got a little better, but he was still basically the same. Very fun-loving and taking care of his pleasures first. So my mom decided to marry someone else.

Then there was a tragedy in the family. My husband died—he took his own life. And when my dad came to the funeral and my mom came to the funeral with her fiancé, Dad asked her to marry him again. Of course, she said no. That made my dad very angry that he didn't get his way. He became very angry with me and ended up blaming my husband's death on me. He decided it was my fault. My dad accused me of running around with other men and that being why my husband killed himself. Nothing was farther from the truth. Actually my husband was running around. But my dad blamed me for ten years, and that was very, very difficult for me. He refused to speak to me for ten years.

My husband has been dead for fourteen years. Ten years after he died, I finally put it back together with my dad. I called him one day. I'd called him before, and I had been told that he didn't have a daughter, that his new wife had two daughters, and they were now his daughters. It hurt a lot.

One time my brother called and said Daddy was in the hospital. I asked him if he thought Daddy would talk to me. He said, "I don't know, I'll ask him. He's right here." So he gave Daddy the phone, and he immediately jumped on me, and I was in tears, "Daddy that's not true. Daddy that's not the way it is. I love you, and I need you." It got nowhere except making me feel worse. I finally just said, "To hell with him. I don't need him. It's his loss. I hope he never calls me for anything because I'll tell him to go to his friends."

But there's always that draw. A girlfriend of mine kept saying, "I know you're angry, and I know he didn't treat you right, but keep trying." I said, "No. To hell with him. I don't need him." She said, "Yes, you do. Keep trying." Well, it took her four years or so to convince me. I had just been thinking about him lots.

So finally I called my dad, and I just talked to him, but I didn't tell him who I was. I asked him all kinds of questions, and he didn't know who it was. He kept trying to guess. He must have guessed a hundred women's names, and he never ever guessed my name. After thirty minutes, I finally told him who it was. I felt comfortable enough. He said, "Is this really you?" He'd talked to me for so long by that time that he wasn't angry. I knew if I told him it was me in the beginning, he'd hang up on me. So I just kept talking. I asked him if he would come and see me if I would send him a plane ticket. He said, "You would do that for me?" I said, "Of course I would do that for you. I'd love to have you come visit me."

So I sent him the money for a plane ticket. Nothing was said about any of our problems. When I told my kids that Grandpa was coming, my oldest son said, "Grandpa who?

We don't have a grandpa." I said, "Yes, you do." He said, "I'm going to tell him how mean he's been to you." I said, "No, you're not." I finally got it across to him that this was a meeting to put things back together, not to tear them apart further. That we wanted to convey to Grandpa that we loved him and that we wanted him as part of us, not to give him trouble and hurt him for hurting us.

Everything went very well. There was always tension. There was the feeling, "I want to tell him how bad things were." I did tell him some of the things that had happened, but I didn't ever bring him into it. Never, "You did it wrong," or anything. I think he kind of got the idea that things were pretty bad before my husband died.

Daddy just worked like a beaver. He fixed all the doors in the house. He did this and that for me. He was having a ball. I kept telling him to slow down. He had emphysema and was always using his inhaler.

He went home and everything was great. We'd call each other, and he'd tell me he loved me and how much he missed me and he'd like to be there. Then he got really sick and was in the hospital. I went down to see him and met his new wife and loved her.

Later on, I think Daddy knew things were getting pretty bad for him, so he and my stepmom decided to come out and visit me. Daddy came out with his oxygen tanks. He couldn't sleep at all. It was really sad. Yet he enjoyed it. He went places with me. And my kids came over, and they played cards, and Daddy told them stories about me. They thought that was wonderful. That was probably the closest they had ever been to my dad.

One day I was cooking and Daddy was sitting on the bar stool. I turned around to say something to him and he had great big tears running down his cheeks. I asked him what was wrong. He said, "I feel so bad that we missed the last ten years." I said, "Me too, Daddy." That was the closest my dad could ever come to an apology. That was really hard for him.

When Loretta's father was rushed to the hospital during his final illness, he called for her right away. She flew in and was with him the night he died. She will always be glad she made the phone call that finally broke down the barriers between them. As she thinks back over their years apart and together, Loretta says, "I don't have regrets, but I feel real sad. I didn't have him very long. It would have been real tough if we hadn't worked it out."

NOTES

CHAPTER 1

[1] Samuel H. Preston, "Children and the Elderly in the U.S.," *Scientific American* 251 (December 1984): 48.

[2] Statistics on the aging of the American population are from the United States Bureau of the Census, *Statistical Abstract of the United States: 1986*, 106th ed. (Washington, DC: U.S. Bureau of the Census, 1986); American Association of Retired Persons, *A Profile of Older Americans: 1989*, (Washington, DC: American Association of Retired Persons, 1989); and, Preston, op. cit., 44.

[3] S. K. Wisendale and M. D. Allison, "An Analysis of 1987 Family Leave Legislation: Implications for Caregivers of the Elderly," *The Gerontologist* 28 (1988): 779–785.

[4] Gunhild O. Hagestad, "Demographic Change and the Life Course: Some Emerging Trends in the Family Realm," *Family Relations* 37 (1988): 409; and Edward F. Ansello, "A View of Aging America and Some Implications," *Caring* (March 1988): 5.

[5] American Association of Retired Persons, op. cit.

[6] Lillian Troll, "New Thoughts on Old Families," *The Gerontologist* 28 (1288): 590–91.

[7] Jeffrey A. Giordano, "Parents of the Baby Boomers: A New Generation of Young-Old," *Family Relations* 37 (1988): 413.

[8] Marvin B. Sussman, "The Family Life of Old People," in *Handbook of Aging and the Social Sciences*, ed. Robert Binstock and Ethel Shanas (New York: Van Nostrand Reinhold, 1985): 415–449.

[9] Lois M. Tamir, *Communication and the Aging Process* (New York: Pergamon Press, 1979): 112–122; and Lillian Troll, Sheila J. Miller, and Robert C. Atchley, *Families in Later Life* (Belmont, CA: Wadsworth Publishing, 1979): 92–99

CHAPTER 2

[1] For discussions of family rules, see Katheleen M. Galvin and Bernard J. Brommel, *Family Communication: Cohesion and Change* (Glenview, Illinois: Scott Foresman, 1982): 45–53; Daniel Goleman, *Vital Lies, Simple Truths* (New York: Touchstone, 1986): 174–179; and R. D. Laing, *The Politics of the Family* (New York: Vintage Books, 1972).

[2] Galvin and Brommel, op. cit.

[3] Carl R. Rogers, *A Way of Being* (Boston: Houghton Mifflin, 1980): 14–22.

CHAPTER 3

[1] For a review of research on the feelings adult children and parents report about each other, see Lillian Troll, Sheila J. Miller, and Robert C. Atchley, *Families in Later Life* (Belmont, CA: Wadsworth Publishing, 1979): 94–95; and: Jon F. Nussbaum, Teresa Thompson, and James D. Robinson, *Communication and Aging* (New York: Harper & Row, 1989): 134–135.

[2] Rosemary Blieszner and Jay A. Mancini, "Enduring Ties: Older Adults' Parental Role and Responsibilities," *Family Relations* 36 (1987): 178–1798.

CHAPTER 4

[1] Vernon E. Cronen, W. Barnett Pearce, and Lonna M. Snavely, "A Theory of Rule-Strucutre and Types of Episodes and a Study of Perceived Enmeshment in Undesired Repetitive Patterns," in *Communication Yearbook 3* ed. Dan Nimmo (New Brunswick, NJ: Transaction Books, 1979): 225–240; Vernon E. Cronen, W. Barnett Pearce, and Linda M. Harris, "The Logic of the Coordinated Management of Meaning: A Rules-Based Approach to the First Course in Interpersonal Communication," *Communication Education* 28 (January 1979): 22–38; and W. Barnett Pearce, Vernon E. Cronen, Kenneth Johnson, Greg Jones, and Robert Raymond, "The Structure of Communication Rules and the Form of Conversation: An Experimental Simulation," *The Western Journal of Communication* 44 (Winter 1980): 20–34.

[2] Cronen, Pearce, and Snavely, op. cit.

[3] For discussions of balance theory, see Fritz Heider, *The Psychology of Interpersonal Relations* (New York: John Wiley

& Sons, 1958): 174–217; Robert B. Zajonc, "Cognitive Theories in Social Psychology," in *The Handbook of Social Psychology*, 2d ed., vol. 1, ed. Gardner Lindzey and Elliot Aronson (Reading, MA: Addison-Wesley, 1968): 338–362.

⁴ For a discussion of dissonance theory, see Roger Brown, *Social Psychology* (New York: The Free Press, 1965): 584–608.

⁵ Arthur P. Bochner and Eric M. Eisenberg, "Family Process: System Perspectives," in *The Handbook of Communication Science*, ed. Charles R. Berger and Steven H. Chaffee (Newbury Park, CA: Sage, 1987): 544; and John Weakland, "Communication Theory and Clinical Change," in *Family Therapy*, ed. Philip J. Guerin, Jr. (New York: Gardner Press, 1976): 122.

⁶ Samuel Vuchinich, "Arguments, Family Style," *Psychology Today* 19 (October 1985): 40–46.

⁷ Virginia Satir, *Peoplemaking* (Palo Alto, CA: Science and Behavior Books, 1972): 59–79.

CHAPTER 5
¹ William V. Haney, *Communication and Organizational Behavior*, 3d ed. (Homewood, IL: Richard D. Irwin, 1973): 55–72.

² An interesting series of survey-based studies examining the attitudes of Baby Boomers toward themselves and the opinions corporate personnel executives have about them is discussed in D. Quinn Mills, *Not Like Our Parents: How the Baby Boom Generation Is Changing America* (New York: William Morrow, 1987).

CHAPTER 6
¹ Gunhild O. Hagestad, "Continuity and Connectedness," in *Grandparenthood*, ed. Vern L. Bengston and Joan F. Robertson (Beverly Hills: Sage, 1985): 36–41.

² J. H. Britton and J. O. Britton, *Personality Changes in Aging* (New York: Springer, 1972). Cited in Lois M. Tamir, *Communication and the Aging Process* (New York: Pergamon Press, 1979): 119.

³ Karen Payne, *Between Ourselves: Letters Between Mothers and Daughters, 1750–1982* (Boston: Houghton Mifflin Co., 1983): 99.

[4] Allan N. Press and Lynn Osterkamp, "Advice vs. Facilitation: Individual Differences in Assisting Others in Solving Interpersonal Dilemmas," Unpublished paper presented at the National Conference on Social Cognition and Interpersonal Behavior, 1983.

[5] Joan Aldous, "Parent-Adult Child Relations as Affected by the Grandparent Status," in *Grandparenthood*, ed. Vern L. Bengston and Joan F. Robertson (Beverly Hills: Sage, 1985): 117–132.

[6] Alison Leigh Cowan, "Parenthood II: The Nest Won't Stay Empty," *The New York Times*, 12 March 1989, 1.

[7] J. M. Fitzgerald, "Actual and Perceived Sex and Generational Differences In Inerpersonal Style: Structural and Quantitative Issues," *The Journal of Gerontology* 33 (1978): 401.

CHAPTER 7

[1] Graham Allan, "Kinship, Responsibility, and Care for Elderly People," *Ageing and Society* 8 (1988): 252–254.

[2] Paul C. Rosenblatt and Cynthia Meyer, "Imagined Interactions and the Family," *Family Relations* 35 (1986): 319–324.

CHAPTER 8

[1] Vimala Pillari, *Pathways to Family Myths* (New York: Brunner Mazel, 1986): 10.

[2] Steven J. Wolin and Linda A. Bennett, "Family Rituals," *Family Process* 23 (September 1984): 401–402.

[3] Wolin and Bennett, op. cit., 414.

CHAPTER 9

[1] David J. Schneider, Albert H. Hastorf, and Phoebe C. Ellsworth, *Person Perception*, 2d ed. (Reading, MA: Addison-Wesley Publishing, 1979): 175–188.

[2] Ibid., 76–77.

[3] For an overview of contemporary symbolic interactionism, see Sheldon Stryker, *Symbolic Interactionism* (Menlo Park, CA: The Benjamin/Cummings Publishing Co., 1980): 55–85.

[4] Eileen M. Crimmins and Dominique G. Ingegneri, "Interaction and Living Arrangements of Older Parents and Their Children," *Research on Aging* 12 (1990): 8.

CHAPTER 10

[1] For a discussion of dyadic interactions within triads, see William W. Wilmot, *Dyadic Communication: A Transactional Perspective* (Reading, MA: Addison-Wesley Publishing, 1975): 20–30.

CHAPTER 11

[1] Allan N. Press and Lynn Osterkamp, "Family Relationships of the Middle Generation: Adults' Frustrations and Satisfactions With Parents and Children," Paper presented at The Gerontological Socity of America's 43rd Annual Scientific Meeting, November, 1990.

[2] American Association of Retired Persons, *A Profile of Older Americans: 1989*, (Washington, DC: American Association of Retired Persons, 1989).

[3] American Association of Retired Persons, *A National Survey of Caregivers: Final Report* (Washington, DC: Health Advocacy Services Secton, AARP, September, 1988): 2–4.

[4] Lynn Osterkamp, "Family Caregivers: America's Primary Long-Term Care Resource," *Aging* 358 (1988): 3.

[5] American Association of Retired Persons, *A National Survey of Caregivers: Final Report* (Washington, DC: Health Advocacy Services Section, AARP, September, 1988): 7.

[6] Judith Rodin, "Sense of Control: Potentials for Intervention," *Annuals AAPSS* 503 (May 1989): 29–42.

[7] Shelley E. Taylor and Jonathon D. Brown, "Illusion and Well-Being: A Social Psychological Perspective on Mental Health," *Psychological Bulletin* 103 (1988): 193–210.

[8] Lynn Osterkamp, "Caregivers Cognitive Coping Strategies: 'These are Things I'm Talkin' to Me About,'" Eric Resources in Education, ED#313634 (1990).

CHAPTER 12

[1] Dan Greenburg, *How To Be A Jewish Mother* (Los Angles: Prince-Stern, 1965).

[2] Michael E. Roloff, "Communication and Conflict," in *The Handbook of Communication Science*, ed. Charles R. Berger and Steven H. Chaffee (Newbury Park, CA: Sage, 1987): 489.

[3] Liz Smith, *The Mother Book* (Garden City, NY: Doubleday, 1978): 52.

[4] "A Slice of Life?" *USA Weekend* (February 16–18, 1990): 10–11.

[5] See Barbara L. Fisher, Paul Giblin, and Margaret H. Hoopes, "Healthy Family Functioning: What Therapists Say and What Families Want," *Journal of Marital and Family Therapy* 8 (July 1982): 273–284 and Nathan B. Epstein, Duane S. Bishop, and Sol Levin, "The McMaster Model of Family Functioning," *Journal of Marriage and Family Counseling* 4 (October 1978): 20–21.

[6] Dolores Curran, "What Is A Healthy Family?" *Redbook* (June 1985): 87–89.

[7] Nathan B. Epstein, Duane S. Bishop, and Sol Levin, "The McMaster Model of Family Functioning," *Journal of Marriage and Family Counseling* 4 (October 1978), 19–31.

[8] Frederick Steier, M. Duncan Stanton, and Thomas C. Todd, "Patterns of Turn-Taking and Alliance Formation in Family Communications," *Journal of Communication* 32 (Summer 1982): 150–153.

[9] Eric Berne, *Games People Play* (New York: Grove Press, 1967): 48–107.

[10] Ferdinand Van Der Veen, "Dimensions of the Family Concept and Their Relation to Gender, Generation, and Disturbance," in *Advances in Family Psychiatry,* Vol. I ed. John Howells (International Universities Press, 1979): 171–190.

CHAPTER 13

[1] Albert Ellis and Robert A. Harper, *A Guide to Rational Living* (Hollywood, CA: Wilshire Book Co., 1972): 44–51.

[2] Paula J. Caplan, "Take the Blame Off Mother," *Psychology Today* 20 (1986): 70–71.

[3] See Edwin G. Boring, *A History of Experimental Psychology* 2d ed. (New York: Appleton-Century-Crofts,1957): 706–714; and Duane Schultz, *A History of Modern Psychology*, 3d ed. (New York: Academic Press, 1981): 315–340.

[4] See Edwin G. Boring, *A History of Experiemntal Psychology* 2d ed. (New York: Appleton-Century-Crofts, 1957): 641–653; and Duane Schultz, *A History of Modern Psychology*, 3d ed. (New York: Academic Press, 1981): 203–270.

[5] Philip J. Guerin, Jr, "Family Therapy: The First Twenty-five Years," in *Family Therapy and Practice* ed. Philip J. Guerin (New York: Gardner Press, 1976): 2–22.

⁶ Melody Beattie, *Codependent No More* (New York: Harper/Hazelden, 1987).

⁷ C. R. Snyder, Raymond L. Higgins, and Rita J. Stucky, *Excuses* (New York: John Wiley & Sons, 1983): 4–8.

⁸ Eileen G. Pendergast, "Following the Trail into the Extended Family: Doing Individual Therapy with Male Distancers," *The Family* 13 (1985): 31.

REFERENCES

Aldous, Joan. "Parent-Adult Child Relations as Affected by the Grandparent Status." In *Grandparenthood,* ed. Vern L. Bengston and Joan F. Robertson, 117–132. Beverly Hills: Sage, 1985.

Allan, Graham. "Kinship, Responsibility, and Care for Elderly People." *Ageing and Society* 8 (1988) 252–254.

American Association of Retired Persons. *A Profile of Older Americans: 1989.* Washington, DC: American Association of Retired Persons, 1989.

American Association of Retired Persons. *A National Survey of Caregivers: Final Report.* Washington, DC: Health Advocacy Services Section, AARP, 1988.

Ansello, Edward F. "A View of Aging America and Some Implications." *Caring* (March, 1988): 4–8.

Beattie, Melody. *Codependent No More.* New York: Harper/Hazelden, 1987.

Berne, Eric. *Games People Play.* New York: Grove Press, 1967.

Blieszner, Rosemary and Jay A. Mancini. "Enduring Ties: Older Adults' Parental Role and Responsibilities." *Family Relations* 36 (1987) : 176–180.

Bloomfield, Harold H. *Making Peace With Your Parents.* New York: Ballantine, 1983.

Bochner, Arthur P. and Eric M. Eisenberg. "Family Process: System Perspectives." In *Handbook of Communication Science*, ed. Charles R. Berger and Steven H. Chaffee, 540–563. Newbury Park, CA: Sage Publications, 1987.

Boring, Edwin G. *A History of Experimental Psychology* 2d ed. New York: Appleton-Century-Crofts, 1957.

Britton, J. H. and J. O. Britton. *Personality Changes in Aging.* New York: Springer, 1972.

Brown, Roger. *Social Psychology.* New York: The Free Press, 1965.

Caplan, Paula J. "Take the Blame Off Mother." *Psychology Today* 20 (1986): 70–71.

Cody, Michael J., Margaret L. McLaughlin, and Michael J. Schneider. "The Impact of Relational Consequences and Intimacy on the Selection of Interpersonal Persuasion Tactics: A Reanalysis." *Communication Quarterly* (Spring 1981) : 91–106.

Cohler, Bertram J., and Henry U. Grunebaum. *Mothers, Grandmothers, and Daughters.* New York: John Wiley & Sons, 1981.

Cottle, Thomas J. *Like Fathers, Like Sons: Portraits of Intimacy and Strain.* Norwood, NJ: ABLEX Publishing Co., 1981.

Cowan, Alison Leigh. "Parenthood II: The Nest Won't Stay Empty." *The New York Times* (Sunday, March 12, 1989): sec 1A, p.1, 22.

Crimmins, Eileen M. and Dominique G. Ingegneri. "Interaction and Living Arrangements of Older Parents and Their Children." *Research on Aging* 12 (1990) 3–35.

Cronen, Vernon E., W. Barnett Pearce, and Lonna M.Snavely. "A Theory of Rule-Structure and Types of Episodes and a Study of Perceived Enmeshment in Undesired Repetitive Patterns." In *Communication Yearbook 3* ed. Dan Nimmo, 225–240. New Brunswick, NJ: Transaction Books, 1979.

Cronen, Vernon E., W. Barnett Pearce, and Linda M. Harris. "The Logic of the Coordinated Management of Meaning: A Rules-Based Approach to the First Course in Interpersonal Communication." *Communication Education* 28 (January 1979): 22–38.

Curran, Dolores. "What Is A Healthy Family?" *Redbook* (June, 1985): 87–89.

Ellis, Albert and Robert A. Harper. *A Guide to Rational Living.* Hollywood, CA: Wilshire Book Co., 1972.

Epstein, Nathan B., Duane S. Bishop, and Sol Levin. "The McMaster Model of Family Functioning." *Journal of Marriage and Family Counseling* 4 (October 1978): 19–41.

Fisher, Barbara L., Paul R. Giblin, and Margaret H. Hoopes. "Healthy Family Functioning: What Therapists Say and What Families Want." *Journal of Marital and Family Therapy* 8 (July 1982): 273–284.

Fisher, Celia B., James D. Reid and Marjorie Melendez. "Conflict in Families and Friendships of Later Life." *Family Relations* 38 (1989): 83–89.

Fischer, Lucy Rose. *Linked Lives.* New York: Harper & Row, 1986.

Fitzgerald, J. M. "Actual and Perceived Sex and Generational Differences in Interpersonal Style: Structural and Quantitative Issues." *The Journal of Gerontology* 33 (1978): 394–401.

Framo, James L. "Family of Origin as a Therapeutic Resource for Adults in Marital and Family Therapy: You Can and Should go Home Again." *Family Process* 15 (June 1976): 193–210.

Galvin, Kathleen M. and Bernard J. Brommel. *Family Communication: Cohesion and Change.* Glenview, IL: Scott Foresman, 1982.

Garms-Homolova, Vjenka, Erika M. Hoerning, and Doris Schaeffer, *Intergenerational Relationships.* Lewiston, NY: C. J. Hogrefe, Inc., 1984.

Giordano, Jeffrey A. "Parents of the Baby Boomers: A New Generation of Young-Old." *Family Relations* 37 (1988): 411–414.

Goleman, Daniel. *Vital Lies, Simple Truths*. New York: Touchstone, 1986.

Greenburg, Dan. *How To Be a Jewish Mother*. Los Angles: Price Stern, 1965.

Guerin, Philip J., Jr. *Family Therapy*. New York: Gardner Press, 1976.

Gundlach, Julie Kettle. *My Mother Before Me*. Secaucus, NJ: Lyle Stuart, Inc., 1986.

Hagestad, Gunhild O. "Demographic Change and the Life Course: Some Emerging Trends in the Family Realm." *Family Relations* 37 (1988): 411–414.

Hagestad, Gunhild O. "Continuity and Connectedness." In *Grandparenthood*, ed. Vern L. Bengston and Joan F. Robertson, 31-48. Beverly Hills: Sage, 1985.

Haney, William V. *Communication and Organizational Behavior*, 3d ed. Homewood, IL: Richard D. Irwin, 1973.

Headley, Lee. *Adults and Their Parents in Family Therapy*. New York: Plenum Press, 1977.

Heider, Fritz. *The Psychology of Interpersonal Relations*. New York: John Wiley & Sons, 1958.

Herman, Nini. *Too Long a Child: The Mother-Daughter Dyad*. London: Free Association Books, 1989.

Hill, Reuben. *Family Development in Three Generations*. Cambridge, MA: Schenkman Publishing, 1970.

Hinde, Robert A. and Joan Stevenson-Hinde (Eds.). *Relationships within Families*. New York: Oxford University Press, 1988.

Howard, Jane. *Families*. New York: Simon and Schuster, 1978.

Kahn, Michael D. and Stephen Bank. "In Pursuit of Sisterhood: Adult Siblings as a Resource for Combined Individual and Family Therapy." *Family Process* 20 (March 1981): 85–95.

Laing, R. D. *The Politics of the Family*. New York: Vintage Books, 1972.

Mancini, Jay A. and Rosemary Blieszner. "Aging Parents and Adult Children: Research Themes in Intergenerational Relations." *Journal of Marriage and the Family* 51 (May 1989): 275–290.

Marotz-Baden, Ramona and Deane Cowan. "Mothers-in-Law and Daughters-in-Law: The Effects of Proximity on Conflict and Stress." *Family Relations* 36 (1987): 385–390.

McCormack, Mary. *The Generation Gap: The View from Both Sides*. London: Constable & Co., 1985.

Mead, Margaret. *Culture and Commitment: A Study of the Generation Gap*. Garden City, New York: Natural History Press/Doubleday & Co., 1970.

Miller, Arthur. *Death of a Salesman*. In *A Treasury of the Theatre* ed. John Gassner. New York: Dryden Press, 1950.

Mills, D. Quinn. *Not Like Our Parents: How The Baby Boom Generation Is Changing America*. New York: William Morrow, 1987.

Nussbaum, Jon F., Teresa Thompson, and James D. Robinson. *Communication and Aging*. New York: Harper & Row, 1989.

Osherson, Samuel. *Finding Our Fathers*. New York: The Free Press, 1986.

Osterkamp, Lynn. "Caregivers Cognitive Coping Strategies." ERIC Resources in Education, ED#313634, 1990.

Palazzoli, Mara Selvini, Luigi Boscolo, Gian Franco Cecchin, and Giuliana Prata. "Family Rituals: A Powerful Tool in Family Therapy." *Family Process* 16 (December 1977): 445–453.

Payne, Karen (Ed.) *Between Ourselves: Letters Between Mothers and Daughters, 1750–1982*. Boston: Houghton Mifflin Co., 1983.

Pearce, W. Barnett, Vernon E. Cronen, Kenneth Johnson, Greg Jones, and Robert Raymond. "The Structure of Communication Rules and the Form of Conversation: An Experimental Simulation." *The Western Journal of Communication* 44 (Winter 1980): 20–34.

Pendergast, Eileen G. "Following the Trail into the Extended Family: Doing Individual Therapy with Male Distancers." *The Family* 13 (1985): 30–38.

Pillari, Vimala. *Pathways to Family Myths*. New York: Brunner Mazel, 1986.

Preston, Samuel H. "Children and the elderly in the U.S." *Scientific American* 251 (December 1984): 44–49.

Press, Allan N. and Lynn Osterkamp. "Advice vs. Facilitation: Individual Differences in Assisting Others in Solving Interpersonal Dilemmas." Paper presented at the National Conference on Social Cognition and Interpersonal Behavior, 1983.

Press, Allan N. and Lynn Osterkamp. "Family Relationships of the Middle Generation: Adults' Frustrations and Satisfactions With Parents and Children." Paper presented at The Gerontological Society of America's 43rd Annual Scientific Meeting, November, 1990.

Rodin, Judith. "Sense of Control: Potentials for Intervention." *Annals AAPSS* 503 (May 1989): 29–42.

Rogers, Carl R. *A Way of Being*. Boston: Houghton Mifflin, 1980.

Roloff, Michael E. "Communication and Conflict." In *The Handbook of Communication Science*, ed. Charles R. Berger and Steven H. Chaffee, 484–534. Newbury Park, CA: Sage, 1987.

Rosenblatt, Paul C. and Cynthia Meyer. "Imagined Interactions and the Family." *Family Relations* 35 (1986): 319–324.

Salk, Lee. *My Father, My Son: Intimate Relationships*. New York: G. P. Putnam's Sons, 1982.

Satir, Virginia. *Peoplemaking*. Palo Alto, CA: Science and Behavior Books, 1972.

Schneider, David J., Albert H. Hastorf, and Phoebe C. Ellsworth. *Person Perception*, 2d ed. Reading, MA: Addison-Wesley Publishing, 1979.

Schultz, Duane. *A History of Modern Psychology* 3d ed. New York: Academic Press, 1981.

Sieburg, Evelyn. *Family Communication: An Integrated Systems Approach*. New York: Gardner Press, 1985.

Sloan, Bernard. *The Best Friend You'll Ever Have*. New York: Crown Publishers, Inc., 1980.

Snyder, C. R., Raymond L. Higgins, and Rita J. Stucky. *Excuses*. New York: John Wiley & Sons, 1983.

Steier, Frederick, M. Duncan Stanton, and Thomas C. Todd. "Patterns of Turn-Taking and Alliance Formation in Family Communication." *Journal of Communication* 32 (Summer 1982): 148–160.

Steiner, Claude M. "The Seven Sources of Power: An Alternative to Authority." *Transactional Analysis Journal* 17 (July 1987): 102–104.

Stevenson, Joanne Sabol. *Issues & Crises During Middlescence*. New York: Appleton-Century-Crofts, 1977.

Stryker, Sheldon. *Symbolic Interactionism*. Menlo Park, CA: The Benjamin/Cummings Publishing Co., 1980.

Suitor, J. Jill and Karl Pillemer. "Explaining Intergenerational Conflict When Adult Children and Elderly Parents Live Together." *Journal of Marriage and the Family* 50 (November 1988): 1037–1047.

Sussman, Marvin B. "The Family Life of Old People." In *Handbook of Aging and the Social Sciences*, ed. Robert Binstock and Ethel Shanas, 415–449. New York: Van Nostrand Reinhold, 1985.

Tamir, Lois M. *Communication and the Aging Process*. New York: Pergamon Press, 1979.

Taylor, Shelley E., Bram P. Buunk, and Lisa G. Aspinwall. "Social Comparison, Stress and Coping." *Personality and Social Psychology Bulletin* 16 (March 1990): 74–89.

Taylor, Shelley E. and Jonathon D. Brown. "Illusion and Well-Being: A Social Psychological Perspective on Mental Health." *Psychological Bulletin* 103 (1988): 193–210.

Troll, Lillian. "New Thoughts on Old Families." *The Gerontologist* 28 (1988): 586–591.

Troll, Lillian, Sheila J. Miller, and Robert C. Atchley. *Families in Later Life*. Belmont, CA: Wadsworth Publishing, 1979.

Turner, Ralph H. *Family Interaction*. New York: John Wiley & Sons, 1970.

United States Bureau of the Census. *Statistical Abstract of the United States: 1986*, 106th ed. Washington, DC: U.S. Bureau of the Census, 1986.

Van Der Veen, Ferdinand. "Dimensions of the Family Concept and Their Relation to Gender, Generation, and Disturbance." In *Advances in Family Psychiatry*, Vol. 1, ed. John Howells, 171–190. International Universities Press, 1979.

Vuchinich, Samuel. "Arguments, Family Style." *Psychology Today* 19 (October 1985): 40–46.

Wasserstein, Wendy. *Isn't It Romantic*. Garden City, NY: Nelson Doubleday, 1984.

Wilmot, William W. *Dyadic Communication: A Transactional Perspective*. Reading, MA: Addison-Wesley Publishing, 1975.

Wisendale, S. K. and M. D. Allison. "An Analysis of 1987 Family Leave Legislation: Implications for Caregivers of the Elderly." *The Gerontologist* 28 (1988): 779–785.

Wolin, Steven J. and Linda A. Bennett. "Family Rituals." *Family Process* 23 (September 1984): 401–420.

Zajonc, Robert B. "Cognitive Theories in Social Psychology. In *The Handbook of Social Psychology*, 2d ed., Vol. 1, ed. Gardner Lindzey and Elliot Aronson, 320–411. Reading, MA: Addison-Wesley, 1968.

Zwerling, Israel. "A Single Intervention: A Visit to the Family." *Family Process* 19 (December 1980): 349–353.